Animal House on Acid

The Barrington Hall Saga

A Memoir

Beverly A. Potter, PhD
—Docpotter

RONIN
Berkeley, Ca
www.roninpub.com
www.docpotter.com

Other Books by Docpotter

Overcoming Job Burnout:
How To Renew Enthusiasm For Work

Finding A Path With A Heart:
How To Go From Burnout To Bliss

The Worrywart's Companion:
21 Ways to Soothe Yourself And Worry Smart

From Conflict To Cooperation:
How To Mediate a Dispute

Get Peak Performance Every Day:
How to Manage Like a Coach

High Performance Goal Setting:
Using Intuition to Conceive & Achieve Your Dreams

Brain Boosters:
Foods & Drugs That Make You Smarter

Drug Testing At Work:
A Guide For Employers and Employees

Pass The Test
A Guide for Employees

Marijuana Recipies & Remedies

Healing Magic of Cannabis
It's the High That Heals!

The Way Of The Ronin:
Riding The Waves Of Change at Work

Turning Around:
Keys To Motivation and Productivity

Preventing Job Burnout:
A Workbook

Youth Extension A-Z

Beyond Consciousness:
What Happens After Death

Patriots Handbook

Spiritual Secrets for Playing the Game of Life

Simple Pleasures

Question Authority to Think for Yourself

Managing Yourself for Excellence

Heal Yourself
Harness Placebo Power

Healing Hormones
Turn on Natural Chemicals to Reduce Stress

Chlorella

Animal House on Acid
The Barrington Hall Saga
A Memoir
Beverly A. Potter, PhD
—Docpotter

Animals House on Acid
ISBN: 978-1-57951-193-7

Published by
RONIN Publishing, Inc.
PO Box 3436
Oakland Ca 94609
www.roninpub.com

Library of Congress Card Number: 2013945846

Distributed to the book trade by PGW/Perseus

Dedication

For Juan Mendoza and Christian Soto, beautiful spirits who got lost in the Rabbit Hole.

Acknowledgement

Thank you to Sheldon Norberg, Reid Stuart, Steven Whitacre Sam Quinones, Doug Whitman, and Stew Huntington who shared their stories and to Bill Griffith for Zippy. Thank you to *The Daily Cal, Slingshot, The EastBay Express, The Berkeley Voice, The Oakland Tribune, The SF Examiner,* and *The Reporter* for giving permission to reprint your news stories—and to the Barringtonians who lived it and, in some cases, died in the process.

A special thanks, Dear Reader, to you for picking up this book. May you enjoy this amazing, amusing, disturbing tale.

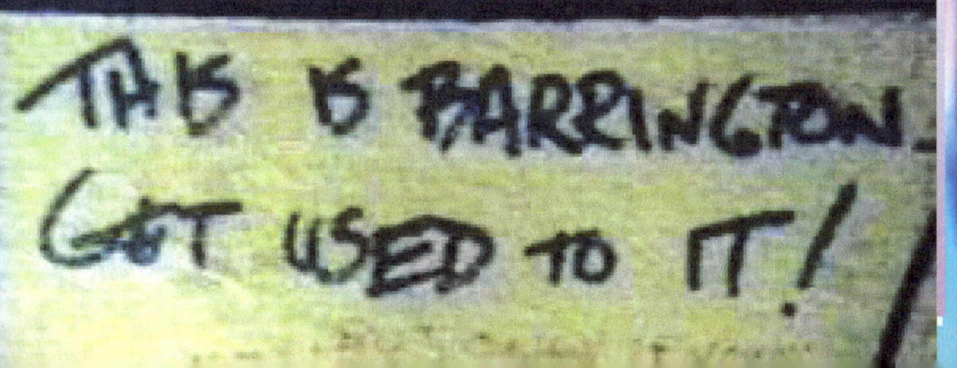

Table of Contents

1.Beverly 8
2.Sebastian 30
3.Haiku, the Fastest Mouth in the West 35
4.23 Skidoo 37
5.Barrington 38
6.Dinner at Barrington 44
7.How I Learned the Punk DIY Ethos 46
8.The Barrington Bull 52
9 History Onngh Yanngh 54
10 Bug café 57
11 Workshifts 58
12 Pink Cloud 60
13 Barrington 62
14 City of Berkeley Memorandum 65
15 We Are Not Circus Animals 71
16 Charles Spinosa Letter 72
17 Elsmere Arbitration 74
18 Supermarket of Dope 78
19 Hanging Out with My Big Brother 79
20 Bev as Junkie 80
21 Hell Summer of '85 83
22. Lucy in Hell with Heroin 84
23 Hard-Core Drug Use Is Uncooperative 87
24 Rodent Liberation 88
25 Slimy Decadence 90
26 Barrington House Charter 91
27 Drug Woes May Close UC Co-op 92
28 International Solidarity 98
29 Teenage Refuge in . . . . . Barrington 99
30 Barrington Hall . . . . Chronology 101
31 Special Report 102
32 Anti-Barrington Activist Publishes Drug Guides 104
33 Always a Scene Downstairs 106
34 Gello Wrestling 107
35 Code of Silence 108
36 John Harmon 109
37 Bombarded 110
38 Feeling No Pain 112
39 Day-Glo Rat Goes to City Hall 113
40 Sea Haggs 130
41 666 131
42 Wine Dinner 134
43 Seven Hospitalized After "Acid Punch" Party, House Chief Quits 136
44 Letter to Donald Biiiingsley 138
43 Seven Hospitalized After "Acid Punch" Party, House Chief Quits 136
44 Letter to Donald Biiiingsley138
45 New Member Disorientation Party 139
46 Acid Party Tosses Troubled UC Hall into Hot Seat Again 140
47 Barrington Bash or Barrington Bashing? 142
48 My Barrington Gig 143
49 Letter to Shirley Dean 144
50 Letter to Don Biliingsley . . . 145
51 Letter to Loni Hancock 148
52 The City Council Reacts . . .150
53 Field Trip 151
54 UC Neighbors Edgy About Housing Co-op 152
55 Readymades 157
56 Melissa Marshall 158
57 Barrington Hall Meeting Minutes 159
58 Lettert to George Proper 163
59 Primus 164
60 Co-ops Evict All Residents of Barrington 166
61 Now U.C. It 168
62 Co-op Represents Civil Liberties 171
63 Letter to Don Jelinek 174
64 Letter to George Proper 176
65 Tradition of Protest 177
66 Who is going to stand up for Barrington? 178
67 John Harmon 183
68 Glenn Lynch, Health Dept 185
69 Acid Rain 186
70 Witches Sabbath–June 23 190
71 Berkeley Fire Dept Memo 191

Table of Contents

72 Suit Filed Against Co-op Association 192
73 Press Release RICO Suit Filed Against Student Co-op 196
74 Use Immunity Order Granted 197
75 Letter to Don Jelinek 198
76 Dildo in the Door 199
77 Letter to George Proper .. 213
78 Complaint to Police Review Commission 214
79 War on Barrington 221
80 Taking Acid 224
81 The Suicidal Iguana 228
82 The Rap Master......... 230
83 Flying Appliances 236
84 Neighbors Skeptical of Barrington Closure 242
85 A Long Strange Trip 246
86 Barringtonians Pelt Board 269
87 Barrington Injunction 270
88. Onngh Yanngh 272
89 Better Living Through Chemistry 274
90 Berkeley Bob 284
91 The Secuirty Guards 286
92 Barrington Hall Event Chronology 287
93 Mystery of Barrington's Missing Doors Stumps Police 88
94 From Poetry to Rioting .. 289
95 I'm On Sound 290
96 Bev, The Cop Trainer 92
97 Cops Hate Poetry 295
98 The Blues 305
99 We Own It; George Runs It 306
100 The Holdovers 310
101 Poetic Injustice 311
102 Police Press Conference . 318
103 Sebastian, What's That Smell? 20
104 Barrington Death Still a Mystery; Probe Urged . 321
105 Letter to Shirley Dean .. 322
106 Did He Fall Or Was He Pushed? 324
107 Who Killed Juan Medoza? 326
108 Moms Tell Barrington Horror Stories 328
109 My Daily Fix 332
110 Suicide blamed on New Bridge 333
111 What a Racket! 334
112 Ninth Circuit Court of Appeals 335
113 He had Agreements 348
114 Books 357
115 Ronin Books for Independent Minds 357

Yours truly

Beverly

Born to Millburn and Maplewoor (NJ) High School drop-outs who eloped to secretly marry because I was on the way. Campbell, "Cam", my father came from a long line of mechanical genius. "Dad", Mark Hopkins Potter, his father was an engineer (which was about as common as astronaut in "those days") with Buick. Earlier he invented a car. Daddy was a "real man" with an incredible "can-do" attitude. At 19, after having spent a tour of duty at the end of "The War", he acquired a lot to build us a house from lumber of a barracks he was paid to dismantle, hauled on his Model-T flatbed truck. WHatever money came from selling the cube windows as coin banks.

Daddy was always hanging cars by wires in the garage to rebuild them, while making "Little Bevy" work on her trike next to him. Being an early F-84 jet pilot, I was a military brat, constantly moving every few months, on a two-lane road, going at a high speed—non-stop, in our *Rain Man*-like yellow roadmaster convertible with dynaflow, pulling the jeep, where Mickey, our Springer Spaniel, rode, often sitting in the driver's seat with paws on the steering wheel.

I was raised as an Officer and Gentlemen: Integrity, character, and honor is foremost. I must do the right and honorable thing - *always.* Daddy was a hard task-master. He was charismatic in a JFK way —I have at least two half-siblings—and a rebel, who con-

House Daddy built at 19 years old with no money.

stantly skirted military rules in flamboyant ways. I was his side-kick. He teased me well into abuse and allowed no slack. He beat me, put me on restriction for days, sometimes weeks, and spoke of how he'd probably kill me one day—by mistake—then would be sorry. Like my father, I could barely read—reading at the second grade level when starting high school.

Daddy on T-6 which he flew recon in Korea with only hand-held machine gun. He was awared the Bronze Star posthumously.

We had airplanes. The first was a Stetson that had the call letters N97555. Saying. "Seven Triple Nickel" to "the Tower" was Daddy's thrill. He traded it for the Howard, which was known to be hard to take off and land. When starting, he'd jump out with a fire extinguisher to quell the flames. It had two gas tanks and smelled of gas fumes in flight. Daddy always had a cigarette hanging on his lower lip—Chesterfields. There were five seats and I sat in the back on the right. He'd take me to the Caribou Airport (Maine) to work on the Howard, where I waxed the top of the wings, which were too high to cimb down from. At home in the garage he was building a Piper Cub with two control panels—skiis and pontoons— with the plan to teach all of us to be pilots. You can figure who would be the first student, i.e., victim. Had he not died, I'm sure things would have become sexual. How could they not? We'd be off in the wild somewhere having flown in and landed on skis on some remote lake, filled with flesh-eating piranhas, sleeping in a tent, ten below outside, chopping wood and cooking. Did I mention I'm a closet survivalist?

Moving constantly, driving non-stop at high speed pulling the jeep.

I see myself as "average" —average height, average intelligence, etc— but *not* usual. Clearly it is due to my not having a usual childhood, moving constantly, living in funny places where people didn't like me. My parents were far from supportive. My mother was covertly hostile. All bad things were my fault, which continues.

We always lived in town with "the locals", except in Caribou, where we had to live on the base because of the heavy snow fall.. I was in Roswell when the alien UFO crashed. I love looking at those black and while movies with the Army hats, all crunched up —that's the "fifty mission crush", my mother explained. There are three types of aliens: the little gray, the lizards, and the blond Nordic humanoids. I may be an alien, which would explain many things.

Then we moved, against "orders", to Nome, which was a "territory", and where my father was stationed. We dependents were not permitted to live on the base, since we were not allowed to be there. Instead we lived in a house on skis in an encampment with the other nonconforming rebels. One day Daddy dragged home with his jeep a better three-room house with an in-door out-house, with a fur-lined seat where a "honey" bucket hung underneath. A man would open a small door from the outside to get the bucket to empty it. I recall peeing on a gloved hand. I dressed like an Eskimo and my best friend was an Eskimo girl. We'd pull her sled, made of bones and seal skin, to the top of the house, which was covered with snow, and slide down from the roof.

Mommy, Daddy, Auntie Ann and Little Bevy

We had no electricity and thus no refrigerator. Instead, we had an unheated, closet-sized room where food was kept frozen "like a rock". There was no running water. Water was bought from an ice man who sold it in blocks, which we kept in the cold room. To brush teeth, Mommy had to chip the ice with a pick and warm over stove. I was young, being primitive, seemed natural. It was what we did.

The Howard

Daddy was always off somewhere on a “mission”. One winter night we ran out of fuel and nearly froze. It was 50 below. Mommy dressed us in many layers and got us into bed to be warm, while hoping someone from the base would bring oil. Dishes in the closet began exploding as it got colder and colder, Fortunately, someone came with fuel.

Wolves and wolf-dogs ran freely around our house. One time, when playing in the walkway—where the snow was piled up over the height of the door—I looked up to a wild wolf-dog looking down at me.

In the second grade I went to five different schools in funny towns like Radium Springs, Quitman, and Moultrie, GA; Enid, OK. where I was miserable, and San Antonio TX, where my bratty little brother was born. I experienced serious discrimination and abuse from the town teachers who hated the AF.

My father was always on the edge and he took us, especially me, with him. It wasn’t optional. At the end we were in Caribou, Maine. Daddy would fly us to Boston and Quebec in the Howard. Mostly Mark and I stayed in the hotel while my parents went on a “date”. Hey? How cool is that?!

Dolly & Gus Modersohn

We crash-landed twice. First time was in Montreal, where we did a “ground loop”. The wind grabbed us and we spun with my side-wing down. Everything in the cockpit was flying around, the tower and my mother screaming, my father was in his element. Adrenaline full-bore in the moment, on THE EDGE. Almost trance-like, I

Jet pilots are the rockstars - this is F-84. One time two flew in formation with us in the Howard as a sign of "brotherhood"

focused on the wing out the window, I calmly concentrated all my attention on the right wing going up and down to as close as an inch above the ground -> and our death.

When we finally came to a stand still we were in foam, surrounded by emergency vehicles. Recently a theoretical physicist agreed that my consciousness was at work, pulling the Quantum Strings, as my father *and I* brought the plane in. My father died at 31 in a plane crash—what else? He was "*The Great Santini*" (who was a Navy jet pilot) only not as mean.

Gustaf Adolf Modersohn, my mother's father, was a banker. Fifteen-year-old daughters of bankers are not suppose to get pregnant. Ceres, my bird-like grandmother, was 80 when she changed her name to "Dolly", was mortified and nailed the marriage license on the front door.

My mother was an obsessive cleaner, on her knees every day scrubbing the kitchen floor with a Brillo pad. All things were extremely neat with hand-printed tags reading "Bev's scarfs" and Mark's gloves" below the stacks in closets and drawers. All except Beverly's room, which was a complete disaster. Mother was very dependent, helpless, and whinny. Until my father was killed—then she transformed into the Air Force's nightmare—a lot like the wife of the test pilot in *After Burn*.

It was my first night of freedom—December 20. I was twelve and had taken the blue Air Force bus to the Teen Center for the first time where I played ping pong with some boys. Arriving home at about 9 pm, I immediately "knew" my father was dead. Mark, my baby brother, was whimpering *"I want my Daddy."* Col.

Williams, my father's CO—Commanding Officer, the Chaplan, and a Medic were upstairs trying to control my mother, Alice, who was screaming, thrashing, and refusing to submit to the needle.

As a "Gray Lady" volunteer she had been sent to help the wife of the first man at LAFB to die and saw first hand what the Air Force does. They shoot the widow up with drugs. Then she lies unconscious on the bed in her slip, as the neighbors arrive with the food and peep in "to see the widow", like in *Zorba, The Greek*. While keeping her drugged, she and all possessions are moved. The poor widow wakes up in another state in her home town with her parents.

Suddenly an aggressive superwoman emerged from Mousy Mommy. She chartered a plane and flew to the crash site. She refused to move out of the apartment and flew back to Loring AFB, after depositing my brother, Mark II, and me with our grandparents in Milburn NJ.

Eventually we ended up in Plattsburgh NY, which was near an AF base, where I went to High School—all four years in ONE school—Wow!. Mother had many boyfriends who I had to suffer. While she had never had any paying job before, she got into Radio and later TV, starting off as "*Alice in Slumberland*" airing nightly at 11:15 pm where she did her best to "talk dirty" like a "shock jock". This in a *Payton Place*-like town that passed laws as to how long a girl over 14 shorts must be above the knee. They actually arrested and deported women for wearing "short shorts." It was triggered by that old pop song: *Short Shorts*: "*Who likes short shorts? Da da da da da da. We like short shorts. Da da da da da!!!* I was in high school and my mother was the uptight town's sexual provocateur!

Amazingly, I went to college—Syracuse. I had "war orphan" benefits, similar to the GI Bill—$110 a month, because my father died in an Air Force plane. The checks went to my mother. She always put on a show of being "the good mother" while

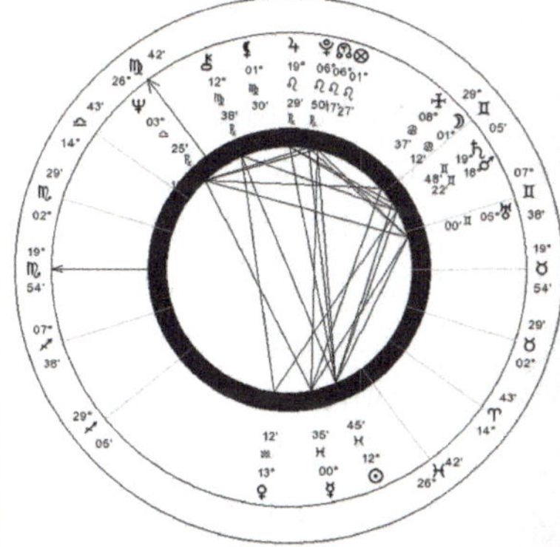

Bev's birth chart

Alice, my mother, the sexiest Mommy of all.

covertly sabatoguing me. People often said, *"With a mother like yours."* I never knew what they meant, but I did know that she was a hostile rival. *Snow White and the Seven Dwarfs* is my story. Mother had a four-foot-tall portrait of herself in a peignoir on her mantle. *"Picture, picture, on the wall, who's the sexist Mommy of all"*. But I digress.

College was a challenge. I still had major reading issues—being educationally-challenged due to all that moving from school to back-water school. Syracuse was my "one shot". I wrote outlines of every textbook and lecture and then memorized the outlines because I was so scared I'd fail and have to go back to Plattsburgh.

Mother paid Syracuse slowly, so I was threatened with being excluded from class. I wrote her pleading letters, with *"Don't let Denny read this"* at the top. My brother told me that, laughing, they would read my letters togethers.

Mother moved to Sioux Falls, SD to host a daily afternoon TV show. I met a handsome Ensign, Phil Dennis, on a train from Syracuse to Souix Falls at Christmas, who filled me with stories of San Francisco. That was when *I Left My Heart in San Francisco* was on the charts. Those were the free-wheeling days in California, when college was practically free—something like $12 a unit, when "liberal" meant anti-establishment and not group-think and government control.

At the end of my sophomore year, I fled to San Francisco to get away from my mother who was constantly setting me up. She had no idea where I was. It was her fervant desire that I become a prostitute and alcholoic, with illegitimate kids, in the gutter. When I called her from Oakland—it was Summer 1963—the first thing she said was—not "Where are you?" or "Are you okay?", but, *"I don't want to read about you in the paper like that Caroline Keefer"*—a call-girl passed around the English Parliment, as my mother put it. Of course, nothing could have delighted her more.

I had to call Mother every month to beg her to send me my $110, which often took her weeks. Finally, I made a complaint to the VA, after which they sent the check directly to me, only it carried her name. So I still had to send Mother my check, then beg and plead for her to sign it and send back. Then the strangest thing happened. Someone stole the check and somehow it was got deposited —sans endorcement—into my checking account. Wa! La! I was FREE. I had my own money! Free at last! Or so I thought.

Upon visiting "home" in Souix Falls, I found my brother, Mark, now 12, in his rocking chair—in the closet. A sign on this bedroom door said: *"Keep out! That means YOU!"*

Now that I was no longer at home, my mother's boyfriend was abusing Mark, the favored one. While I was extremely obedient, having been raised like a dog ("Sit", "Stay"), my brother often threw fits to get what he wanted and got away with it. I learned much by watching his tantrums. But with Denny, Mark was cowed. Mark called him, *"Denny, the Deviate"*.

Denny and I were always nose-to-nose, immediately upon my arrival home. If he walked into the house without knocking, I would roar, *"You knock before entering!",* then stand in front of him, pointing to the door to make him go out and knock. Then I would let him in. And this is how I was *expected* to behave, by the way. I was my father's stand-in.

Mark did baby sitting and bought a shortwave radio with his earning. Denny stole it!. It was a bad situation. I immediately began thinking of ways to get my brother out of there. The initial plan was my mailing him a bus ticket and he giving a series of lies to account for his whereabouts over a weekend—as my father had done when he and my mother eloped. He'd be in California before anyone knew he was gone. Should have followed that plan.

Instead, I got him out of there by marrying Sandy McCann, a self-proclaimed "Mama's Boy". He was Catholic and we got married in the Catholic Church. I went through a bunch of Catholic stuff so that Sandy could have his wish of a church marriage.

Sandy McCann a self-professed Mama's boy

My mother and brother had to attend the wedding. My brother was sent out first, to live with me.

I had been diddling my neighbor, Gene Koziol, about my mother for months. I had 4 or 5 other men in the wings. My mother had become a sexual predator—to "show" my father. Waving a man in front of her was like waving a bone for a dog. She came out about a week before the wedding, but wouldn't stay in my apartment due to my many cats and dust and her allergies—so she moved in with Gene. After the wedding, she immediately went back to Sioux Falls, quit her "big time" TV job and moved to California. She and Gene lived together for fifteen years.

I paid for everything for the wedding. With my tiny money I had a wedding dress custom made for $100. I used my father's ID card for the reception at the Officer's Club on Treasure Island, where I could afford one plate of horderves. I had one guest at the wedding. Mark walked me down the isle. I manifested engagement and wedding rings—both old rings from my grandmother, Dolly. Our union lasted about a year, when Sandy broke my nose over a milk shake. Soon after he was granted an annulment (so he can be buried in a Catholic cemetery) that I arranged, with my mother being his witness against me.

Gene Kozoil

Whatever! I got Mark out of Souix Falls and away from The Deviate. Mother quit her job, to start over at KRE-KBLX in Berkeley, working up from copywriter to General Manager. I worked there as the traffic clerk in Summer of 1964. The station is now a Radio Museum,

KRE with Bev's Red VW in front.

I found my name painted on the wall at a recent broadcasting event held there.

As the first woman in radio sales, Mother out-sold all the men. She always used sexual allure. For example, in pursuit of boating accounts, she first sent out a sexy card to the owners that said, "*There's a woman in your life.*" Nothing more. A week later she sent an equally provocative follow up. Finally, when their interest was peaked she sent a third note with her business card, saying "*Call me!*" Needless to say, she easily got an appointments and sold every account.

Mother worked with the FBI when receiving the Patty Hearst SLA messages sent to KRE. Another time, some folks "took over the station" to broadcast: *"Alice Potter is a Racist"* and satirical ads about cops—all in violation of FCC. Alice roared out to the station and threw them out. (I switched to calling her Alice rather than Mother in the early 1970s)

I got very good at going to school. And I followed the money. At "State"—S.F. State—Gene was in a 2-year intense masters program in Vocational Rehab Counseling" that PAID!!! $180 mo the first year and $200 mo the second. Wow!!! I told my boyfriend, Chris Cunningham and another friend,

Me as hippy with peace symbol I made.

John Rossovich, who was wheelchair-bound, and we all got in.

Every penny above $110 month and I've been rich! I actually saved money from that VA stipend!!! My internships were in criminal justice. I interned in a drug halfway house. In the second year I spent three days a week in an agency for county jail inmates. I and the Salvation Army man were the only "civilians" permitted into the Men's Jail in San Bruno. I was a hippy, with long sun bleached hair, 3 inch skirt and braless. I had many harrowing experiences and was stalked by men (plural and simultaneously) who wanted to do bad things to me. I was so scared that I locked myself with my dog, Little Dog, inside the bed room at night.

When I was moving I found a magazine back cover glossy picture hanging in the tree by my front door, that looked like me with numerous pik-like holes in it. I didn't go in and left. When I came back later, there were more pictures hanging in the tree—women in bras—with numerous holes. The bad guy, one of my several stalkers, had been there. Maybe he was inside the house at that very moment. I left all my possessions in the house.

Later during my first year at Stanford when my boyfriend, John Marry, a classics doctoral student, and I were driving into the city about 10 pm one night, I remembered that old house and asked, *"Hey, do you want to see a weird place where I use to live?"*

The house was abandoned. All the windows removed, leaving gaping holes. Inside the toilets were gone—taken, tile pried up. The walls were filled with graffiti—a little like Barrington's, some of which I'd painted. It was the local teenager fuck-house with a mattress on the floor. There was piles of "stuff" everywhere. I was reminded of old derelict houses I'd come upon when on a drive in the back country. A house abandoned for years—just a hulk. There would always be a lot of "stuff", some times ankle-deep. That's how that old house was. I bent down in the dim light to pick up something lacy that caught my eye, with my extended finger. Then I recognized it,. *"Oh!!"* I gasped. *"My wedding dress!"* I have always thought that was very funny. Just like those country abandoned houses —only it was my stuff!!!! But, hey, I got away from the lunitic, didn't I?

I lived in the Haight as a "hippy". Unlike my roommates, I had a job, working from 6 am to 2 pm at the Army Education Center on the Presidio. Every day I went through a weird transition from hippy to Army. I was assigned as a teacher, called tutor, for men who were below education standards, McNamara"s Project One Hundred Thousand brought in 100,000 men below standards. It was our job to bring them up to standard so that they could be sent to "Nam". Actually, our guys had already all been to Nam and had survived. We'd search out the dumb-bell guys to induct into our Program.

I and two Army Officer wives were the teachers. The class was outrageously out of control, with guys throwing spit wads and setting fires in waste baskets. I developed ways to get these guys to perform while keeping the class under control. I started the guys a grade below their level, which we assessed by asking them questions. Their math questions were in pictures, like "*2 jeeps plus 3 jeeps =*". I kid you not. These guys were remedial!!! However, they were not necessarily "stupid". Most had learning "issues". We gave them "pre-tests" in the "testing environment" and then tutored them and tutored them on items they missed. By the time they got to the "real" test, they would ace it—and they knew we would not give them the test until we were sure they would ace it! Many of the guy began accelerating as they succeeded in school—for the first time. I intuitively understood this.

At the end of 3 months, our remedial guys were given the Army General Classification Test (AGCT). Based on the their score on this test, they received certain post-Army training opportunities. Patty, one of the other tutors, stole the Army classified test. These guys were wrongfully drafted, had survived the war. I had no problem with this "fraud". Zip!! Our guys deserved a break.

Most IQ-type tests are heavily biased toward vocabulary—which I knew. We extracted 100 vocabulary words from the test. I invented the class game: Vocabulary Bee. It was like Spelling Bee, only the up-guy could choose between a new word to

Bev in front of comic store

define or giving a second definition of the previous guy's word and, if they got it wrong, they were not "out" but went to the back of line to continue in the "Game". Winners got candy bars. We three tutors—all 23-24ish—cheered on "our"guys in a competitive manner. Being a bra-less hippy with a 2-inch skirt and streaming long blond hair, a "sex pot"—it was motivating. Amazingly we'd get to school at 6 a.m. to find guys already sitting in their groups, drilling one another on vocabulary! Wow!!!! Sex sells!

Well, the day of the test came. The very quiet, tense environment, with Army proctors walking around, previously would have sent our guys into catatonic shock. It was intense. Everyone of our guys had learned those 100 words with at least 2 definitions, so to a man, they all aced the test!!!!

News traveled fast and the Sixth Army sent officials to investigate. No one mentioned the stolen AGCT or the vocabulary drilling. The guys went into a room and took a test and aced it. We tutors were lauded and given raises to $6.50/hr! Not long after that I left for Stanford. Later I found out that all my lessons and processes had been institutionalized as the program went on for years and years.

Linda Raffel, a classmate in the Rehab Master's program and daughter of a Stanford big wig professor, urged me to apply to Stanford, which I thought was ludicrous. But WTF! Somehow I got an appointment with John Krumboltz, the head of the Stanford Counseling Psych doctoral program.

It was 1970. I sat in the chair across the corner of the desk from John, who was polite, nodding with Rogerian unconditional acceptance, obviously found me uninteresting—until he asked in voice verging on boredom, *"What else have you done?"* I mentioned being a volunteer coordinator for David Fisher's Behavior Therapy Institute, at which John's face brighten and his interest sparked.

Hummmm? I called David as soon as I got home to ask him to write a letter of recommendation. *"Oh, I just declined to write a chapter in his book, so it'll probably not help." "No! No! Please write a letter, David. Write a letter!"* He did. Later when we PhD students sat around speculating how we had been chosen among so many—I was one of four (!!!) in my year, with only 12 active doctoral students in the Department—with two highly lauded Stanford full professors. We concluded that the letter is key—someone they personally knew.

I was invited to an interview to consider my acceptance into the Program. I imagined that everyone who applied would be interviewed. So I showed up in my going-to-town hippy-garb. I wore a leather dress that I had made—I was artsy-fartsy and made everything, which is how I was "rich". I'd bought the leather very cheaply at the tannery. I wore handmade leather sandals, crafted for my feet, with color coordinated tights, and a pottery medallion that I had made on a leather strip. My California hippy sun-bleached long blond hair was combed. All the other applicants wore business garb. One was a school principle, for example. This was the kind of person I was competing with.

The interview was a series of performance tests lead by the doctoral students. Tho shy in public speaking, but thinking all the others were, well, so "up-tight" and I had no chance anyway—so WTF! I basically "played" each exercise like a game, maxing out on the drama—improv. I would place myself in the power spot, or stand when others were sitting. I didn't realize it at the time, but I made quite an impression..

Speaking afterwards with Carl Thoresen, who was co-chair with John, and a big deal in academia (only what did I know?), *"What are my chances?" "We got 3000 applications. We're interviewing eight, and will accept four,"* he explained. Then I "freaked". *OMG!! What have I done?*

I called David Fisher to tell him about the interview. David was a behavioral psychologist who talked like Lenny Bruce—even looked a little like him. He said, *"Yeah, after the lies I wrote about you, I* ***knew*** *they would be interested."* I freaked again. What lies? He didn't say. Perhaps I'd not been the best volunteer coordinator, so he may have exaggerated—lied. OMG!!

Bev at Stanford

I was accepted. Me, one of a class of four, at Stanford University—and with money: some kind of Teaching Assistance at about $200 monthly. Carl sent out a list of books we might read over the summer in preparation for Fall, and write "Reaction Forms" on each. Taking David's comment to heart, I knew I was a fraud, soon to be discovered and ejected. So I read every book, wrote the Reaction Forms, which I deposited in Carl's box upon arriving at Stanford—just before going off to The Orientation Retreat in Santa Cruz, lead by the doctoral students. The Forms were gone when I tried to get them back to redo.

Sometime early in the Retreat, I ran into Carl, who looked down at me very seriously through his bushy Norwegian eyebrows, saying, *"We need to talk."* I've been exposed. I "knew" he had read my Reaction Forms and found them totally lacking. He was going to invite me to leave. For the remainder of the weekend I avoided Carl, who I expected was going to send me packing.

At that time, the Counseling Psychology Department had a one-year Masters Program of about 25 student, that we doctoral students "ran". Early on in one of Carl's classes he brought up the Reaction Forms, saying, "*One person did what I consider to be a model and that person is Beverly Potter.*" Whoa! I'd gotten over fearing I would "be found out" as a fraud; but my Forms being the best? That came as a shock. And such was my experience at Stanford—frequent unexpected affirmations. I was THE Sunshine Girl!

Being one of only four, it was a kind of "apprenticeship" experience. We did everything. Develop material. Ran classes. Wrote the professors' papers. Set up internships. Since I had been in a "women's" group and in Synanon as a "square player" Carl picked me to work with him in developing "behavioral group counseling". He and I sat in Carl's office, brainstormming what a behavioral group was, how it could be used in counseling, creating modules to teach it. I got really good at this "model creating".

Getting a PhD is a political process. As long as I was working with Carl on behavioral group counseling, or with John on something that fit into his research, I was sailing along and there was always some sort of TAship with money included. But then I decided to do my dissertation on a subject having to do with sexism. I became a black sheep. Steve Zifferblatt, a third professor who came on for a few years, with whom I had a bit of a 'love-hate" (platonic, of course) relationship. Actually, he constantly harassed me. He said one day, *"Bev, you're free trip is up. There's no money* ***for you*** *next year."*

This is the first sign of doctoral-student death. Later I had a boyfriend, Michael Loceff, a doc student in the math department, who invited me to a department party that his professor Karel de Leeuw and wife also attended. Whispers told me "who" they were. He was a funny looking man, like a character from *The Hobbit.* Not long after, the important professor met with a struggling 19-year doctoral student, Ted Streleski, who murdered him with a sledge hammer in his office!!! This is what happens to doctoral students who lose the financial support, i.e., fall out of favor to become politically incorrect. They aren't thrown out, they just can never finish. When he turned himself in to the authorities, Strelecki claimed the murder was justifiable homicide because de Leeuw had withheld departmental awards from him, demeaned him in front of peers, and refused requests for financial support

Michael Loceff was a Math doc student, later he was the Exec Writer for the popular TV serial "24"

I saw the handwriting on the wall. Pivot. Scramble. I applied for a dissertation fellowship in Women's Studies from the Ford Foundation, which, if won, would pay all my fees and give me a stipend. To complete my application, I had to be "nominated" by

Bev

the Dean of my School. Counseling Psychology, which grew out of school counseling, was housed in the School of Education. The Dean was Dr. Arthur Coladarci. I got an appointment with him. His office was huge and all wooded, with a large desk at one end. I sat in the chair, with arms across, from him. Dr. Coladarci was an intimidating figure. I'd never even seen him close up. He was the image of an Italian mafioso, with a cigar and as frightening.

Speaking slowly, he asked, *"What can I do for you?"* I explained that I was applying for the Ford Dissertation Fellowship and needed to have him "nominate" me. Gruffly, he asked if my proposal for my dissertation had been "approved". I said "*No, but* ..." explaining that the Ford Foundation did not require an approved proposal. Coladarci retorted, *"Well, I require it!"* That was that.

That's it! Without financial support, that was the end of my getting a PhD. I imagined standing in White Plaza with a sign saying *"Will do tricks for tuition."* Figuring I had nothing at all to lose, I looked right into Dr. Colardarci's eyes with determination, and, as I took hold of the arms on the chair, I said, *"Dr. Coladarci, I am not going to leave this chair until you agree to nominate me."* I kept looking at him with chin up, while imaging the Campus Police carrying me off in the chair, which is why I was holding on to the arms. He looked at me for a long pause, then said, *"Okay!"*

I won the Fellowship and received a letter with gold embossing from Dr. Colardarci, congratulating me, *"It is an honor for the School, as well, and we thank you for making us look good."* I became The Golden Girl again, only now with my own money, with all expenses paid. I finished my research and wrote my dissertation fairly easily—if writing can ever be "easy". The next and final big hurtle—Orals. I'd heard stories, horror stories. They always revolved around statistics. A professor on the committee asks a challenging question, which is probably invalid, about the Chi Square of the bla bla. (I had five graduate courses in stat and that's what I remember!!!) Next thing the candidate knows she's doing another year of "research" to try to satisfy the prof—and another year, and another year.

So I prepared. It was a "behavioral" program. John always asked, when would a professional psychologist go into a room to write answers to a test for eight hours? So our Exams, were behavioral—competency-based. We had to "show" skills. Make a speech at a conference; teach a class, and so froth. I'd gotten a tip from an advanced student, Michael Dansker, that hiring a statistician was acceptable. After all, were I leading a research project I would have a statistician doing analysis, which I would have to interpret and show its relevance.

So I hired the top graduate student, Chuck Dunbar, of the top statistician on the faculty. Every time I had a question about how to proceed in analysis, if Chuck couldn't answer it, well, he could quickly get the best answer available. This cost me $100. A hundred dollars was a lot of money back in 1974, say $1-2000 now. Money well-spent.

My Orals may have been the shortest in history, just barely 30 minutes. Every time a professor went after something statistical, designed, of course, to trip me up, I answered with, *"According to my consultant, Chuck Dunbar,. . ."* which to them was synonymous with the great Dr. S, herself—I've forgotten her name. I sailed across the thin ice.

I never realized that I was a "punk" until working on this project because I didn't know the connection with DIY. I did everything myself. I sewed all my clothes. I made jewelry, including lost wax, soldering silver, built a slik screen and printed cards, changed oil and tuned up my Fiat that I'd painted yellow and orange. I stretched that $110, now $200, to amazing lengths.

Bev and brother, Mark, with Fiat I painted to look like an Italian taxi

At Stanford, I lived in the servants quarters behind a mason

The Free Swin was a basic orgie.

on University Avenue. My landlord and his family, who lived in the front house, were "swingers" and nudists. There was a pool and a peacock and large orgies, with about 250 naked people around the pool and throughout the house. Opulent food tables. All kinds of decadent goings-on. John, my landlord, was into "gas", which he sucked constantly and eventually died on it, as did another gas freak from the artificial intelligence who was sucking gas under water. I was a participant-observer.

Tony Clendenin, one of the most likely to succeed from my high school class was working in Reno as a cook and coming to Bay Area to visit his Auntie. *"Hey, sure come see me!"* I saw my opportunity for an innocent "get back" on Tony who was very superior and who's mother looked down her nose at me. *"Just come down to the back where there's a gate into the back yard."* I didn't mention that it was the day of the "free swim" where everyone was naked.

When Tony arrived, he saw the gate and then looked up where he saw Jennifer, John's big busty 12-year-old daughter on the porch roof looking down on him, wearing only a bra and cowboy boots!! I'm laughing remembering his expression when he opened the gate to a sea of naked bodies. I leaped up and rescued him.

Eventually John went to the Spirit World on gas. I thought Nancy, his wife and son Charles altered the gas and oxygen mix. John often announced to all around that he would be the first to "deflower" Jennifer.

John was an attorney of the worst mentality and Nancy had a court-reporter business. I'd often hear them upstairs going over depositions when I went into the front house to get my mail. After John died, a big horsey woman named Lee moved in and began training as a court reporter, practicing on those old tapes.

There was a huge mirror on the wall behind Lee's large ground bed, where she sat naked, wearing only her silver necklace, with back to mirror, holding court spread eagle, exposing her enormous pussy—which was hard to not gape at. Lee was the mistress of SF State President "S. I." Hayakawa, who she bragged left $100 bills on the bedside table.

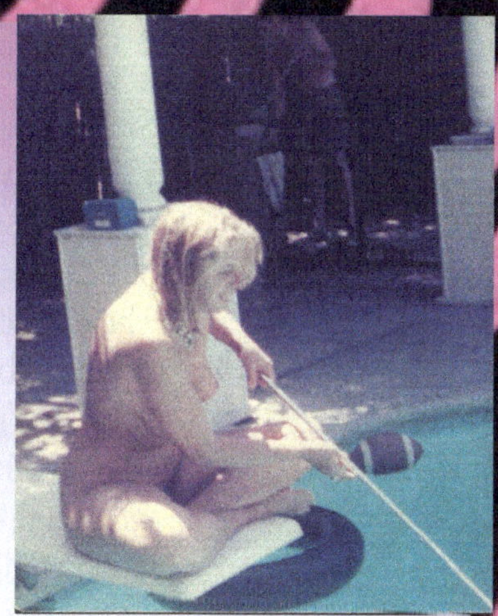
Lee was always naked

Lee was a cigarette pusher and would lure me over with smokes. One night she played a tape she found in the box of practice tapes of John and Nancy arguing about Jennifer's deflowering and Nancy said, "*I'll kill you*!" She sure sounded like she meant it!

One of my personas is Agatha Christine's Miss Marpel. When people are murdered, I seem to be around. Of course, John's death was considered a drug overdose. He was cremated so fast! I didn't win friends when expressing my theory of John's demise. For Christmas, Nancy gave me a pin-doll with my pic on the face in a small toy coffin. Do you suppose that was a message?

Fortunately, the first time I was evicted I had taken all my money—$4200—and bought two houses on one lot in South Palo Alto, for $28,500. I always send kisses to John when I mentioned this as those houses are the cornerstone of my security and fortune. Now under pressure again, I had a place to move, only it was occupied by a Section 8 tenant. I moved into my tin shed in the backyard in the winter rain.

It was "The Carter Years" when I got my PhD. Half of the engineers in Silicon Valley were unemployed. I did have a possibility at Fordham University but I didn't want to move. So I had nothing. I was like a high-powered computer, unplugged. I spent most days on campus in the Stanford Coffee House, later in Printer's Inc, on academic skidrow working on "my book".

All I knew was teaching and writing. Vicky Katz, from the masters program was the head of Short Courses at Deanza. My in!! I created 4-5 courses in which I translated counseling techniques

D'Art

management methods. I lead full day workshops for Silicon Valley professions once or twice a month for $200 a day. The rest of the time I hung out in coffee houses. I saw a newspaper article about Police Burnout. "*Ah,*" I thought, "*great topic for a workshop*". Then I realized that I was burning out.

I described what I was experiencing as burnout, developed a model on how to beat it, like I'd learned with Carl, taught it at Canada College on a Saturday, then wrote it up in a book, *Overcoming Job Burnout*, which I managed to get published. Next thing I knew I was a national expert on job burnout and touring the East Coast on a PR trip, which was great fun. It was January. "*It'll be cold and I don't have a coat,*" I worried. Then I remembered my hippy fir coat that I'd bought for $3.00 in the 60's in Ashland. I pulled it out and off I went.

It was January 1980. I stayed at the Mayflower Hotel, where Reagan had just given his inaugural speech. It was filled with "Washington suits" who all stared at me as I, in my fir coat, pulling my luggage, made my way to the check-in. *"Who is **that** woman in the fur coat?!!!"*

I published my two first books in 1980: *Turning Around: Keys to Motivation and Productivity* by AMACOM—American Management Association and *Overcoming Job Burnout*. I was plugged in and productive—again. Soon I penetrated most of the schools in the Bay Area, which evolved to corporate training. I went to Martha's Vineyard and a dude ranch in Colorado.

I found the NCBPMA—Northern California Book Publishers and Marketing Association in San Francisco, which is how I entered the Bay Area publishing scene and found Sebastian.

Spring of 1982, I was at SF International to fly to LA to visit D'Artagnan. D'Art was a high school drop out and a vagabond. I was "The Vagabond Apprentice". I could "be" with D'Art so long as I wasn't "with" him. We'd go to Castro Street, for example, and so long as I acted like I was alone and danced in the street uninhibitedly, we could go together. If a predator

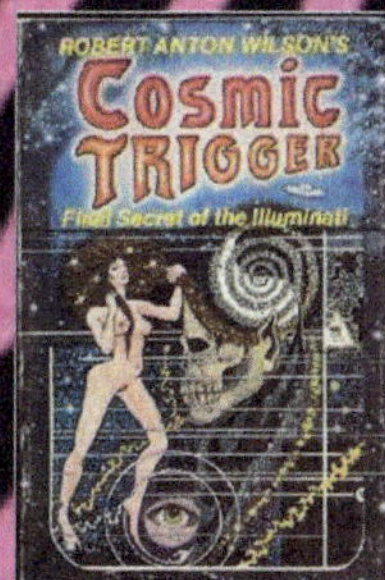

I picked up the *Cosmic Trigger*

approached me, D'Art would appear. We went on many adventures, like a Hell's Angel's party. But at any provocation, D'Art would take a off, such as when I had to get out of Death Valley, with no public trans— picked up with outlaws, and who I then narrowly escaped.

While waiting in the airport bookstore I picked up the *Cosmic Trigger* by Robert Anton Wilson and published by And/Or Press. It was a conspiracy with us in the future on Sirus, the Dog Star,

By the time we landed, I had been captured by the conspiracy and D'Art looked like a character from the book. Pulling the Quantum Strings, within 6 months, I met Sebastian and everyone in the book, including RAW, Tim Leary, Jacques Valley, the scientist in *Encounters of the Third Kind.* The original art from the book cover hangs above my desk.

Original art for *Cosmic Trigger* hangs on my office wall

Hanging out with Sebastian, he was always talking about "the house that got away". *"House smouse. If you want a house, I'll get you one!"* I had a friend who was a Berkeley realtor, Jim Cord. He had a house at 2310 Haste Street where the tenants, five Mexican guys, were holding a rent strike. If he sold the house to a homeowner, then they could be evicted. The Mex guy said to me, *"For Jim we never give up; but for you we move."* It was March of 1983.

We saw '23" on the door and knew it was an ominous sign.

As we walked up to the door for the first time, Seb noted the address and said *"23 Skadoo!"* The house was a dump. Ceilings falling in. Windows sliding down like guillotines. The downstairs bathroom was like a garden shed. It was $80,000. It was our house next to Barrington Hall, three blocks from campus. Barrington was low profile and under the thumb of Elsmere Arbitration. What did we know?

Sebastian

Born Joseph Peter Orfali, "Joe", in Jerusalem, Palestine to Steffie, a flaming red-headed escapee from the Weimar Republic, and Jacob, a Christian Armenian helping Jews escape, which is how they met. When Steffie missed her train to school, her professor met her at the station. *"They've come for you."* She fled to Palestine immediately, with only the clothes on her back.

When pregnant with their third child, Steffie had a dream about St. Sebastian, who said *"You will have a boy. Name him after me and I will always protect him."* When she awoke she saw it was St. Sebastian's Day. They didn't name him as directed, but Steffie told Seb the story, i.e., your basic mindf--ker!! Obsessed, as a ten-year old he began, secretly at first, changing his name. Seb's boyhood school notebooks said "Joseph S. Orfali". Eventually Sebastian emerged.

The Orfali family fled to Beirut because one could not live easily with a German Jew in Palestine. Then they fled to San Palo, Brazil, where Jacob worked as an engineer at a dam.

When Sebastian was a toddler in Jerusalem, Bev was in a house on skiis in Nome Alaska.

Seb rode across town alone on the bus to his job with a sandel-maker. At some point they acquired a bar/restaurant where Seb and his siblings all worked and Seb learned to cook. They migrated to Zion, Illinois when Seb was about 13

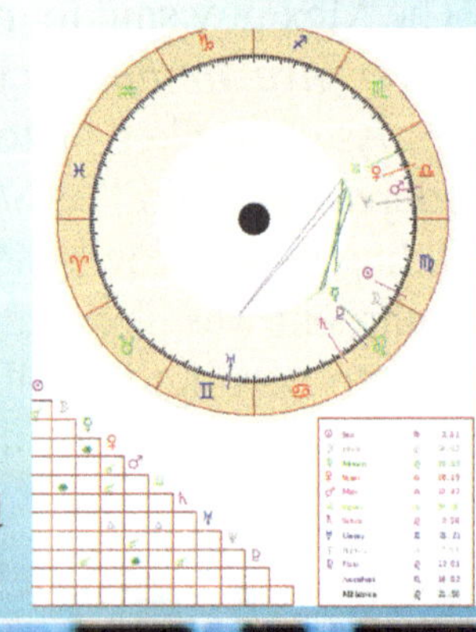

Jacob and Steffie, Seb's parents

Cooking served him well, as he got a coveted job cooking for a sorority. Sebastian was always cooking. He'd take over. There was no resisting. Steffie had become a "large" woman. Seb began making me into a large woman with his double-sized, delicious portions at each meal.

Seb was a philosophy PhD candidate at U of New Mexico in Tao, but eventually bailed with a Masters. He loved telling of being busted on the Ides of March by the Border Patrol in Truth or Consequences, NM, for three pounds of pot.The attorney who extracted him from this debacle, became a Buddhist priest, and curiously, had the exact same name as our attorney in this tale: Donald Driscoll.

Seb made fantastic meals everyday

From his earliest days, Seb was always creating fringe, in-your-face publications. At Schimer College as Publisher of the school paper, he was often called into the Dean to account for something that had outraged the faculty, such as when he published the word "testicles". OMG!! He loved telling of an issue printed in large print, *"You've heard of the New-Age. Move over Pepsi Generation"*—turn the page—*"for the Pill-Age"*.

So it should have been no surprise that Sebastian played a

One of And/Or's Banned books

Sebastian deal making

significant role in birthing "West Coast Small Press Independent Publishing." Seb worked at Last Gasp in the early 1970s and started People's Comix, an underground comic book store, in North Beach in 1973. He and his roommates founded And/Or Press in the 1970s, which published several national best-sellers, including "*The Holistic Health Handbook*" and "*Marijuana Grower's Guide*." by prominent authors like Timothy Leary, Paul Krassner, Robert Anton Wilson, Colin Wilson, David Wallechinsky, Terrence McKenna and Jacques Vallee.

Some And/Or Press books were banned in several countries, including "*The Young Lust Reader*," denied entry as an import in England and marijuana guides that were seized in Canada.

And/Or soared. The sharks arrived for a "hostile take over" and a bilking of And/Or. These things take place on the Board of Directors—like the way that Steve Jobs got ousted from Apple in the late 1980s. They decided to create a consortium of publishers, to handle distribution and marketing, called Network Inc. And/Or's assets supplied the engine and cash and credibility. In relocating to a new building, Sebastian was moved from

Are we having fun yet?

Seb was ridiculed in Bill Griffith's Zippy, the Pinhead cartoon.

the corner office with large window, into the mop room, literally.

On Seb's good word most small presses on the West Coast had signed on and had their inventory in a Navato warehouse. When the warehouse didn't get paid, the doors slammed, threatening the existence of the publishers. Sebastian was blamed. Outnumbered and voted over, everyone began grabbing what they could. Someone even allowed the mainframe computer that had one last payment due, to be repossessed. Duh? The head mail clerk managed to make off with some $50K. Even Seb's car was repossessed. But he always smiled and didn't "grouse"

And/Or Press broke ground with a series of pot books

That's when Bev showed up. It was during our first year at 2310 that I got on And/Or's Board, so Seb had an ally. The predators hated it. Some things that went on were off-the-grid, such as when, in the ninth month of her pregnancy, Ginger lost her employee health care because of the bankrupcy. It was a crisis. A predator in the drama left the Board meeting to propose to Ginger in the hallway that he and his wife pay Ginger a fee to buy her—ah, adopt—her baby. I was scandalized.

Ronin Publishing emerged out of And/Or's ashes at 2310 during our first year. I'd developed a career strategy that I initially called

Bev & Seb at Book Show

Sebastian & Timothy Leary

"The Vagabond Psychologist" that became "the Way of the Ronin" *Ronin* is an uninden-tured samurai thrown into the "waves of change". Ronin translates from Japanese as *ro* = wave, and nin, like *ninja*, = man or person. Wave-man. The concept was to use work as a "trip ticket". I was highly influenced by Hunter Thompson's *Hell's Angels,* which told of how he joined the Hell's Angels for two years. But being an author, it was a "trip" he took, then left behind.

Funny thing, as I was writing about Sebastian here, I received an email from Jennifer of Bob and Jennifer, formerly Mushroom People in

Jennifer & Sebastian

Inverness, now Orchid People in Hawaii. I hear from Jennifer every few years. So seeing her message in my in-box was an "*Oh!*!" which became an "*Oh Wow!!*" when I opened it to see Seb looking out at me with an enigmatic smile.

Haiku, fastest mouth in the west

BABBINGTON HALL
2315 DWIGHT WAY
BERKELEY

Basic Rhythms of Nature

The physical biorhythm cycle is said to be 23 days. It takes 23 seconds for blood to circulate through the human body. The male and female each contribute 23 chromosomes during conception. A full turn of the DNA helix occurs every 23 angstroms. The number of joints in the human arm is 23. There are 23 vertebrae in the human body.

23 Skidoo

"It's time to get while the getting is good".

American slang for getting out of somewhere popularized by the arcane usage by Allister Crowley, William Burroughs and Robert Anton Wilson.

Around 1960 Burroughs spoke with a certain Captain Clark in Tangier who bragged that he had been sailing 23 years without an accident. That very day, Clark's ship wreaked, killing everybody aboard, including Clark. While musing on the irony, Burroughs heard a radio news flash that a Florida airliner, piloted by another Captain Clark had crashed and everyone perished. It was Flight 23.

9/11/2001 9 + 11 + 2 +0 + 0 + 11 = 23

2/3 = .666

23 Enigma

There is something deeply mysterious, extremely special and wonderfully interesting about 23.

2310 Haste ST.

Sebastian said, "23 Skidoo!" the first time we walked up to the house, I had a "knowing" something extreme was coming.

ANCIENT EGYPT'S NEW YEAR WAS JULY 23, THE DAY SIRIUS RISES BEHIND THE SUN.

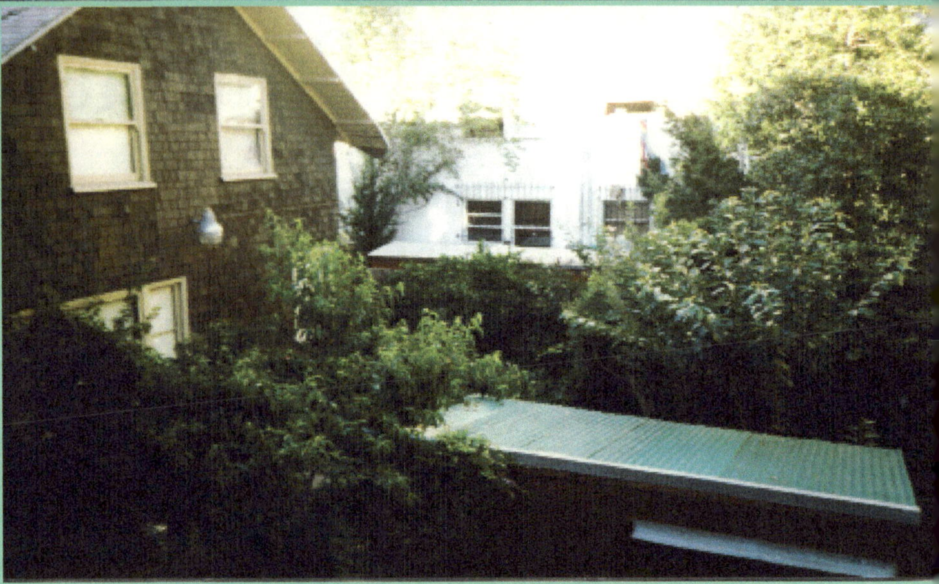

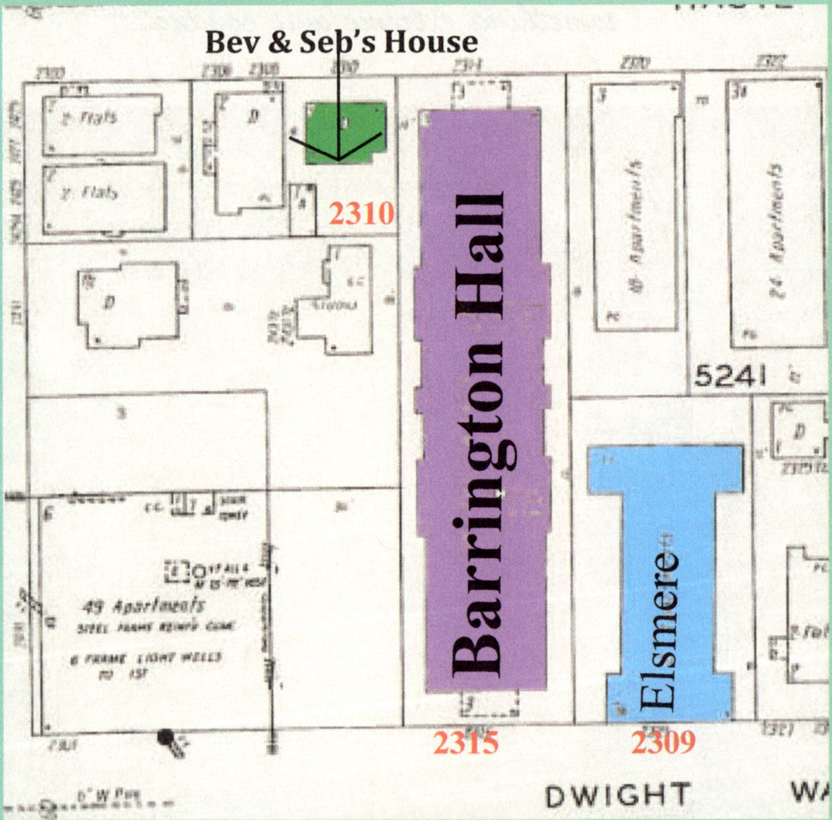

Bev & Seb's House

2310

Barrington Hall

Elsmere

2315

2309

DWIGHT

1929 Plot Map

Barrington was a block long with two entries, one on Haste Street and one on Dwight Way. The Haste opened to a long hall of doors going into private suites. The Dwight entrance led to the basement, or "Subterranean," as Narrintonians call it. "The Rogues Gallery", on the wall inside the Dwight door, featured photos in a glass display box of PNG (persona non-Grata) members. Across from the photos to the right upon entering the building was a switchboard station.

Suites

Barrington had three floors–each a block long–with 15 suites on each floor. Suites included two to four rooms–usually three–doubles or singles and a bathroom. Bathrooms had classic claw-foot bathtub with a shower. Each suite had a phone connected to a switchboard.

Sunday Meetings

Barringtonians met on Sunday evening in the room on the left after the Rogue's Gallery to discuss house issues. They tacked up white butcher paper from ceiling to floor outside the meeting room. This was the"Bitch List". During the week, they wrote things to discuss at Sunday's meeting. The bitch list was usually long and about the house or other Barringtonians or neighbors. Anything not on the list by Sunday morning was not on the agenda and pushed to the next week. Gripes focused someboy be-

Dwight Side

Looking up at Barrington from Bev & Seb's yard

Looking down from Barrington into Bev & Seb's yard

Bev in backyard telling reporter about being bombarded with bottles in the yard and how a rat and an ijuana from Barrington ran into the kitchen.

ing PNG-ing, like Berkeley Bob, Ice-pick Al , Skateboard Kenny, or Hella Fuckin' Rockin' Ronny Raw. Hoarding dishes was an issue discussed. Bitch sessions were democratically run, requiring a quorum. Nitch sessions were pushed by a core group. Most of Barringtonians paid them little attention and never attended.

PNG

PNGing was the practice of excluding specific people, called "PNGs" (persona nonGrata) is reputed to have begun in the Winter of 1970 when the Central Level first got involved in Barrington issues. The USCA President kicked out street people hassling women in the house and members involved in heroin deals.

The Store

There was a Store was on the right, next to the switchboard. Running the store fulfilled work shift hours for Store Managers. The job had perks, like a personal Cost Co membership and 24-hour access to the store. Store managers had to have a car. The store was open from six to eleven pm daily and sold cigarettes, candy bars, gum, snacks, and sundries along with beer and soda..Smokers. soda junkies, alcoholics and stoners lusting chocolate constantly hassled the Store Managers when the store was closed.

There was a stairway next to the Store leading up to a vestibule area opened to Subterranean—the dining commons. A cafeteria with Formica tables, chairs and benches. The commercial kitchen was on the other side of the dining area. The dish washing area consisted of several sinks. A notice on the sanitizer screamed in black ink: "I *am Sanitizer!*"

The kitchen featured a large fridge with steel doors, a locked walk-in fridge, and a huge wooden chopping table.. The store room, which was supposed to always be locked, for keeping dry, non-perishable goods. Kitchen Managers had keys. Keys were atatus..

To the left beyond the stairway was The Maintenance Room where there werevarious tools, including a table saw, various wood to make shelves or build a loft for Barringtonian's rooms. Next came The Band Room that held a drum set and big amps. Just bring drum sticks for a good time.

To the right of the Band Room came the north stairwell which featured brightly colored murals, words painted on the walls and ceiling, with am awesome vampire shadow portrait at the top of the stairs.

The Hidden Stairwell

There was a hidden staircase, unknown to most, that went between the first and third floors, while the other stairs went to the roof. The doors to the hiddent stair were always closed.. Charlie Manson was stenciled on the walls with spray painted writing over: GGFH—Goat Gods From Hell. Time stopped when entering the hidden stairwell. It was quiet and creepy

Shitty's

The Roxy Market was a small neighborhood grocery store a half block away, on the corner of Dwight and Ellsworth. Barringtonians called it "Shitty's".

Barrington was a cross between an eyesore and the most awesome building you've ever seen. Barringtonians hung out and run around on the roof. One night they threw a washing machine off the roof onto my house.

Dinner at Barrington

Barringtonians did everything to run the building, as did all the Co-op houses—ordering food, preparing meals, and cleaning. There was very little cleaning done, so the place was a dump.

Dinner was a group meal where Barringtonians gathered in the dining room, hungerly awaiting the grub with dinner-demand music: a drumming cacophony, banging together plates, silverware, bongs.

Serving dinner could be dangerous venture. Often there was not enough food for everyone—especially crashers. Servers would take out large bowls of steaming something-or-the-other to the tables, to face a wild feeding frenzy as Barringtonians pushed one another aside to pounce on the food.

It was a nightly struggle—a mad rush to get to the serving bowl. You had to be nimble and quick to eat. Hippies and punkers can be aggressive. After being pawed at by a few grueling homeless guys, one wondered if the food was safe to eat.

Servers brought out baked chicken on hot trays pulled from the oven at one dinner. The trays burned their hands, so the servers ran to the tables, only one server tripped. The chicken flew off the trays and slid across the grime-encrusted floor. No matter to the hungry! Barringtonians pounced on the filth-spiced chicken.

Fried pot stickers in oil on the griddle and dipped into soy sauce mixed with cayenne pepper, or vinegar was a Barringtonian favorite. Sometimes they added ramen noodles. Quesadillas were a nighttime favorite, with tortillas, big blocks of cheese and salsa.

A German punk who had a zipper tattoo on his arm was Dinner Manager. It is reputed that he found a road kill—a dead raccoon—along the side of the highway. After they debated the ethics of not letting the meat go to waste, they skinned carcass and boiled in a large pot for a stew.

The Alternative Kitchen provided only vegetarian and vegan meals every day except for Sunday. The A K was a converted lounge with the big cheese "last supper" painted on the entire wall, except the postulates are vegetarians and Christ is a carrot.

—*Slingshot*
November 1989

Rasputin Music on Telegraph Avenue, Spring 2014.

How I Learned the Punk DIY Ethos

Here's the way it happened: A guy named Ken Friedman, sometimes Cal student, lived at Barrington and was very into promoting shows and getting into the music biz. (He's now a successful restaurateur in NYC — The Spotted Pig)

Ken learned to do it by promoting punk shows. He did the *Readymades,* which was the first show I remember him doing. I didn't help on that show. Eventually Ken did *Talking Heads* on Sproul Plaza for free several times. He worked at Cal's student production company and used Pauley Ballroom, where he did the *Ramones, Iggy Pop, Siouxsie* and the *Banshees*, etc. I have posters of those shows. I worked on all these shows as a stage hand/promo type minion.

One of Ken's best shows was later at the American Indian hall in San Francisco with *Gang of Four*. That was fantastic. *Ramones* and *Iggy* were also just great shows.

Anyway, I learned to promote shows from Ken. I can't remember how I started with him, but I did help with the *Mutants* show at Barrington Hall in the Fall of 1979, which was my first foray into working as a kind of gopher/stage hand/promo guy.

"Barrington Hall remains for me one of the great liberating experiences, a place that encouraged me to create a life of my own design."

From there, Ken moved on to Bill Graham Presents and then did a lot of shows at the Market Street Cinema—*Toots* and the *Maytals, Grace Jones, English Beat*). Meanwhile, I began doing shows at Barrington Hall. This was in the winter, spring and summer of 1980.

I and a friend, Harald Hope, put on the *Dead Kennedys* with the *Zeros*. That was probably the best show Barrington ever had. It was utterly packed—350 people in a place really meant for 150. The crowd was like a hurricane and the DKs were

BARRINGTON HALL

Before legal arbitration with the neighbors in 1984, Barrington was the launching pad/petri dish of Bay Area Punk, and bands played frequently.
The song "Frizzle Fry" by the band Primus as well as the theme of their album, Tales From the Punchbowl, was inspired by one of the Barrington's recurring parties, called "Wine Dinners," held at the house where punch laced with LSD was served.
Black Flag, Flipper, X, NOFX, and The Dead Kennedys played at Barrington in the 80s, along with hundreds of other punk rock bands.

Barrington 1989
Originally located nearby at dwight and elseworth, now it is private student housing.

"the launching pad/petri dish of Bay Area Punk".

stunned that they could make money and have such a great show. It was a night I'll never forget.

As we had more and more bands playing, the place began to get busy, we—or someone—made a four-panel stage. It was 10 feet by 15 feet, but only 8-inches high because Barrington's ceiling was very low, 8-feet or something. So the stage barely elevated the band above the crowd. The crowd kept plowing into the band, so a bunch of us had to lock arms and became the bulwark protecting the DKs. That stage saw amazing action over the years!

The music was manic and fantastic and we got pummeled. I was literally pulled out of my shoes by a guy who put me in a neck lock. Another guy at the show saved me from this idiot. I don't know what his problem was.

With that show, I came to view Barrington as a place where all kinds of music could be presented. I put on a show with the *Offs* and *Zeros*, which was pretty good, though I don't remember much about it.

During the summer of 1980 I tried to turn Barrington into a club of sorts—unlicensed, of course, but still selling alcohol, minors welcome —it was completely Wild West, unregulated stuff.

That didn't really work as I put on reggae shows and the music turned out not to be nearly as popular as it was said to be. The musicians were utter flakes and always late. Probably the best show was *Rova Saxophone Quartet*, avant guard jazz...but again, not too many people came. Also, during the summer, students leave and the crowd dwindles. Still, it was a lot of fun.

Then the next quarter or the one following, I put on *Black Flag* and *Flipper* and that was about as close as I came to ruination. We were very lucky no one was injured or killed at that show. *Black Flag* slept on my floor at my Rochedale apartment, where I was then living.

Somewhere in there, Michael Lang, a friend I've lost touch with, put on X. That was another great show. I don't know the date of it. He's a history professor somewhere now. But by 1981, Barrington had been a venue for some of the top west coast punk bands: X, Black Flag, Flipper, Zeros, Mutants, the Dils, Ready-mades, and some others.

I had moved out of Barrington by then, and soon some house managers were elected who had a dim view of these shows. So I moved on and happily was never really part of the music business, such as it was, after that. I do think that later folks in Barrington began to see that it was, in fact, a perfect music venue and had other shows. The downstairs had been a parking garage and was utterly indestructible.

I went on to other things, but I have to say that punk ethos of just doing it yourself, self-reliance, not asking permission, having an idea and building it to fruition, not worrying what people will say, trusting your own instincts, and above all, doing it—all that has been part of my life ever since and probably some of the most important things I learned at Cal Berkeley.

Sam Quinones
Journalist & Author
www.samquinones.com

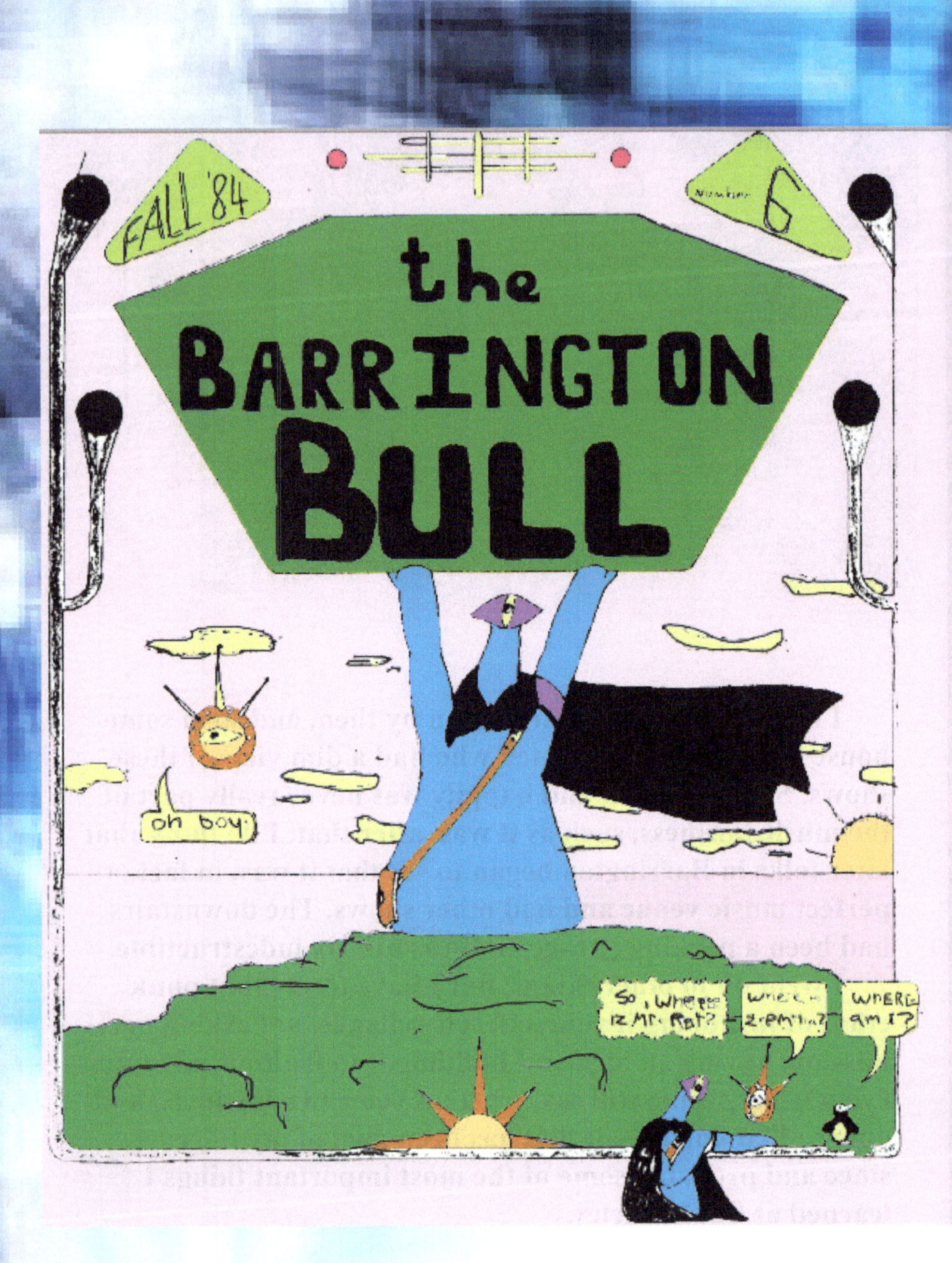
FALL '84
6
the BARRINGTON BULL
oh boy.
So, Where iz Mr. Rat?
WHERE am I?

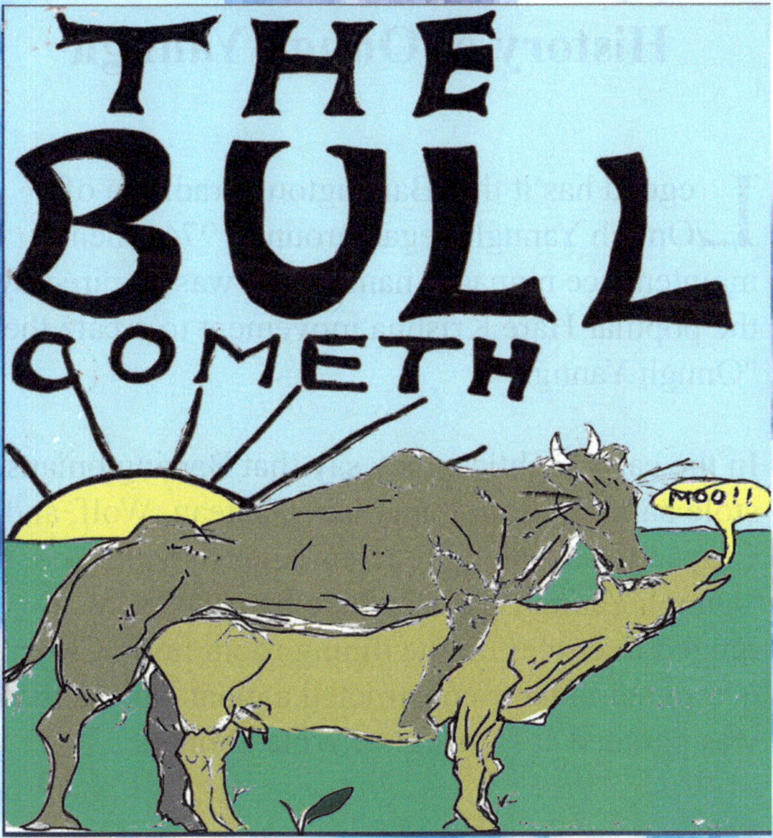
THE BULL COMETH
MOO!!

THE BULL COMETH
FALL 1984
BARRINGTON

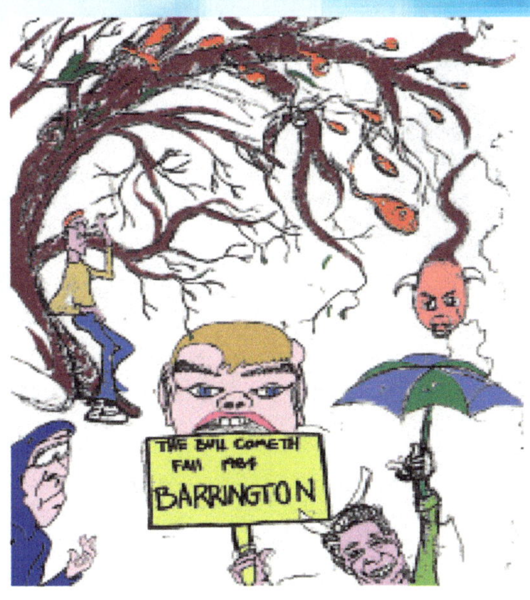

The Barrington Bull was an in-house publication of Barrington Hall, published from 1936 to 1989.

History of Onngh Yanngh

Legend has it that Barrington's tradition of Onngh Yanngh began around 1974 when a maintenance manager named Bill was inspired by the popular Hare Krishna movement to create the "Onngh Yanngh".

In the early eighties, they say that Barringtonians stole bananas from Kingman, Chateau, Wolf, and Cloyne for candlelight ceremonies they dubbed, "Onngh Yanngh Days" where bananas were arranged in circles on the dining room floor. Cloyne is reputed to have constructed a giant banana that was paraded at Barrington Wine Dinners.

Onngh Yanngh Spoke

And these were his words:

1. **Thou shall make no T-shirt for thyself; sell them.**

2. **Thou shall not bow down to Iceman or worship him, for Iceman is Onngh Yanngh**

3. **Thou shalt not made wrong use of the name of Onngh Yannge, such as verbs, adjectives, adverbs, or (Onngh Yanngh forbid!) exclamations.**

4. **Thou shall keep the Sabbath day holy: PARTY!**

5. **Honor thy father and thy mother, that they might give the money.**

6. **Thou shall not commit murder, except at C.O., or at Sproul Hall or at California Hall or at University Hall.**

7. **Thou shall not commit adultery, except when you feel like it.**

8. **Thou shall not steal except from street people if they have good weed.**

9. **Thou shall not give false dope to thy neighbor.**

10. **Thou shall covet thy neighbor's house, his wife, his slave, his slave-girl, his ass, etc.,–after all, this is a cooperative! —** *Barrington Bull*, 1984

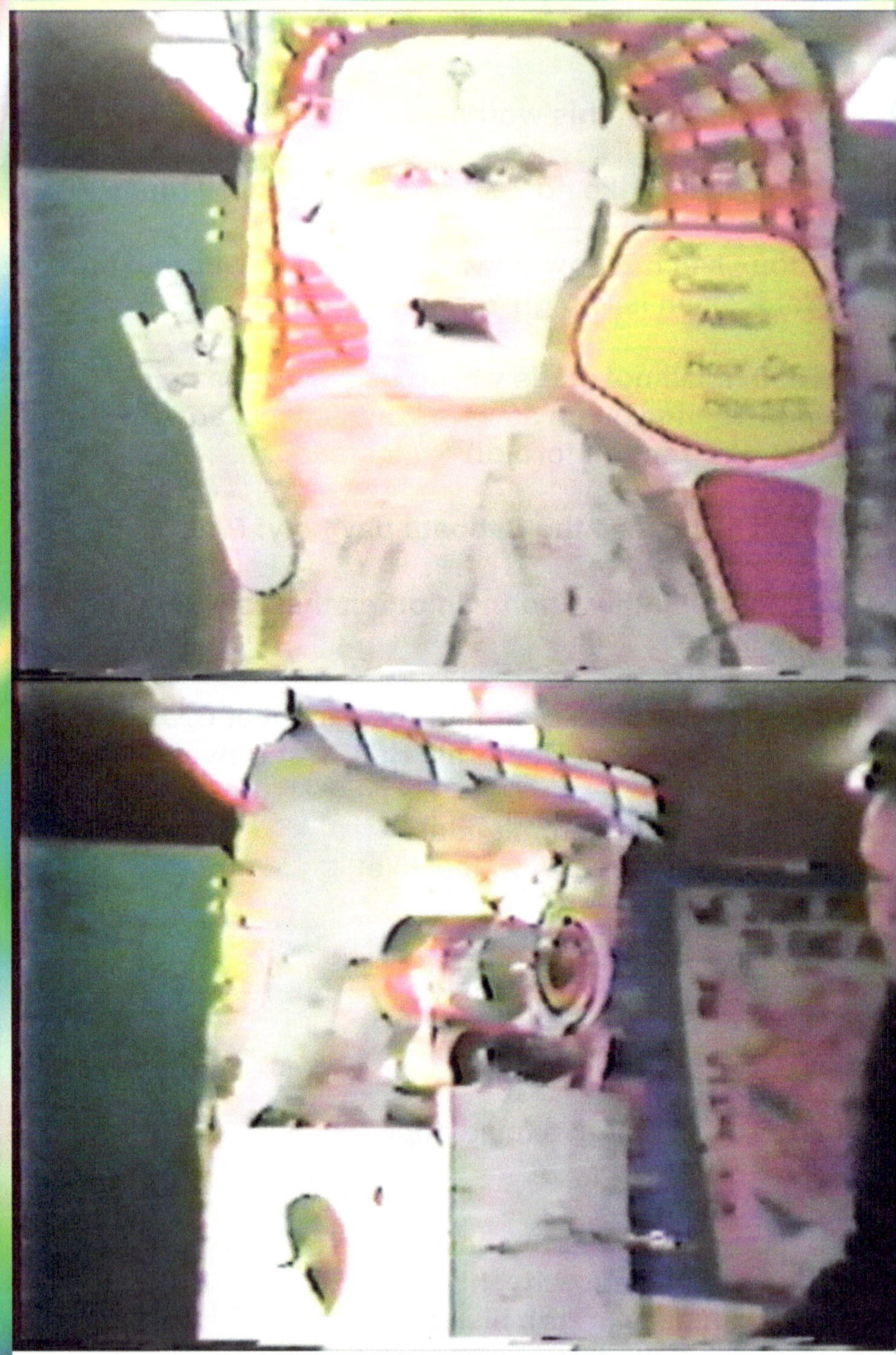

Mechanical Onngh Yanngh-Atrong
from Christian Soto video

The Barrington ·· Menu

Evening of 16 February 1982

~ Les Insectes ~

Courses

— Served with fine wines imported from —
· Modesto ·

1. Escargot a la mushroome façon du chef
2. Chocolat Chirpies
3. Petites ailes et jambonneaux de jeunes criquets.
4. Garlic fried mealworms
5. Jeunes criquets sans ailes ni jambonneaux.
6. Applesauce Surprise Cake
7. Paté de petits vers
8. Jumping guacamole dip
9. Jeunes abeilles noyeés dans leur miel.

When you think of fine food, think of "The Barrington"

There was a "Bug Snack" that was the brainchild of Doug Whitman, a PhD candidate in entomology who is now a professor of entomology at Illinois State University. Maggot pate, fried bee larvae, crispy crickets….name the bug, and Doug would find a way! Most people stayed on the sidelines, but there were many adventurous, or stoned residents who happily munched away. There was a larger point than shocking our parents. The protein available to us in the insect world could feed the world (maybe), if only we could stomach it.

If you have lived in a co-op before, it may seem strange to you that a house as large as Barrington doesn't have worked shift managers, but that is, in fact, the case. Oh, Barrington has had work shift managers in the past, like almost every other co-op, but not long ago it was realized that "Workshift Managers" are, especially for Barrington, and an outmoded and inefficient device, not unlike the Altar computer or the Reagan Administration. So Workshift Managers simply ceased to be. We took their place. We are the Administrators of the Department of Love.

YOUR DEPARTMENT OF LOVE

We are people, just like you. Our feelings are hurt when we are addressed as "Hey, Administrators" (sometimes, for short, "Hey, Adlove"), or, even worse, when we are mistakenly referred to as "The Workshift Managers." We have names like Mike Simon (who lives in the walk-through single in 202), Hendricks Davis (in the walk-through single in 302), and Eric Vogt (non walk-through, 103). Placed at one per floor for <u>your</u> convenience, we try to be always available to talk to, to try to explain things or answered questions, and, unavoidably to be bitched at. Find us, also, for those commodities like light bulbs, toilet paper, shower curtains, roach motels, vacuum cleaners, miscellaneous clean-up supplies, or etc. However, if your toilet isn't working, <u>that's</u> maintenance...

HOW TO MAKE IT THROUGH THE SEMESTER DOING AS LITTLE WORK AS POSSIBLE...

Is not the name of the game, here. Cooperativeness this is. This is *your* house, and the home of some 185 other people. It needs love and work. As they say, the Co-op is not just a cheap place to live. Barrington is a home, and it is very large home at that, with absolutely incredible potential for filth. Because of this potential Barrington can is distinguished from the other Co-ops in yet one more detail–we're the only house that has been placed on a 12-month probation period by the City's Department of Health. In fact, we came dangerously close last semester to losing our license to operate a kitchen, so if at times we seem a little demanding or meticulous, please understand why that is.

So there is work to be done–5 1/2 hours of work per week for each member. This includes cleaning, cooking, cleaning, running to the switchboard, cleaning, maintenance, cleaning, and cleaning.

WAIT ... THERE'S MORE!

Yes, in addition to the 5 1/2 hour weekly shift, our house has something called a "House Improvement" hour obligation, like most of the houses, except we often refer to it as your Onngh Yanngh Hours. This obligation amounts to 2 1/2 hours of extra cleaning or whatever done at any time during the semester.

Work parties are using a good time to get your Onngh Yanngh Hours out of the way. Every once and a while, your Department of Love will called a Work Party, usually on a weekend afternoon. These are called before inspections, after wine dinners or whenever else there is a lot of work to be done. Work Parties amount to a bunch of people getting together and working. Often, I keg or two of beer is available for workers. Work Parties can also be a good time to make up any down hours.

Pink Cloud
Fall 2013

Pink Cloud

Pink Cloud, birth name unknown, was Barrington's beloved acid dealer. Long stringy white hair and dressed in tie-died thermal underwear, Pink Cloud would creep along the side of Barrington, under the windows and in a loud whisper meow to signal he had product to sell: "Meow. Meow". Looking ancient in thc mid-1980s, Yet, at this writing, Pink Cloud can be found hanging out on a corner on Telegraph Avenue. Pink Cloud crashed in Barrington for years, no for decades!!

AD-COM ALLOWS PINK CLOUD INTO THE USCA. June 30, 1976. Case #10 Pink Cloud has lived in Barrington for 23 quarters without ever having being on contract. This summer, Barringotn wants to put Pink on contract so that he will have the same obligations and rights as any other member. VOTE ON MOTION PASSES 7-0-1

AD-COM SEES MORE OF PINK CLOUD September 28, 1977. Case #12. PC is a summer resident who owes the USCA $269 for summer contract. Would like to extend his indebtedness for approximately six months, by making $10/wk payments, due to financial hardship. Usual policy is to not to extend loans beyond the end of the contract

Nightly Snack

Four nights a week—school nights—snacks like freshly baked cookies or brownies were served at 10 p.m. It was the Snack Manager's responsibility to coordinate this feat.

The Switchboard

Barrington Hall had one phone number. A live person was expected to answered when calling between 9 a.m. and midnight until the mid-1980s. The Switchboard Operator put the call through to the room. If not answered, the Operator took a message and put it into a bin for Residents. Barringtonians could call out from a phone in their suite, via the switchboard when an Operator was on Shift Duty and could call other suites without Operator assistance.

Hallways

The long graffiti covered halls were a hang out where anyone might show up. During "Wine Dinners' mattresses were often dragged out into the halls to create a massive "slumber party" atmosphere.

The Co-op was a group-living situation—a blend of dorm and commune, where everyone chipped in on the work. Each resident had to perform 5 hours of work per week for their keep in the "house", such as cooking or cleaning duty. There were 18 separate houses in the USCA system. The co-op was half the price of the dorms.

The co-ops attracted the extremes and funkiest, so it was no surprise that a cooperative housing system in Berkeley was on the bizarre side—off the grid. The 18 USCA houses were themed. One was vegetarian, another encouraged African American culture, another was women-only—then there was Barrington. Although not specifically stated, its theme was drugs. Barringtonians were the hardest-core hippies at UC Berkeley.

PIG
FREE
ZONE

CITY OF BERKELEY
Memorandum

TO: KATHERINE KLEINE, Assistant City Manager

FROM: GLENN LYNCH, Chief of Environmental Health

SUBJECT: BARRINGTON HALL

The following is a detailed documentation of conditions at Barrington Hall commencing in February 1978:

2-20-78	Complaint by Bill Benthowsky, a Barrington resident, about filthy conditions in food service area.
2-24-78	Inspection confirmed many deficiencies in food service operation.
2-28-78	Reinspection found little improvement; kitchen area still dirty and poorly maintained.
3-1-78	Kitchen inspection still not satisfactory; maintenance and sanitation poor. (Prop 13 intervened in our ability to inspect)
6-4-80	Complaint from Carol J. Russell, 2501 Haste, 845-6370, reported filthy conditions in the kitchen at Barrington. They do not have any soap or detergent, milk not being refrigerated, garbage overflowing in kitchen, perish¬ables not being refrigerated, floors filthy.
11-18-80	Dr. Gay, Health Officer, contacted about a case of hepatitis A (non-aerum) in food handler.
11-20-80	Kitchen inspection - generally poor and dirty, a problem.
3-24-81	John Johnson, 644-1469, called expressing concern about Mike Gavin, a Barrington resident admitted to Herrick emergency with diagnosis of hepatitis B (serum).
4-3-81	Jan Cooper, 2344 Dwight, 548-4059, reported large accumulation of garbage on both sides of building.
6-23-81	Complaint from Helen Johnson, 2320 Haste #7, 481-5696; observation of rodents coming from Barrington.

SUBJECT: BARRINGTON HALL (cont'd.)

7-6-81 Trash and garbage accumulation around Barrington.

9-28-81 Anonymous call - garbage scattered around Barrington.

9-28-81 Anonymous complaint regarding Barrington—cockroaches, halls filthy. Kitchen floor covered with slop, paper scattered in hallways. Garbage scattered around outside of building.

1-11-82 Complaint from Jennifer Cherniss, 2491 Ellsworth, 841-8659. Garbage scattered all over outside of Barrington for last two weeks.

4-30-82 1) Anonymous complaint regarding garbage problem and "free box".

2) Complaint from Sandra Bessler, attorney for 2321 Dwight, complaining of garbage and "free box" at Barrington.

5-11-82 Complaint from Isaac Medich, 841-4539, regarding garbage problem at Barrington. Called also regarding same problem on 5-18, 5-24, 6-15 and 6-22.

8-17-82 Kitchen facility not in full use, found to be very poorly maintained.

9-9-82 1) Complaint from Sandra Bessler, 642-1828, regarding garbage problem at Barrington.

2) Complaint from Charles Spinosa regarding garbage problem at Barrington.

9-15-82 Recheck inspection - no change. Kitchen still very poorly maintained.

9-29-82 Complaint from Renee Quintana, 841-3277, regarding garbage, rats, roaches and a very unsanitary kitchen.

10-1-82 Complaint by Lee Faberman, 530-8322. Barrington unfit for living, bathrooms filthy, rooms filthy, kitchen filthy.

10-5-82 Citation issued to Eric SUllivan for filthy conditions, garbage and trash accumulation.

10-19-82	Kitchen filthy; advised that if not cleaned, permit could be suspended.
SUBJECT:	BARRINGTON HALL (cont'd.)
11-4-82	Reinspection - no change noted.
11-11-82	Kitchen cleaned up.
2-3-83	Hepatitis A (non-serum) at Barrington. Patient Joseph Kanala - several other cases reported - no detail. Barrington identified as Drug Kingdom #1, and Cloyne Court as Drug Kingdom #2.
3-25-83	Complaint from Charles Spinosa regarding garbage.
8-4-83	Noise problem from generator during construction.
1-9-84	Complaint from Charles Spinosa regarding garbage.
1-23-84	Complaint from Charles Spinosa regarding garbage.
1-31-84, 2-7-84, 3-2-84, 3-7-84	Kitchen condition found to be very poor, extremely dirty, etc.
4-6-84	Kitchen still in very poor condition.
4-14-84	Complaint from Jennifer Cherniss, 2491 Ellsworth, regarding garbage problem at Barrington.
4-19-84	Administration hearing with George Proper regarding conditions of food service facility. Permit suspen¬ded, but allowed to operate for two weeks pending complete cleaning and repair.
5-18-84	Reinspection of kitchen at Barrington. In reasonably good condition.
8-31-84	Complaint from-Mary Kennedy, 2491 -Ellsworth #30, 548-2950 regarding garbage.
9-4-84	Accumulation of garbage. Auto blocking driveway and dumpsters cannot be emptied.
10-1-84	Anonymous complaint regarding roaches in kitchen and bedrooms. Flies, fleas, stray cats and mice in kitchen. Refrigeration not adequate.
1-23-85	Complaint from Beverly Potter regarding broken sanitary sewer, at Barrington. Complaint from

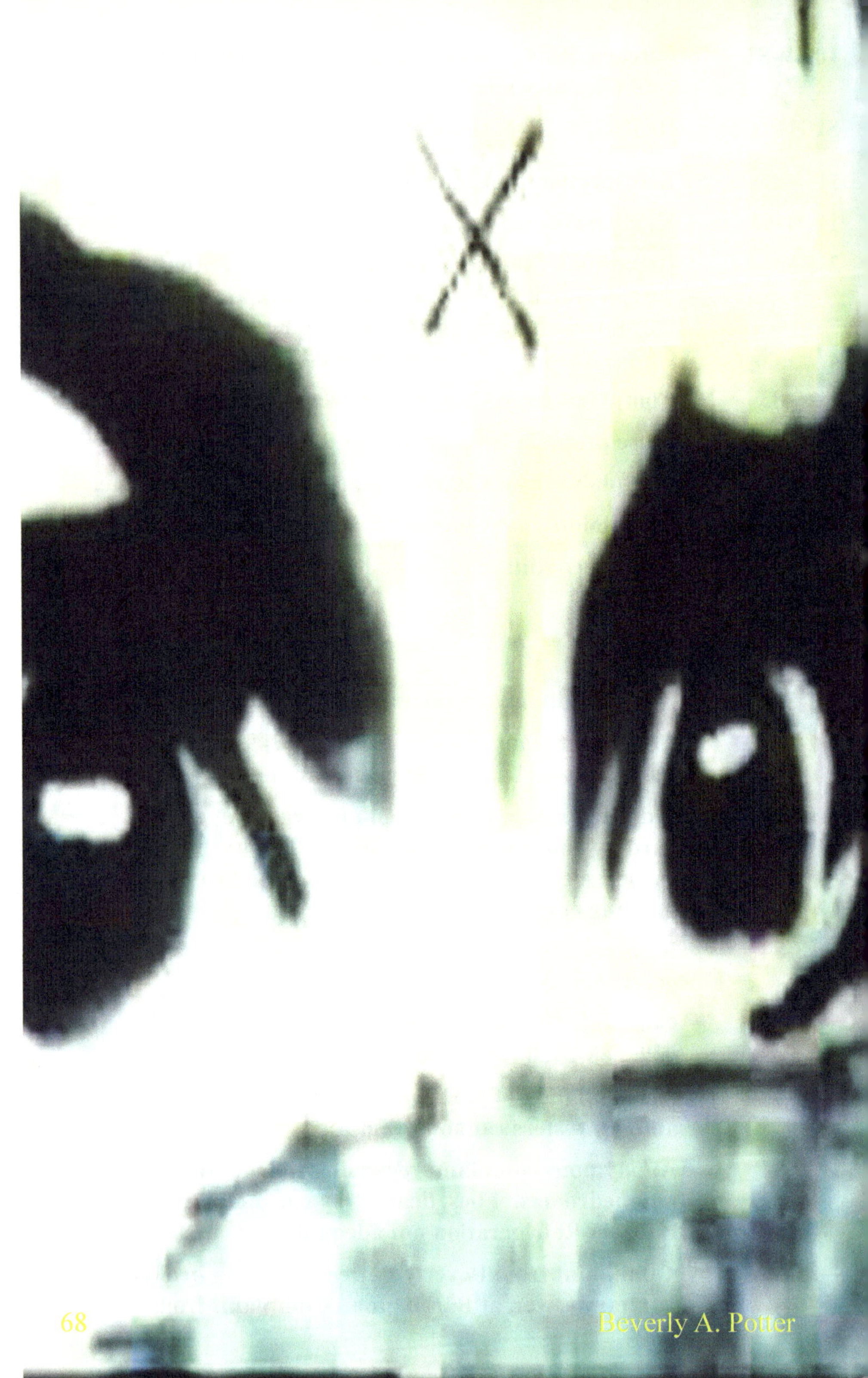

	Sebastian Orfali, 2310 Haste, regarding overflowing sanitary server. Ms. Huston of Barrington said that sewer, had been cleaned but overflow not cleaned up.
SUBJECT:	BARRINGTON HALL (cont'd.)
	1) Complaint from Tom Brienes, 2491 Ellsworth #30, 231-9470 regarding accumulation of garbage in parking lot.
	2) Complaint from Mary Kennedy regarding rats and garbage in parking lot.
3-28-85	Complaint from Jennifer Cherniss, 2491 Ellsworth #52, 841-8659, large accumulation of garbage being scattered by animals.
6-7-85	Referral from Ron Littley, Fire Department regarding large accumulation of garbage. Issued citation H-600252. Also noted unsanitary conditions throughout the interior. It was reported that there was improper disposal of human and.animal feces, with smell of urine in hallways. No human or animal feces found. There was a bad odor in the entire building .
9-3-85	Letter of complaint from J.S. Felton, M.D. regarding filthy conditions at Barrington.
10-2-85	Anonymous complaint from concerned parent regarding filthy conditions at Barrington.
4.0-25-85	Anonymous complaint about filthy condition in kitchen at Barrington.
10-30-85	Health and Safety Inspection requested by City Manager.

The remainder of the history to date you are familiar with. Let me know if there is anything further I can do.

The Rabbit HOle

We Are Not Circus Animals

Barrington's history includes complaints by tenants of rats, drugs, broken windows, garbage and the Co-op's "own unique smell—a bad nursing homes smell," according to Co-op Association reports.

"The place has always been a place that people's parents were never really excited about," said Ed Wells, 31, lived Barrington from 1972 to 1975 and is now a legal aid lawyer in San Francisco, "But there was never any harrowing years that I was aware of."

Barrington Pres. James Dashe acknowledged the Co-op is a mess. "By virtue of the fact that we live here, it's OK for us," said Dashe, a music composition major. "The bottom line is we're students, and cleanliness is not necessarily next to godliness."

He said residents are fighting to preserve an environment that is "a fascinating place to live, rather than just a place to live." "We're not a circus animal," Dashe said, "not something for the entire world to look at it all and wonder, "How can we live like this?" We are something to understand. We are not animals."

Barringtonians did not take authority seriously.

6 Minute Burn Time

When the fire department inspected the building and declared that, structurally, it bordered on being a fire hazard and could burn to the ground in six minutes, the residents of the building ordered thousands of matchbooks printed with the phrase "6 Minute Burn Time".

Elsmere Apartments
2321 Dwight Way, Apt. 30
Berkeley, California 94704
October 31, 1983

Mr. John Denton
Berkeley City Council Member
2130 Milvia
Berkeley, California 94704

Dear Mr. Denton:

I have called your office recently to inform you of the long and severe noise problem we have been having with our neighbors and to ask you for your assistance in this matter. I want to thank you for whatever efforts you have already made in our behalf and ask you for even more assistance, since our neighbor Barrington Hall still makes so much noise that we may not count on using our apartments to sleep, study, or even watch television at a normal volume.

Last Saturday night, October 29, 1983, serves as a good example of the noisy behavior we suffer from. At approximately 8:30 p.m., the members of the Barrington Hall student cooperative started drumming on the tables in their large ground floor dining hall. The noise was so loud that I could clearly hear it more than a block away. By 9:00 p.m., at least four tenants in my building had called the police department to complain. And by 9:30, this noise stopped, because the residents at Barrington Hall started helping a live band set up for the party they were going to have that evening.

The band began to play at around 10:00 p.m., and it was loud enough to make conversation difficult in apartments on the west side of my building. More tenants called the police, and around 11:00 p.m., a police sergeant arrived (badge number 21) unfortunately while the band was on break. But even during the break, Barrington Hall had a stereo playing which I could hear in my apartment on the northeast side of the building (on the opposite side from Barrington Hall). The Sergeant said that this stereo music was acceptable for this part of town. And I told him that the other residents and I had called because a live band was performing at Barrington Hall. I also added that even that stereo music would probably make sleeping difficult for those people in my building who live closest to Barrington Hall.

Page 2

The Sergeant said that he would talk to the Barrington Hall students about their noise level and left.

About 20 minutes later, the live band started playing again. And again, the police were called. But the sound level was not reduced markedly until 1;30 a.m. Today, residents of my building who live on the Barrington Hall side have been telling me that the noise continued on keeping them awake until after 3:00 a.m.

I believe that residents in my building should not have to suffcr any longer because of Barrington Hall's noise. It has been over a year now since we began writing and petitioning City and County officials. And we are not the only neighbors of Barrington Hall who have been trying to get the City to do something to quiet Barrington Hall down. (Please see the enclosed copies of petitions.)

We would like to be able to count on living in peace and quiet in our own apartments, and I would like to know what Berkeley will do to help us reach that goal.

I look forward to receiving hopeful news from you, which I could pass on to the residents of this building. I am giving copies of this letter to those residents who have informed me that they called the police last Saturday night to get Barrington Hall quieted.

Sincerely,

Charles Spinosa
Resident Manager

enclosures

cc: Nancy Gordon
Chris Grandy
Robert Moore
Robert Powell
Mary Volkmann

Elsmere

Arbitration

At the end of 1983, neighbors in Elsmere filed a complaint with the City of Berkeley, accusing Barrington of being a public nuisance. Elsmere residents complained that filth, unruliness, drug activity and noise tormented them. The exterior of Barrington was covered with graffiti. “Terrorist” and “This is Barrington, get used to it.” was spray painted in large letters. In the middle of Haste Street “LSD” was painted in twenty-foot tall yellow letters, as an in-your-face statement about the rampant drug use inside.

The dumpsters were over-filled and over-flowed all around, attracting rats. Blasting stereo in the downstairs kitchen the windows of Elsmere west side was reported at all hours of the day, and especially late at night. Neighbors had had it with the huge unruly parties, several every month that lasted often all night and into the wee hours of the morning. Neighbors saw Barrington as a den of wild drug activity, attracting homeless and criminals. One neighbor dubbed Barrington “a noisy, unsafe, unsanitary, rat trap”. Police were constantly at the Hall and City officials had stacks of complaints in their files.

We moved into 2310 in March of 1983 shortly before the Elsmere Apartments filed suit with the City of Berkeley's district attorney in an attempt to shut Barrington down. Suddenly Barrintonians were on their "good behavior", so Seb and I wondered what the big brouhaha about Barrington was all about. They didn't seem so bad as neighbors. We didn't come under siege until Hell Summer of 85. In response to the suit, the City set up an Arbitration Committee in January 1984. The Joint Tenants' Council was made up of three Barringtonians, three Elsmere residents, George Proper, USCA's General Manager, and the U.S.C.A student president. The Council arrived at a set of guidelines after several meetings for how Barrington and the Elsmere Apartments would interact.

Barrington agreed to follow several agreed upon rules. There could be no more than one party a month, which was to shut down at 2 A.M. or earlier. Parties had to be kept completely indoors. The radio that blasted music from Barrington's kitchen had to be kept at least 30 feet from closed windows. The Barrington managers were required to carry a pager so that Elsmere residents could contact them when there was a pressing issue. Barringtonians agreed to the terms of the Arbitration and based upon that promise Elsmere dropped the suit and agreed to be more tolerant of the Barrington lifestyle. A five-member Barrington Action Group was established to enforcement of the Arbitration Agreement.

Pretty quickly Barringtonians, especially the incoming ones, disregarded their promises and ignored the Agreement and their promises from the day it was signed. Barringtonians continued to act in an unruly fashion and neighbors continued to complain.

AMERICAN ARBITRATION ASSOCIATION

In the Arbitration Matter of	)	
	)	Case # 874-44-0018-83
ELSMERE APARTMENTS	)	
Claimants	)	<u>AWARD OF ARBITRATION</u>
		)
and	)	(AMENDED)
	)	
BARRINGTON HALL	)	June 29, 1984
Respondents		)
	)	

<u>AWARD</u>

<u>Joint Tenants Council</u>

BARRINGTON HALL and ELSMERE APARTMENTS will form a Joint Tenants Council (hereafter referred to as JTC) for the purpose of continuing a dialog between the parties, to be an avenue for settlement of all outstanding issues and issues which may arise during its lifetime. The JTC is a permanent committee. The JTC will meet at least four (4) times per year; dates and times to be determined by the parties. The JTC will also meet whenever either party has a need for communication with the other, or for negotiations and settlement of legitimate complaints.

The main points of the Agreement:

- Barrington must limit the number of parties;
- Parties cannot be advertised outside the house (in-house parties only);
- Elsmere must show tolerance during a party;
- Barringtonians must play stereos at no more than a reasonable volume;
- Various rules regarding must be followed in the kitchen;
- Barringtonians cannot park in the driveway between Elsmere and Barrington;
- Barrington members must keep the area around the Hall trash-free (esp. the Elsmere driveway);
- Barrington Action Committee is responsible for enforcement of the Aware;
- Barrington will install a permanent beeper system to receive complaints from ELSMERE;
- Parties agree that violence and vandalism are unacceptable behavior.

This Award is as binding as a Court Judgment on Barrington and Elsmere, and if it is broken, either side has the right to go back to the DA for enforcement of the Agreement. Hopefully the Joint Tenants Council and the Barrington Action Committee with prevent a necessity for DA enforcement.

Tanya Batte-Thomas
Arbitrator
Walter Merlino
Arbitrator

Supermarket of Dope

I had a friend from the debate team, Ben Brainerd, who worked in a bank. He was always studying the stock market & shit, and had several hundred in a savings account, so I said to him, "Look, you've got your money in a savings account at what, 5 percent or something? I could make you 25 percent a year."

"Doing what?" he asked. "Selling drugs." I smiled back. Ben didn't smoke pot, so he was reticent at first, but the allure of real capitalism tied to my solid business plan won him over. Basically, he trusted me. He knew I was smart, had things figured out, and could keep my mouth shut. So around Thanksgiving I borrowed 300 bucks in cash. My parents let me take my vacation down to Berkeley, which they recognized for the educational Mecca that it was, (although they may have just wanted to get rid of me), and I met Dave at Barrington.

Dave brought me up to see his friend Stymie, whose room was entirely painted like the cover of Dark Side of the Moon. I had met him before, but not under these circumstances. He was definitely leery of selling dope to a high school kid, and I could respect that. But I was Dave's kid brother, and had been partying there for years without getting busted or doing anything stupid, soooo I was allowed to shop at Barrington, the supermarket of dope. This was just about the time that Humboldt County put itself on the map, and there was orange bud and red bud and gold bud and the occasional purple bud all for the taking. Stymie had everything.

So I bought a couple ounces of this beautiful pot, which was only $140 an ounce, and proceeded to get high! I went down to the Avenue and bought myself a funky little postal scale, the kind you clip your bag to and hang, got some baggies, and when I took the bus back home I was a businessman.

Of course, my weekend was not without its introductory lesson in dope dealing ethics. You see, the folks at Barrington had a pretty well developed science of dope dealing. Pink Cloud, the ancient hippie, who I had bought my first lid from when I was in eighth grade, made sure that everyone knew the score.

"Keep it cool! Simple as that. Don't sell drugs to people you don't know! Don't buy drugs from people you don't know! Don't hang out places looking to sell dope. Don't sell dope to people who ask you on the street. Just sell dope to your friends and things will take care of themselves."

Hanging Out with My Big Brother

I took BART out to Berkeley, and got out at the bubble, that landmark of urban architecture. I remember all the vendor carts parked there, selling smoothies or coffee & donuts, back before Odwalla and Starbucks were even a dream. Dave met me there, and we walked back to the co-op where he lived, the infamous Barrington Hall!

It was an amazing place, a playground for big kids. All the hallways were painted in murals. So were most of the rooms. Dave took me up to the top floor, the 3rd floor, where we went to his friend's room. He put "Mars Hotel" on the stereo, and got out some Thai weed. He had this poster on his wall of a corner in Ann Arbor, Michigan, where these two streets cross, Nixon and Bluett. They fired up a pipe, passed it to me, and I nervously took my first of a lifetime's worth of hits. I don't think it quite affected me the way I was expecting though. I still felt pretty clear. I wasn't tasting the music or seeing trails, but I had the most curious sensation going back downstairs, like I weighed 300 pounds, and it was kinda cool.

Dave and I talked about LSD too, and he promised to take some with me when I turned 21, but that was a long way off. I started making weekend jaunts to Barrington every month or so, smoking pot, and hanging out with Dave and his college buddies. What more could you ask for in seventh grade? I kept it together at home though. I realized I couldn't tell anybody what I was doing. My friends were still completely straight, and the cool kids who smoked dirt weed had me pegged for a narc, which was fine by me. The one decision I made about smoking weed was that if it ever affected my health, I'd quit.

Sheldon Norberg
Confessions of a Drug Dealer
Healing Houses

Bev as Junkie

My masters (MS) in Vocational Rehabilitation Counseling was a two year degree, with one day weekly internship the first year, and three day internship in the second year. We were paid a stipend. I always followed the money. I liked a meeting of the minds with clients, so working with the mentally challenged was out. I also didn't like physical deformity.

One time at State in the cafeteria the man sitting next to me was severely deformed, probably from an explosion. He held his sandwich in a hook and this face was massively scared, with freaky looking eyes. I could hardly sit there or eat. After graduating, I went to a job interview and when I walked in there was the same man sitting at the desk. I'm sure he read my shock and repulsion on my face and that it happened often. I'm sorry.

So I gravitated towards psychopaths and the criminal element, like drug addicts, men in the county jail, and criminal justice: cops, cons, jails. As graduate students we, I and my boyfriend Chris Cunningham, wanted to "experience" various modalities. Synanon was hip at that time. Synanon was for drug addicts, primarily heroin. They had "square games" wherein non-drug addicts were invited in for group process games. Unlike T-groups, which were 6-8 and supportive, square games were 15 screaming, attacking harpies. There were two rules: No drugs and no violence or threats of violence. Then they would start and we had to figure out WTF was going.

Looking at Chris with his mustash and small beard, one would start, *"What's that? Pussy Mouth!"* Then the harpies would scream, *"Pussy Mouth! Pussy Mouth!"* Looking at me, who was shy, *"What are you, a sponge?"* Then the harpies: *"Sponge! Sponge!" "So you are just a garbage can, letting everyone dump on you!!" "Garbage can! Garbage can!"*

I quickly figured out that they focused on reactions, then the pack would drill down. I managed to be a dope smoker and never let it out! Eventually, I got over shyness, learned how to deflect them, and could lead the pack myself. I gained a great skill—being able to withstand attack, with hardly a reaction, and still be able to "hear".

A Stanford colleague, Rick Bale, had a gig at the Menlo Park VA Mental Hospital Drug Wards. One ward had a very bad recidivism rate. I was drafted to go in as a heroin addict, live on the ward to diagnosis the problem.

I wasn't undercover. They all knew I was a psychologist and not a junkie. Still I had to show my "commitment" by going through intake, and attack. Then I stood on the chair and yelled for "help!" I had to live on the ward. At night there was no staff. Just about 30 male drug addicts and me!!! I had a private room about the size of a jail cell. I wore hospital blues, gave urines, got up at 6 am for jumping jacks, and was escorted everywhere—for two weeks. I do NOT like being locked up. After that I went to the ward every day. This is where I learned to swear like a drunken sailor, Old Salty, as Jeff Mishlove described me.

The first night, I was sleeping with my back to the door—I was so relaxed, yet alert. Someone creped into my room. Still asleep, speaking in a low growl-like slow voice—My Voice of Authority—*"WHAT are YOU doing coming into my room without knocking?!!"* as I rolled over to see one am inmates halfway across the room, frozen in shock. Then he dashed out. I was a machine, like the Terminator. Later a woman vet junkie was assigned to the ward. In her first night, an inmate sneaked in, put a pillow on her face and tried to rape her.

Hell Summer of '85

By the summer of 1985, things had devolved and deteriorated in Barirngton to a near crisis. Barrington was open at a reduced capacity of 40-50 residents for the summer. Each resident had an entire suite with a bathroom and several bedrooms—all for the price of one room. Illegally subletting the spare rooms to transient, drug dealers and other questionable characters became a fabulous source of cash flow.

By mid-summer, occupancy in Barrington had grown to around 125 people, with only about fifty being members of the Co-op and legal tenants. No one was accountable. Anarchy reigned. Barringtonians ran a muck—wild alcohol and drug consumption, blasting noise at all hours especially around 3 a.m. Heroin was back in vogue and found its way into Barrington. Few residents did their required workshifts. Crashers moved in and took advance of the lax atmosphere. The House was unkempt as trash, filth and sewage flow from every opening and off of the roof into our yard. There were thefts and other uncooperative happenings. Rumors circulated around Berkeley about sex slaves and selling drugs to kids.

The CO-Central Office took action to kick subletters but were handcuffed by the prohibition against infringing on members' privacy by entering their rooms without permission. Barrington was trashed by the end of summer. "Hell Summer" underscored Barringtonians' "do want you want" attitude because U.S.C.A. could not recover debts for the damage done by the illegal subletters.

A sensational *Oakland Tribune* story exposed Barrington's ugly underbelly, which sent shock waves South Side community. The insurance company was threatening and the City Council was barraged with complaints and demands to shut it down. The Central Office of the USCA adopted a "kids will be kids" defense, suggesting that college students be they in dorms, fraternities, sororities or apartments' experimented with drugs. It was part and parcel of the college experience, they said. Barrington was no different, they claimed. The U.S.C.A. insisted there was no heroin problem in Barrington and that they had the situation under control.

Under pressure from neighbors and the Central Level, Barrington outlawed heroin in the fall of 1985, but problems continued. Two non-Barringtonians had near-fatal overdoses in the Spring of 1986. Then a house manger not only finally acknowledged heroin was being used by many in Barrington, but that he, himself, was an addict and resigned.

Cool people were doing heroin. It was the 'in' thing.

In a Referendum, the Co-op members voted to sell the building but Barrintonians managed to override it. The House was closed for the summer of 1986 with only eight Barringtonians in residence, who had been hired by the CO to oversee the massive clean up. All walls not muralized received fresh paint, and narrow hallways made the "walk-through" singles accessible from the foyer.

Lucy in Hell with Heroin

Trust Fund Junkies

Lucy, a 20-year old freckled-faced college student from Indiana, became a heroin addict in Barrington Hall. "I didn't get strung out right away," she said. "It sneaked up on me over a few months. I kept my kit on the table next to my bed so I could shoot up in the night. When I woke up because I couldn't sleep the whole night without a 'fix.' I remember looking at the shadow against the wall of my hand holding the syringe. It was horrifying. Me, a junkie!"

"I worry that this thing is going to be on my back for the rest of my life," Lucy said. "Sometimes I feel there's something missing from my life," she went on, "but then I shoot up and everything is good, everything is better, and I'm complete. I stop worrying about my life and just lay there."

"A punker in a suite down the hall who was doing a lot of coke offered me some really good China White. He said it helped to smooth out the coke-ride," Lucy recounted. "It seemed innocent enough. I tried it and it was GREAT! A bunch of us were taking an English course about that time that included studying William S. Burroughs' book, *Naked Lunch* where he describes his life on heroin and seems to legitimize it. We romanced heroin. We romanced the beat authors. It was all sooo cool. No one realized that in just a few months we'd be really messed up."

"My friends were snorting it. We didn't think we'd be hurt. The horror stories sounded like huge exaggerations, like those we'd heard about smoking pot—you know, *Reefer Madness*. After I smoked pot, then snorted a little coke and nothing "happened" I just didn't believe the scare stories anymore."

"I started by just snorting it a few nights in a row. Then I snorted a little in the morning. Soon the time between snorting got shorter and shorter until I couldn't go for more than two hours without my fix—then another fix. Then one morning I woke up *craving* heroin!" Lucy recounted. "In the beginning it was only about $25-a-day to keep 'my habit' going but it quickly became a $300-a-day habit to feed. I am ashamed to say how I did that. I did sell my body to creeps I'd never met out there on the dirty streets of Oakland," Lucy whispered.

"Still I wasn't too worried," said Lucy. "I thought snorting it or smoking a little with pot would be okay. Junkies were those people who use needles," she continued. "Then that great China White heroin

dried up and I was forced to go to the streets to find 'smack' to feed my habit. That's when I began to feel like a lowlife," Lucy said.

"I'd be out there somewhere on a street corner in Oakland with some pusher I'd never met before. I would pay the creep, then step into an alley, and stick out my arm—wondered why am I doing this?" Lucy whispered. "Like I said, sometimes I'd let the creep fuck me to get a 'free' fix. So I became a prostitute—anything for a fix—*anything!"*

"I told myself I would quit—soon. I promised myself I'd quit after finals but I didn't quit—and I didn't make it to two finals and got in-completes. Before I'd been a honor student, then my grades went into the toilet. Still I continued to use heroin until Christmas, when I had to go home to mother.

People who wish to use heroin without becoming addicted do so by limiting their frequency of use. The rule of thumb is that a person should always refrain from use for twice as long as he used. For example, if used for 2 days in a row, you should follow up by not using for 4 days. Another rule of thumb of is that a person should never use more than 2 days in a row. As the hospital studies have shown, 3 days will result in a minor addiction. While such withdrawal is not difficult to get through, it is likely the addict will become more addicted given that the cure for his pains is one easy fix away–a fix that will make him feel better even as it is making the addiction worse.

–Francis Moraes, PhD
Opium

Finally I called. 'Mom,' I said, 'I'm sorry to tell you that I have a problem… I'm addicted to heroin. I'm a junkie,'" Lucy mother shrieked in disbelief! It wow this could have happened to me. I was an honor student. I studied. I had ambition. Now all I think about is my next fix. I don't know anyone from home who has ever used heroin. How did I fall so far to find myself in the Oakland ghetto at 4 a.m. trying to score? How could this happen *to me?* My life is ruined. They call me a "trust fund junkie". I sometimes think of ending it all—maybe I will, but not today." Lucy revealed.

Editorial

A Barrington house manager said last week that he himself had a heroin-use problem, according to city officials. USCA General Manager George Proper said that Barrington's heroin problem -- thought to have been brought under control -- was "more widespread than we thought."

Proper said the number of heroin users in Barrington has been estimated at between eight and 10....

USCA Maintenance Coordinator Neil Houston said last week that "there is a heroin culture in Barrington protected by a code of silence."

According to USCA officials and Barirngton residents, the credo of the hall is "Those who know don't tell and those who tell don't know."—*Daily Cal*, February 24, 1986

Hard-Core Drug Use Is Uncooperative

The co-ops allow - indeed encourage - young adults to take charge of themselves to live life as they see fit in an open-minded atmosphere. But some people cannot be left unsupervised — they abuse independence as they abuse themselves and others. Barrington Hall unfortunately holds numerous examples of such people.

We commend the USCA for its newly announced plans to crack down on illegal drug use at Barrington and to centralize management of the hall under Central Office. Right now, heroin seems to be the biggest concern. Seven alleged dealers have already been thrown out, and USCA officials estimate that some six to eight Barrington and another 20 or so visitors still use the mind and body destroying drugs.

Heroin dealers and users are being threatened with eviction if they refuse full-time drug treatment. And USCA officials say they will seek court orders to bar visitors from Barrington who sell, sue or intend to buy the drug there.

This is uncharacteristically tough talk form the people at Central Office. But their decision was based on convincing testimony -- that a former house manager who has left Barrington. We thank the person for caring enough about their house to risk the repercussions of revealing the extent of the problem.. . ..

Rodent Liberation

Editor:

No one is interested in closing Barrington Hall and even if we were, there is not the chance of a snowball in hell that we could. Closure of Barrington Hall as a public nuisance or public menace is much too time and energy consuming, expensive, politically negative, and generally bothersome for the city to undertake. Were it to happen it would be done under the so called "red light abatement" used to close whore houses, etc. The idea that George Proper, the General Manager of the USCA might close down a place that rakes in over $200,000 per semester is ludicrous.

Secondly, Barrington Hall is not being attacked for the politics of its membership, for their Mohawk hairstyles or their punk clothes or the music they listen to. Barrington Hall is in trouble because they have failed to even marginally adhere to what are the university accepted standards of community conduct, and because their misconduct and mismanagement of themselves has greatly dis-enhanced the lives of people who must live around them. In the light of these facts, Barrington's claim that it is being singled out for punishment by sinister right wing forces, that it has been

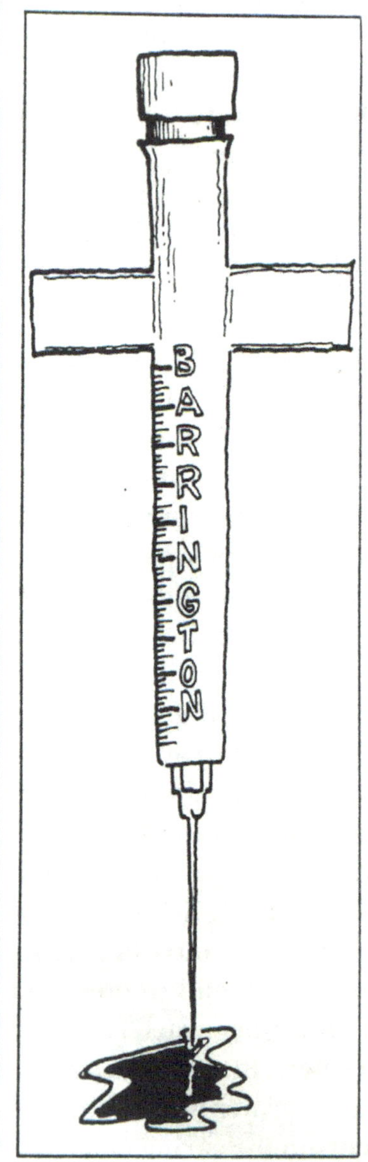

The Daily Californian December 10, 1985

placed under siege because it is a Bastion of New Left values, makes about as much objective sense as saying that Mickey Mouse is a symbol of rodent liberation.

Recently the fire department notified Barrington Hall that they will shut Barrington down if there is one more false alarm. There have been many false alarms. The health department closed down Barrington's kitchen because it was filthy, despite the fact that Barrington has two days notice that an inspection is coming. A letter in the official newsletter of the USCA recently recounted the story of a USCA student who suffered a very bad case of food poisoning as a result of such filth.

The insurance of Barrington was canceled and the Hibernia Bank refused to renegotiate Barrington's loan until Barrington cleans up its act. In the past three months there have been at least three 911 drug overdoses that came out of Barirngton Hall on stretchers. The most recent occurred Wednesday, Nov. 13, at 9:45 p.m.

Thus the idea peddled by Barrington Hall members and its sympathizers and defenders, that what is occurring is a result of the "attention seeking" or "monomaniacal" energy of one "irrational" person (me), or that it is a yuppie-inspired witch hunt, and that if they wore le tigre shirts and drank beer like fraternities, et. al. they wouldn't be under fire, can be seen for the ridiculousness that it is.

The fact that Barrington Hall has tolerated heroin makes all the arguments they are making in their defense specious and communally unethical. As far as their contention that complaints about noise and sanitation and violations of the various city codes have been "overblown and exaggerated" are concerned, I believe that this attitude, which allows them to tolerate heroin makes it patently clear that they are simply not able to make the basic wrong and right, black and white decisions about how to govern themselves. They must change because someday the ambulance will get there too late.

—John Harmon
Community Residents
Against Barrington (CRAB)

Slimy Decadence

Editor:

How would you feel if you were spit upon in your backyard? If you were nearly missed being hit on the head with a bottle while gardening? If you had to spend $2,000 on a security system on your home so you didn't have to worry about being robbed or mugged by a junky in the night or when you stepped out for a minute? If you had three inches of human wastes in a puddle under your kitchen window? Well, that's what life is like when you live next to Barrington Hall!

I live next to Barrington Hall and my freedom and civil rights are diminished by a "de-individualizationed" mentality. It is the process of de-individualization that allows the KKK and soldiers at war and mobs to act without conscience.

I am accountable to my actions. You are accountable for your actions. But the residents of Barrington Hall are not accountable by virtue of de-individualization. Why are the heroin pushers and the chaos makers of Barrington exempt?

I say NO! Barrington should be accountable, just like the rest of us. Barrington has demonstrated (along with the USCA) that it can NOT manage itself. It's time for external management and accountability. Or, maybe, it's time to close Barrington down.

I pay my taxes. Why do my taxes (and I pay, pay, pay) go to paying for the fire inspections, the police calls, the health inspections, etc. etc? Meanwhile, Barrington is rent control exempt, low tax paying, multi million dollar machine.

I say shape up or get out NOW.

—Beverly Potter
Homeowner

Barrington House Charter

No guns. No cocaine dealing. Never call the police.

Damaging a murals is a $75 fine.

It is the duty of new members, once they become old members to teach the new members.

—*Dimitria Psyche*

San Francisco Examiner

Drug Woes May Close UC Co-op

April 22, 1986

by Candy J. Cooper
of the Examiner Staff

BERKELEY–The credo of Onngh Yanngh is spray-painted across the walls of Barrington Hall, tie-dyed on the T-shirts and tattooed on the hands of some residents: "Those who know don't tell, and those who tell don't know."

The code of silence, some outsiders say, protects the 161 occupants of the largest student co-op in the country from its latest, most lethal problem—heroin.

The code has obscured the overdose death of a 25-year-old man in the co-op in December, to heroin overdoses reported in the last 2 months, and the emergence of "trust fund junkies"—upper-middle-class students hooked on heroin.

The silence has covered thefts inside the building at 2315 Dwight Way, South of the UC-Berkeley campus, and protected the teenage runaways and drug addict police say were harbored there for months last year.

But as the police file on Barrington thickened and a 22-year-old house manager admitted he and others used heroin, the credo of Onngh Yanngh—a concept borrowed from a Taoist poem—was broken.

The Board of Directors of the University Students Cooperative Association voted last month to close Barrington, an institution noted for its bohemian lifestyle and left-wing politics.

This week the 1400 members of the Association, which owns and operates 18 student cooperatives around the campus, will vote on whether to abide by the director's vote.

Some residents of Barrington, campaigning to keep the co-op open, say they are evicting drug pushers, and forcing users to seek professional help.

"I think if one would believe all the charges leveled against Barrington, then we assume we have both an "Animal House" and a "French Connection" on Dwight Way," George Proper, general manager of the Co-op Association, told the Berkeley City Council in December. "I'd like to assure you, we have neither."

Barrington's tenants want to save a unique environment that allows self-expression, absolute freedom and encourages normally ghettoized students—deadheads, punks, preppies and nerds—to mix.

"We all trade minds here," said Demetria, a 20-year-old art student who did not want to give her last name. "You get to appreciate other people's point points of view, and you're not, so stuck on your own. People come away are very changed people, who will take something with them in life that they could never get anywhere else."

But some students, neighbors and police believe self-expression has gone too far, that the reforms are insufficient and not followed.

A man who did not want to be identified because he was beaten by "thugs" for speaking out in the past. "When public sentiment starts cresting, they claim to get rid of all the dealers, they claim to bring the building up to code, and they claims they are going to sell it. These moves are effective in "quieting opposition."

Berkeley police Capt. Waymon Jenkins, a member of the city's Berkeley Task Force, a group of City officials, neighbors and Barrington students, agreed that public pressure would "slow down the drug activity. But can the pressure be maintained? That's the question."

Jenkins' file on Barrington notes 50 complaints of noise from neighbors over the 4 months last year; 5 searches resulting in 6 arrests and 2 citations from narcotics and incidences of assault and drug overdoses.

Police believe dealers working out of the co-op "supply a large percentage of the drugs sold in the South campus area," according to one memo.

The tax-exempt status of Barrington, which has no formal association with UC-Berkeley, requires only students can live in the three-story building, whose interior is layered with political art and graffiti. Room and board costs $1100 a semester, plus 5 ½ hours of communal maintenance or kitchen work a week.

Critics blame the hard drug problem on the free-spirited unaccountability of Barrington residents, the premium placed on personal freedom that allows the most bizarre behavior to go unchecked.

Neighbors have complained to the city Council that a washing machine, with the word start "anarchy" painted across the side, was tossed off the roof, narrowly miss-

ing a passer-by and several cars.

They describe sewage spawning onto adjacent yard, rotten hamburger thrown on a neighbor's car, and a nonresident living under solar panels on the co-op's move, sexually harassed neighbors for months.

"I live right next door to Barrington Hall," Beverly Potter, a management consultant who works her home, told the council. "It is an experience of constant hassle, of being spit upon, being almost run over on the sidewalk at my house, things thrown, garbage in my yard, and on and on and on."

Potter said accountability at the co-op is "like a marshmallow," blaming inaccessible managers who she contends fail to respond to neighborhood gripes.

Kathryn Kleine, assistant city

manager and chairwoman of the Barrington Hall Task Force, said the Co-op suffers from its own arrogance.

"I think we're dealing with an set of philosophies and a counter-culture that has a kind of egotistical view of itself, which is not believed itself responsible to the larger community."

Heroin use became fashionable in the hall about 15 months ago, Kleine said, with a big increase 6 months ago.

"Curiosity probably started it, transcending limits," one Barrington resident said. "It was something bad you shouldn't do, and became really cool to do it."

Joe McGowan, 22, Barrington House Manager, said "I think there was a certain mystique in heroin use, of being a secret heroin addict."

Those who began to use the drug seemed the most unlikely—affluent kids who became known as "trust fund junkies," McGowan said.

"They're upper-middle-class, to say the least," he said. "A lot of them have trust funds... One of the ways they really get involved in the drug is that they have rich parents."

After heroin got into the building residents were stealing from friends to support $300-a-day habits.

The previous house manager, who confessed to heroin use, told co-op officials in January that 20 or more outsiders frequented Barrington to buy or use heroin.

"We see the heroin thing," he told Barrington critics and neighbor John Harmon in a January 11 taped interview, "when it's bringing guns into the building, when it's causing people to steal within the house, when it basically violates other people's peace, then the major managers this term have made a commitment absolutely follow it to the end."

McGowan said that when he moved into the co-op in the spring of 1985, three kitchen managers and the house managers were using heroin.

A group of Berkeley parents of runaway teens have addressed the co-op association's directors and the City's Task Force about their children, who they say were harbored inside Barrington.

"I think I could say safely that a new 25 to 30 kids spent time at Barrington," said one Berkeley mother whose 15-year-old daughter had lived inside Barrington for several months last year.

The mother, who asked not to be identified, told co-op directors in October that her daughter was given amphetamines, LSD, marijuana, PCP and heroin, "which was injected into her leg…"

"She became strung out on drugs, out-of-control, she assaulted people, she became violent and she was used sexually at Barrington," the mother said.

But McGowan said the mystique of heroin has worn off and its former users now believe that "heroin… turns people into monsters."

The future, McGowan hopes, will not hold nights like last Dec. 11 when Edmund Zablockas, a 34-year-old non-resident, died in his third-floor room from an over-dose of alcohol and tranquilizers.

The tragedy was nearly repeated last month when 21-year-old student John Juarez has almost died in room 307 of a heroin overdose, according to police.

When police arrived, they found the syringe, cooking spoons, cotton balls and heroin on his desktop. Juarez, who had the word "devil" tattooed on the left side of his head, was a guest at the hall.

Ten days later, 26-year-old Ronald Webster of Oakland, another co-op guest, also overdosed on heroin at the hall police said. He also survived.

McGowan said it reflects the "lingering problem of old-timers. We have absolutely no dealing going on in the house."

Others disagreed.

"The information we have is that there still certainly is a heroin problem and a drug problem at Barrington," said Kleine, the Assistant City Manager

Barrington residents said they are on a crusade to keep the hall open and hope the days of heroin use become just another episode in the co-op's colorful history.

During the 1960s according to the student run Daily Californian newspaper. Students for a Democratic Society, the then flagship of the radical political left, met at Barrington, which also served as a "safe house" for draft dodgers traveling to Canada.

More recently, Barrington declared itself a sanctuary for refugees in Central America. During last Spring's apartheid both test that resulted in a lengthy campus sit-in, Barrington residents provided demonstrators with drugs. This spring, as protests and arrests began a new, co-op residents are again among the organizers. "When there is one arrest, someone comes running over to Barrington, like Paul Revere, yelling "the UC cops are coming," said Demetria, the art student. "They pull the fire alarm and everyone goes."

"The place has always been a place that people's parents were never really excited about," said Ed Wells, 31, lived Barrington from 1972 to 1975 and is now a legal aid lawyer in San Francisco, "But there was never any harrowing years that I was aware of."

International Solidarity

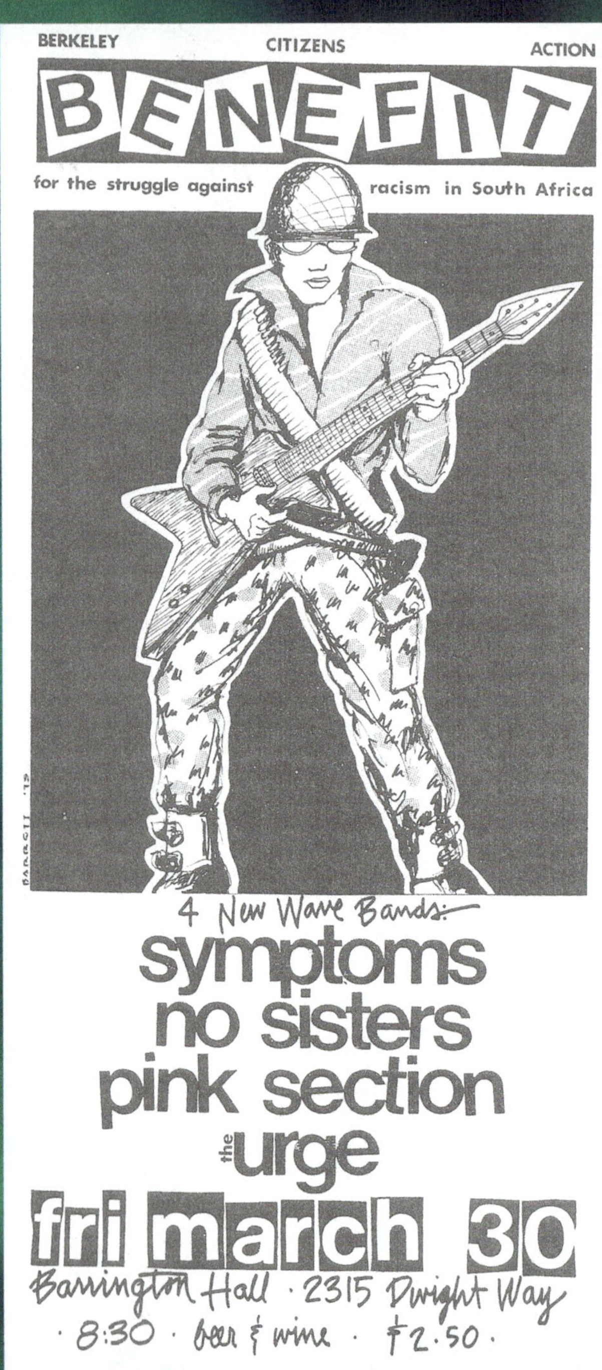

Berkeley Citizens Action Benefit for the struggle against racism in South Africa with Symptoms, No Sisters, Pink Section, and The Urge at Barrington Hall in Berkeley, CA, 1979, by Barrett

Teenage Refuge in Barrington

Not too surprisingly, teen runaways and rebels found their way into Barrington, which is the last place their parents wanted to find them. A pro-family community group known as PACT, "Parents and Children Together" made a presentation to the Co-op Board to voice their grievances with Barrington. They told stories about teenagers who ran away from home to get refuge in Barrington where they were introduced to sex and drugs. One mother claimed that her daughter had become a prostitute because of Barrington.

PACT asserted that Barrington should not be allowed to operate within the community. They wanted immediate action by the Board to deal with the problems at Barrington. Barrington manager denied runaways were "currently" given refuge, but could not account for the past. Given what went on during Hell Summer of '85, the accusations were very believable. Barrington did not deny that teens had stayed in Barrington and used drugs while there.

Under pressure from PACT, *The Oakland Tribune* and George Proper, the Board voted to create yet another Barrington Action Committee to assess Barrington's problems and its future.

Here we go again.

Cool people were doing heroin. It was the 'in' thing. Rumors circulated around Berkeley about sex slaves and selling drugs to kids.

Special Report

To: Glenn Lynch, Dir Environmental Health
From: Lt. Michale A. DeLatour
Date: May 2, 1986

I have been involved in narcotics and vice investigations for over six years. Barrington Hall has always been one location which was know to police officers for drug activity. I have personally participated in various search warrants and I have dialogued at length with various hall monitors and managers of Barrington.

The philosophical view of many of the students in the building is that narcotics is a personal issue and okay and not something that government should be involved in regulating. While this may be an interesting academic point to argue, the reality is this type of view facilitates a permissive open environment where drugs are consumed and where drugs are openly consumed, they must be openly sold.

As a result of this permissive view regarding drugs, a certain type of student and street person has been attracted to Barrington Hall which has created an environment which allows dealers to sell drugs either directly by themselves or through a particular sympathetic student.

There is an attitude of covering for both the drug dealers as well as for individual students who are consuming narcotics. During the service of all search warrants, the various managers and Hall monitors presented an image of hostility towards our actions and what we were doing. Instead of being concerned with the drugs and what it was doing to the fabric of the neighborhood, as well as Barrington, they were more concerned about our intrusions into their private little world and what that intrusion would do to their belief that they had a right to act in a totally free way even through it was irresponsible and counterproductive to the health of the community.

The internal and moral deterioration which occurred as a result of all of this drug consumption was dramatized by the condition of the building which was strewn with litter, debris along the west side of the building from day to day.

It will probably not be possible to stop the drug problems that occur in Barrington. I am sure you are all aware of the manager who was supposedly trying to solve the drug problem but while he was involved in this attempt, he was hooked on heroin.

A few weeks ago, one of our undercover officers entered Barrington with the intent of attempting contact with drug dealers to try to buy some drugs. This operative residents. The individual asked the operative if he knew what was going on, and the operative said that he did not. This resident then told the operative that they were presently having a big meeting regarding the drug problem and that "now would not be a good time to try to make contact with someone". This resident then told the operative to "come back later".

We received information from an informant that a specific individual who was living in the Barrington is using a variety of drugs, including LSD, cocaine, and speed. Whenever someone uses drugs, it is naive to believe that they are simply just using drugs. Generally they are selling a variety of drugs to support their particular habit.

While I welcome attempts by the cooperative to try and control the problem at Barrington, it is only gloss on the surface of a serious problem, which goes very deep. Unless the student population is totally changed and/or their attitude changes which is not possible, Barrington will remain a location where drugs will probably be used and sold with the concomitant deleterious effects upon the neighborhood surrounding it.

THE DAILY CALIFORNIAN
Berkeley's Independent Daily; Established 1871
VOLUME BERKELEY, CALIFORNIA

'Cannabis Alchemy' 2/16/87

Anti-Barrington Activist Publishes Drug Guides

By Carolyn Jones
Staff Writer

One of the Barrington Hall neighbors suing the University Students' Cooperative Association for "permitting drug sales" at Barrington is the publisher of a series of books on growing marijuana.

Sebastian Orfali, who filed a $375,000 lawsuit against USCA last Thursday, is the Project Editor and only employee of And/Or Press, which publishes such books as "*Marijuana Potency*," "*Marijuana Grower's Guide*," and "*Marijuana Botany: The Propagation and Breeding of Distinctive Cannabis*."

Orfali's suit, which he filed last Thursday with another Barrington neighbor, Beverly Potter, charges USCA with "intentionally" distributing LSD-laced wine at a Sept. 25 "wine dinner" party at Barrington, and with permitting LSD, cocaine, heroin and other illegal drug sales at the coop.

"Isn't that the 'pot' calling the kettle black?"

—Commentator
KCBS Radio

Following the hospitalization of four people who allegedly took LSD at the "wine dinner," the City Council established the Barrington Task Force to investigate allegations of drug use at Barrington since the Sept. 25 party.

Orfali, who publishes out of his home at 2310 Haste St., next-door to the 170-member South Side Co-op, said yesterday that his occupation does not conflict with the nature of his lawsuit.

"The books we publish are not, in any way, encouraging the use of marijuana, or in any way involved in illegal activity," Orfali said.

And/Or Press offers a "Drug Education Books by Phone" 24-hour telephone number, through which a customer can purchase books such as "*Psychedelic Chemistry*," "*The Stash Book: How to Hide Your Valuables*," and "*Sinsemilla Technique: Sophisticated Methods Revealed*."

Orfali, who headed And/Or Press since he founded it over 15 years ago, said that through his line of work, he has become "very knowledgeable about drugs."

"That's one of the reasons I'm concerned about what's going on in Barrington,'" he said yesterday. "I've seen the harm that can be done." ' And/Or publishing, which Orfali said earned $1.5 million annually "in its heyday,"

Barrington foe publishes how to grow pot books

also offers video and audio cassettes, including *"Marijuana Moonshine Video," "Mary Jane's How To Video,"* and the cassette *"Marijuana Grower's Guide."*

Barrington President Susan Miles yesterday called Orfali's suit "hypocritical."

"He has a hell of a lot of nerve to attack us on something he condones," she said.

But Orfali's attorney, Don Driscoll, said that Orfali's occupation is irrelevant to the suit.

"There's a difference between publishing a book and disturbing your neighbor," Driscoll said yesterday. "I don't think this will affect the case at all."

And/Or Press, which Orfali founded in 1973, has published more than 70 books, including a variety of holistic health books as well as the extensive range of marijuana growing guides.

The *"Marijuana Grower's Guide,"* written by Mel Frank and Ed Rosenthal, is described by *The New York Times* as "extremely clear and interesting" and has sold more than 1 million copies since its release in 1978.

"Some of the books are controversial, but in a way, it's in the tradition of Berkeley's Free Speech Movement," Driscoll said.

Berkeley City Council member Shirley Dean, one of four council members serving on the Barrington Task Force, said she was "taken aback" at the news of Orfali's profession.

"I think it's very ironic," Dean laughed. "Sounds like he's done some extensive research."

Nevertheless* Dean predicted, Or-

Book published by neighbor.

fali's suit would "rise and fall on its own merits."

Council member Fred Weekes, who also serves on the task force, defended Orfali. Weekes is considered by many to be the most conservative member of the council.

"Publishing is a perfectly legitimate occupation, isn't it?" he said. "It's amusing, but I don't think it has any bearing on the case."

Barrington house manager Michelle Todus described Orfali's occupation as "pretty funny."

"I think most Barringtonians will get a kick out of it," Todus said.

USCA Board of Directors President Elaine McCormick refused to comment on Orfali or the lawsuit because the co-op association has not yet received the suit.

In addition to guides to marijuana cultivation, Orfali has published several books that discourage drug use, including *"Marijuana Alert"* and "*The Marijuana Question: Arguments Against Pot Use,*" and the "*Cocaine Consumer Handbook.*"

Always a Scene Downstairs

There was always a scene in the downstairs of Barrington. The politically inclined argued Marxist theory and played Diplomacy, English majors dissected books, everyone got high and engaged with or despised the various types who floated through. A variety of street people hung out there too. They had a history of hanging out there, doing drugs, and moving drugs for those who dealt with them. I didn't deal with any street dealers, so it wasn't my provenance to hang out with them in search of entertainment. But in an atmosphere that thrived on eclectic radicalism, I suppose that was one way to expand one's cultural consciousness.

Berkeley Bob, who lived in the alley outside the kitchen, had to be ejected a few times though, since he appeared to border on becoming violent to others. He had been shooting speed for years, so it came as no surprise, particularly when you heard him ranting. He would go on unbelievable tirades, screaming at his various personalities, who would scream right back. It was his ranting that birthed the phrase, "Nazi Spies crawled on my flesh." It was written on the ceiling, and immortalized in a tape recording someone made of his late-night self-interrogation. Listening to that was always good for a laugh, but as cocaine gave way to freebase, things began to get a little more rugged for everyone.

Reiner was pretty much the first person I saw lose it. He must have had some kind of trust fund to do as much coke as he did, although he dealt so much that he thought he needed to keep a bodyguard. That was a clear sign of his mounting paranoia, since it's no way to be discrete, and no one would have been any less likely to rip him off or do him violence in the presence of Darren, who was actually just a rather large street person. They were something of a comedic sight, and I was told that Darren was a pretty nice guy, despite his cultivated "crazy street-person" look.

The one person who found no humor in it, while adding to it immensely, was Margo, Darren's street-person wife. She would tow her children around Barrington while screaming "Darren and Pete are Fags! Darren and Pete are Fags!"

Reiner, however, was the first person I saw actually searching the entire downstairs for Nazi spies. Apparently they were multidimensional, because he not only looked under the tables, but on the undersides of the tables, before he opened his jacket and began searching his person for them. I was sitting in the hallway with Luigi one day after that, repeating to him the sage advice Art had given me. "You can do anything you want, but you can't Reiner out." Just then Reiner's door opened and Stymie came out, with Reiner thanking him. He had obviously dropped in to sell his old buddy some weed, since Reiner, being on the eight or ten year plan, had been in Barrington almost as long as I. I had to reassess, in that moment, and as much as it scared me, I told Luigi, "Maybe you can even Reiner out." —Sheldon Norberg

Gello Wrestling

I noticed a huge steel vat of red Jell-O® that everyone had forgotten to eat. It sat in the walk-in frig till my buddy Dartanian came up with the clever idea of gello wrestling. We stacked all the tables and chairs in a corner of the upstairs dining room. We covered the carpet with a clear plastic tarp and taped the edges to the sides of the walls. That evening, we tipped the vat upside down in the middle of the floor and lifted up the steel container. The tall round mound of gello plopped out.

A couple dozen Barringtonians gathered around the mound. We took off our shoes and stripped down to our underwear. The gello was cold so people were hesitant to touch it. Somebody put a Butthole Surfers tape on stereo; soon the music was booming through the loudspeakers. One guy tore off a handful of gello and threw it at somebody else. Soon we were slinging gobs of the stuff at each other. People took turns diving into the mount until it was reduced to a slime that spread out in every direction. The gello liquefied as it warmed.

Eventually, everybody writhed together on the floor. We were all slippery. Our bodies swam into each other while squiggling to the rhythm of the music. We hugged each other, slithering around like eels. One guy kept grabbing my penis, prompting me to swim in another direction through a mass of thrashing limbs and wrestling torsos. By the time the gello wrestling was over, the gello had oozed through rips in the tarp and was absorbed by the carpet, which ever afterward was stiff and smelly from the gelatin.

I climbed into a big steel sink in the kitchen and hosed myself off. Some of the other people, who were covered with red slime that resembled blood, went walking around Telegraph Avenue to provide some shock value for other pedestrians.

Reid Stuart
Triumph of the Green Man

Code of Silence

In February 1987, John Harmon, a Barrington neighbor accused the Central Level Management of the U.S.C.A., particularly General Manager George Proper, of negligence in dealing with drug problems at Barrington. He claimed that Proper knew the extent of the drug, especially heroin problems at Barrington but did nothing to curtail it. Proper's inaction, according to Harmon, had endangered the lives of the students of Barrington. Harmon cited the example of Bill Crooks, a drug dealer with AIDS who had hung around Barrington. Crooks indicated on a television news show that he shared needles with three or more Barringtonians.

Harmon fought Barrington for years, drawing other neighbors into his crusade. Harmon accused Barrington members and U.S.C.A. managers of endorcing "a code of silence" called *Onngh Yanngh* to cover up the drug activity at the house. The Onngh Yanngh symbol, a "Y" with an "O" in its crux, was used by Barringtonians to symbolize the spirit of Barrington. Onngh Yanngh motto was, *"Those who know don't tell. Those who tell, don't know."* Barringtonians, Proper, and others in the U.S.C.A. said Harmon's claim was ridiculous. Harmon, they said, was a man determined to shut Barrington down by any means, including making sensational accusations in the press.

John Harmon aka Red Green

Bombarded

April/8/87 11:30 pm Very loud music from Room 208 – very tired – so loud it can be heard in back – start to call Carlos – suddenly silent so I go back to bed. Noise starts again. Start to call – silent again. Go back to be. Noise starts again. Too tired to get up. Finally fall asleep.

April 9 In morning 8 beer bottles and a Wild Turkey bottle strewn across our front area – thrown from window of room 208. We kicked the bottles over to Barrington.

Called Carlos 3 times on beeper over morning. No response until noon. Explained concern about noise and bottle throwing. He said to call when they are in the act. Asked why don't they expel the boys from the Co-op. He said they are "tenants" and it's too hard to get them out in middle of their contract. Asked about summer and Carlos said he's leaving in 8 weeks. They could get their contracts renewed but if they get bad enf he'll recommend they don't get new contract. I expressed my concern about summer.

2:00 pm Working on porch and again extremely loud noise from Room 208. I hear sounds of breaking glass. See Weinhart box on front area and bottles.

n Noise escalated. More breaking glass I call Carlos. Then go out to front and ' bottles – beer and wild Turkey. One has ront steps and broken at bottom of step. nother is all the way into the driveway and broken. Sandy-haired boy and second boy come down fire escape and picked up bottles. They leave earlier bottles in Barrington area. I go around picking up glass.

3:00 pm From upper porch I hear guttural screaming. I keep thinking I hear my name – then I hear in the demonic guttural scream; "Beverly, you fucking bitch, I hate you." *I go to front and call up, "Come down here. Who's calling me?" The sandy-haired boy spits out the window but tried to not be seen.*

Short, brown-haired punk-looking boy leans out window and says he didn't hear anyone calling. I keep demanding that whoever was calling me come down. A red-head boy – punker – looks and says it's his room and no one called. I asked why he doesn't control the boys in his room. He says they are all over 18 and he doesn't tell them what to do. I go in the house.

12:15 am Very loud music in back from second floor. In lull between songs I call up that it's too loud. Boy says he'll take care of it. Then it's quiet.

4/10 2:00 am Loud music, screaming from boy's window – breaking glass noises.

4:15 p.m. Students cleaning up lots of broken glass on fire escape

5:15 pm 2 girls on fire escape. One looks sick and in anguish. She can't stand. Looks like she is on a bad drug trip.

Boy in window with girl He has a toy machine gun and is laughing and shooting water out over our yard. I worry if it's filled with acid or possibly if they have a real gun.

7:45 p.m. Very loud music from back yard form Barrington. Boy in front is screaming weird scream. Feeling very anxious. When we came back from our walk we found a number of items of clothing (shirts, pants, underwear) were strewn in the bushes under the weirdo's window. More bottles are accumulated. As I write this he is screaming a blood-curdling yell like Linda Blain in The Exorcist when possessed by the devil. It is pretty scary.

Feeling No Pain

This is from my first acid trip - purple gel - at a **Special Forces** show at Barrington on what was Prom Night for Berkeley High School in 1985. I was with Jason Lockwood, David Dancy, Johnny Puke, and a host of others. Johnny puke smashed a lightbulb with his head and this story is what I remember of it.

He stumbled into the room, scratching his blondness. He stopped in front of me and offered me his head. I investigated to see why it was bleeding and found small pieces of glass lodged in his scalp. I began to remove them carefully, trying not to cause him any pain. He jerked his head up and grinned at me, his eyes burning with the fire of intoxication.

I showed him the glass and childlike awe spread across his face. He reached a hand slowly to his head, looking like he was playing Simon Says. I giggled. He stared at the pieces he had pulled from his head. I tried to help him take the rest out, but he pushed my hand away, grinning.

He ambled away, seeming embarrassed at having somehow received a scalp full of glass chips. I watched as he staggered up to someone else and displayed his wounds. He laughed at the reaction of horror and wandered off, chuckling.

I giggled more. Someone walked by and looked at me. I began to laugh loudly and they hurried off, not wanting to be affected by my strangeness. He returned; his animated face floating before me, shining like an alcoholic moon.

He presented me with the rest of the pieces that he had extracted from his head. I solemnly accepted them and thanked him. The pieces shone as he did, catching and throwing light, still tacky with blood. I held them tightly until they disappeared into the flesh of my hand.

Circa 1986; April

Day-Glo Rat Goes to City Hall

I woke up at 3:00 am last night, feeling distressed about the weird kid in the room over our front door who has been harassing us by throwing bottles and soiled toilet paper onto our front yard. Since Carlos Cabana, the resident head, seems powerless to do anything without backing from the Central Office, the kid is escalating. I'm worried he will hurt Beverly or one of our pets, or burn our house - or something. We have been under siege, being pelted with dozens of beer and whiskey bottles and screaming, especially late at night. Two days ago Bev wrote in the log:

"3:00 p.m. I hear guttural screaming. I keep thinking I hear my name. Then I hear, in a demonic guttural scream; "Beverly, you fucking bitch, I hate you." I go to front and call up to the weirdo kid's room, "Come down here. Who's calling me?" The sandy -haired boy spits out the window while trying to not be seen."

As we were leaving to meet with the City, Beverly pointed to a brown paper bag on the ground with some weird paint on it. Inside we found a rat. It was curled up, with a bloody nose and a bizarre cut in its belly and some odd object protruding from under its ribs, as if it has been stabbed in the heart. A push pin was stuck on its tail. The poor creature must have been cruelly tortured and its blood drained. It was painted with day-glow paint.

There are stories about devil worshiping cults in Barrington, so I wondered if the rat were the victim of a ritual cult. Will our cats and dog be safe, I worried.

We took the rat to the meeting at City Hall with Council members Shirley Dean and Mary Wainwright. Beverly got it out over their protests, waved it about, and passed the rat around. They were all grossed out, as they quickly passed it on.

When we got home from the meeting we found clothing (shirts, pants, underwear) strewn in our bushes under the weirdo's window - and yet more bottles. The loony kid was screaming in a bloodcurdling yell, like Linda Blain in "The Exorcist" when she was possessed by the devil. It was pretty scary. Incident Log: April 11, 1987: (SEB)

April 11
On our way out the driveway for the after noon walk we noticed two girls on the fire escape in front of B. One of the girls looked ashen (white) and extremely distraught. Her face contorted with nausea as if she were vomiting. The other girl was comforting her. An older looking student came out, talked to them and then left hurriedly.

Then a brownhaired coed wearing a T-shirt began squirting water cannon in the shape of a machine gun out the window of the weirdo kid's room at passers by on the sidewalk. She looked at us and laughed when she noticed I was looking at her.

When we came back from our walk a number of items of clothing - shirts, pants, under wear - were strewn in the bushes under the weirdo's window. More bottles are accumulating. As I write this he is screaming a blood curdling yell like Linda Blair in The Exorcist when possessed by the Devil. It is pretty scary.

April 12 12:25 pm Man and woman across street parked. They see broken glass all around their car. When man using cardboard scrape it up so he can get his car out. He cuts his finger.

1:25 pm Rite of Spring *playing at high volume from second-floor window over solar unit*

5:15 pm Upon coming home redhead boy in window with plastic machine gun. He saw me and said, "it's only water." I asked his name and told him I was going to file a complaint with the Student Conduct Counsel. He called me a bunch of names and said I was a fascist, etc. I challenged him to come down. He did and yelled at me, waving his finger in my face. I kept asking why he was throwing bottles in my yard. He spoke of frustration and freedom, meanwhile a 2nd boy squirted me with water from the window. I kept asking him his name and telling him I was filing a complaint. He said he wasn't a student and had quit 3 weeks ago. His name is Kyle. I couldn't get the last name. Other students watched and periodically joined in. Finally Kyle said he wouldn't throw his bottles in our area but only in Barrington area. The trash and clothes had been picked up.

April 13 10:20 AM
Man yelling from Room 208, "Feels like heroin to me" over and over. Man in parking lot across street yells, "You feel like heroin to me." Kyle walks up from Dana St and by chance looks up and says quote "Charlie! Charlie!" then turns to us and says he has headphones on. He is more polite after confrontation yesterday. Says he'll quit the yelling. I got the impression the yelling man was older black man. Suspect he's a dealer. Quiet shortly thereafter

April 13 1:30 PM
Martin who works Barrington kitchen walked by and asked if Kyle is bothering us I explained. He said he bothered a lot of people and they could do nothing. He said the manager could

throw him out in a short time but had no spine. He said Kyle is not a student and then is bringing a lot of non-student types in. He said he thought the USCA too large and has a problem in all houses.

5:29 PM Kids on fire escape shooting water the machine gun at pedestrians. One is guy who was at the task force meeting.

6:35 PM Sound of breaking glass in front of Barrington. Sounds like a window but can't see what broke. Kid still on fire escape with water gun yelling at people

April 13 We heard a loud noise and went out to see what happened. A red heater radiator had been thrown from the fire escape in front of Barrington and hit a green Chevrolet Caprice and made a dent in the left door. Two Chinese students walking by were alarmed and worried about being hit. While we talked to them a tube of toothpaste was thrown at us. It missed us by a foot or so. Then a cup was thrown, which hit me on the arm. Beverly called the police. (Seb)

Alphie

April 13. We are worried about our cat, Alfie. He always comes to wake us in the morning to bug us. Today he is missing Since we found the tortured and mutilated rat we are worried that the weirdos in Barrington have tortured and killed him

Berkeley Police Officer came and I told him what happened He went to Barrington and a girl named Delane (Room 109) let him in Still worried about Alfie I walked the perimeter of Barrington, calling him and looking in the dumpster. Robert A was talking to the officer in the Barrington parking lot Carlos Cabana was talking to an older couple, carrying a walkie-talkie They looked official An emaciated distraught person, who did not look like a student, was detained nearby Robert A asked us what we were dong in the alley behind Barrington We explained we were looking for our cat When we explained our concern vis a vis the mutilated rat, He said a student, who works in the vivarium, brings home lab rats to skin them He did not seem to think it was inappropriate to mutilate the rats and toss them out the window onto neighbors yard

April 14, 4:30 pm Sandy-haired boy throws paper out window. I tell him to stop. As soon as I walk away he makes snappy remarks.

Broken bottles, broken glass eer where— constantly

Neil Houston of USCA maintenance walks out. I stop him. He says there's to be a meeting at 11: am tomorrow about my letter. I tell him about the problems. He says he doesn't blame me for being annoyed. He says someone has been shooting him with water pistol.

April 14, 5 pm Run into Carlos at Krishna Copy. He is distressed because I didn't call him before letter and calling the police. I tell him I want to go to Student Conduct Committee and he gives me two troublemakers' names: Joel R and John R. in rm 208.

April 14, 11:15 pm (SEB) Blood curdling screams are coming out of Room 208. Very loud music

April 14, 4:20 pm Neil Houston of USCA maintenance walks out. I stop him. He says there's to be a meeting at 11:00 am tomorrow about my letter. I tell him about the problems. He says he doesn't blame me for being annoyed. He says someone has been shooting him with water pistol.

Looking down from Barirngton onto our deck.

Justa Toy Squirt Gun—Or is it?

April 15 9:30 pm Very loud music and screaming out of Room 208 window. Look out and John R is leaning out window screaming. We were leaving. I called to him and he hid at the side of the window. I called up that I was going to file a complaint with Student Conduct. Joel R was on fire escape, just standing there. I called to him and told him I was going to file a complaint. He said he was only shooting a water pistol.

Martin and other boy from kitchen come by and asked if they were still bothering us. I told him I was filing complaints. He apologized for the others.

April 15 not home all day BAP 9:30 PM very loud music and screaming out of Barrington window lookout John Rudolph leaning out the window screaming. We were leaving I called to him any hitter decided window I called up I was going to file complaint with the student conduct still Rane was on the fire escape just standing there I called him and told him I was going to file a complaint he said he was only shooting a water pistol. Martin and another boy from the kitchen came by and asked if they were still bothering us; him I was filing complaints and he apologized for the others

April 16 10:30 am Spoke to George Prober, who says John R and Kyle would be evicted. Said Barrington to be open for the summer for 40-60 kids. Other rooms to be locked. I express my extreme concert over having things thrown.

8:30 pm Very, very loud music.

9:45 pm Still loud when left for dinner. Tenant C Fong who rented room at 2308 Haste moved out. He said he was kept awake <u>every</u> night – two weeks – and was very unhappy.

Seb & Bev with First Amendment

Animal Control brought report on rat.

April 17 1 pm Very loud music with vocal. I was on phone discussing important possible contract. The loud music started and was very hard to concentrate or talk to client. Client could hear the racket and gave very poor impression of my work situation. Music stopped after about 30 minutes.

Magic Words:
File Complaint with Student Conduct

April 18 I go out and call up to the boy and girl. Boy is stomping and girl is dancing vigorously I call and ask, "What is your name?" "What is your name?" He laughs at me. I say, "Student Conduct Committee!" The boy and girl leave the fire escape. Shortly thereafter the boy comes out and tells Room 208 to be quiet.

April 18, 2:05 pm 2 or 3 bottles thrown on sidewalk.

12:20 am Several white boards are thrown from the roof with loud screams. Awaken 3 times between 2 am and 4 am by screaming from the roof.

April 18 11:50 pm (SEB)

More eerie screams from Barrington There have been extraordinarily loud noises, banging The fire alarm has gone off and extremely loud hoots and yelling and banging on the fire escape with a person stomping on the fire escape yelling 'I don't care if you want to sleep. I am going to scream." There is loud music coming from Room 208

April 18 BAP

I go out and call up to the boy and girl boy is stomping his speed and girl is dancing vigorously I call and ask, "What is your name?" "What is your name?" He laughs at me. I say, "Student conduct committee!" *The boy and girl leave the fire escape. Shortly thereafter the boy comes out and tells number 308 to be quiet.*

12:05 a.m.
2 or 3 bottles thrown on sidewalk been one big book one of your box wrote about music.

12:20 am several white boards are thrown from the world coming by loud screams

Awaken 3 times between 2 am and 4 am by screaming for very good

April 19 Call police to make report Re: glass and debris in front of Barrington

7:30 pm car parked on the sidewalk blocking all POD traffic

April 20 3:20 am: Very loud music from 2nd floor and back

April 21 11:55 pm Hear bottle broken in front. A bottle broken on street. When I go out to investigate I see boy come out on fire escape with empty Wild Turkey bottle. I call up, "Are you going to throw that bottle?" *A girl says,* "No, I won't let him." *I photoed the bottle in the street. Boy says,* "We're on your side. We hate this." *I tell them they*

can throw out the USCA. Awoken three times during night by loud screaming.

Bev Gives Good Head

April 22 11 am Coming home from breakfast at NCBPMA for a meeting with Nancy K who was waiting here to discuss projects, I see graffiti on building across from our door under the window of room 208 at Barrington. It says, "Beverly gives good head." *I wonder if Nancy has seen it. I feel tormented. It is no coincidence.*

2 pm After calling Carlos, the manager, and talking with John and Sebastian, I finally decide to call the police to file a complaint (87-23946). The officer says I can file and advise given complaint but because they didn't put my last name it could be anyone so they can't investigate.

April 22 (SEB) I'm extremely offended and insulted by seeing graffiti referring to Beverly scrawled on the wall of Barrington under the window of Room 208. I called Carlos Cabana, house manager. He promised to have it painted over within 24 hours. I can't meet people here at our house due to the embarrassing and offensive nature of the graffiti. Now that these misfit kids are targeting Beverly, I worry about what they will do - will they harm us physically as well as mentally as they are doing now.

April 23 Graffiti at Room 208 painted out and same graffiti with my name in it repainted in the front of the building.

April 24 early am
Kids in back paint
yellow 3 foot high
letters "LSD" in
street. Cars driving
through it splat-
tered paint period

208

April 24–25 early a.m. Get some bank in painting yellow 3-foot high letters "LSD" *in street. Cars driving through it splattered paint period*

Uneasy Feelings Of Apprehension

April 25 2 am Spree of throwing apples off fire escape onto cars and street across case. Also tomato and grapefruit thrown.

April 26 A very large wad of chewing gum was thrown onto the hood of my car very. Melted and stop making a mess. What a drag!

April 26 5:35 pm: Loud electric guitar playing in room over solar heater unit. Started off as somewhat pleasant but is becoming increas ingly annoying because kids can't play is just making noise while I have to listen to this on Saturday afternoon. I want peace

April 27 1:30 am
Very loud crashing noise in front in morning I see a very large -- about 2 1/2 foot tall -- metal ashtray broken and laying on the sidewalk where most of the stuff thrown from the 3rd floor forest lands

April 29 11:15 am: Talked at length with Mr. Axup of the Atty. Gen Office he was very sup portive about audit in involuntary dissolve it

6:30 pm: John Harmon shows up with report- er from The Tribune. We tell our story and give him papers

April 29 5:30 pm George Proper called, a big surprise. He said

USCA met with 2 boys in Room 208 and told them they are kicked out. He said that USCA doesn't want the kind of kids who throw bottles into neighbors yards. Very appropriate and very unusual posture for the USCA. How come the sudden change? How come for last weeks it been so quiet next-door and so clean? I don't think the kids spontaneously changed. USCA must realize that neighbors are up to something heavy and this shows they CAN act and they CAN control the kids if necessary.

It's very out of character for George Proper to respond at all, much else to "initiate" a call to a neighbor. I wonder about his motives. He said the boys were very angry and he was afraid they might try "doing something" to me and he hoped they focus their anger on USCA. Yet, he said not to hesitate to call the police and said he'd be out of town for the weekend. If anything happened to call Gary Spicer at 848-1936. Only he didn't mention that no one is there and there's only a tape at that phone.

It all sounded so filled with concern, which is such a dramatic contrast to all other contact. Makes me very suspi-

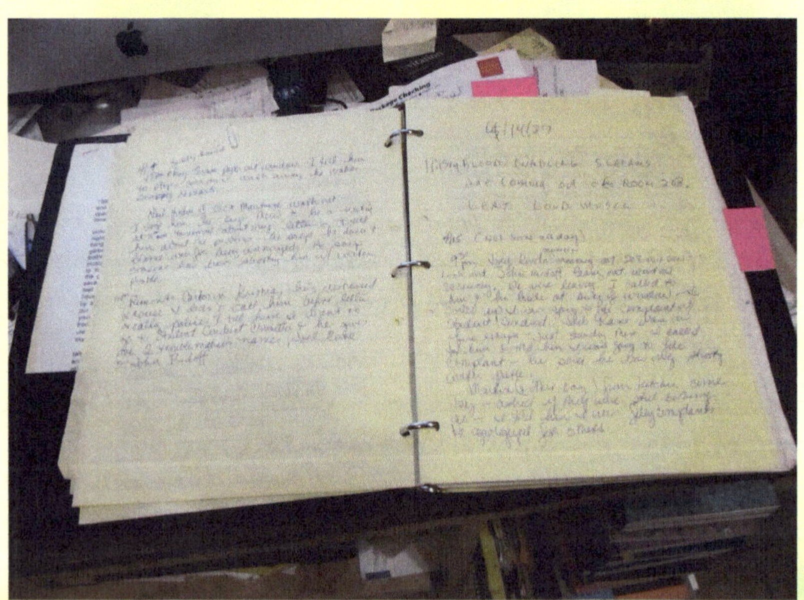

We moved into 2310 in March 1983. Four years later in April 1987, we began keeping an incident log.

cious. After the call we were left with a very uneasy feeling of fear - that we must hide in the house. We fear they could harm our pets so we won't let them out. Or they may tamper with the car or shoot us from the window. We begin speculating that USCA itself could hire a "hit man" to shoot us from that window and those kids to be blamed -- obviously an idea verging on paranoia.

We cannot live in peace in our own home!!

6:30 pm John Harmon shows up with Reporter from Tribune. We tell our story and give him papers.

May 2 : Meet with City Council 12:30 to 2:30

4:30 pm: Very loud 60s music from window in back on 1st floor. Plays for 1 hours

May 2 Sebastian:
Loud party at Barrington I walked by the Dwight Way entrance and saw up 2 young teen agers (about 13 to 14) opening the door peer ing into the party, hesitating and going in No one monitoring entrance to stop uninvited guests from entering

The Party got louder and louder music, laugh ing yelling but did not generate into bottle and wood throwing Front clear in the morning

May 3 2:00 pm Sunday

Three beer bottles thrown into our front area in the middle of theday fortunately Sebastian's car was out

May 3 9:30 PM, Sebastian 3 young men sitting on the curb across the street. They look like high school students 15 years old, or so After sitting on the curb for 10 min, someone comes out of Barrington and whistled to them They got up and crossed the street excitedly and got a small package (rolled up plastic bag) from the older kid who had come out of Barrington Sure looks like a dope deal.

May 8 5 pm (SEB): As I'm going up the front of our house, John R calls out to me from the open window of Club 208, *"I just graduated."* he says. **"Congratulations,"** I reply. *"My senior thesis was about terrorism. Terrorism is okay so long as it is done for artistic, instead political purposes."* Now I realize that there is an a threatening tone in his voice. When George Proper called to warn us to be on guard for retaliation by the boys in 208 - he was making an indirect threat. What a drag to be threatened in our own home. I worry, what will happen to Beverly?

Animal House on Acid

Sleaze metal legends, Sea Hags, played at Barrington on September 25, 1987. They were known for debauchery and decadence at its finest. The party at Barrington was widely publicized, with hand bills posted up and down Telegraph Ave, drawing a huge rowdy crowd anxious "to party"!

The Sea Hags may have evolved into an even better band, but they were hampered by their self-destructive tendencies. As their manager Chris Coyle observed, "There is only so far you can get with three junkies and one alcoholic." Bassist Chris Schlosshardt overdosed on heroin in 1991. They burned out after one album and tour.

Members

- Ron Yocom - Vocals, Guitar (1985-1990)
- Chris Schlosshardt - Bass Guitar (1985-1990)
- Greg Langston - Drums (1985-1988)
- Frank Wilsey - Guitar (1988-1990)
- Adam Maples - Drums (1988-1990)

According to urban legend, "Sea Hags" are found in beach environments around the world. Large breasted at an early age, bleached blond and wearing too much green or blue eye shadow. they have massive egos from attention from horny men. Dressing 20 years below their age, with caked on makeup, Sea Hags are attractive in a cheap "hooker" way. They are loud, over-dramatic, gossipy and usually are recovering alcoholics or coke heads. All Sea Hags are trouble-makers—they love pitting men against one another and will befriend you only to betray—selfishly betray you.

Hours and hours of audio tapes from City metings

5/8/87 Friday evening
Just leaving for the movie and see Kyle on the fire escape, acting very weird. No one else is throwing bottles but he is out there very exaggerated swinging a bottle over the side in his hand. Sebastian's truck is in front. We fear another night of bottle throwing and they surely will break the truck window. We decide to put the truck in the driveway but become concerned that the moving and switching of cars in and out of the driveway will call Kyle's attention and alert him that we are going out and that the house will be empty.

So we decide to both pull out and for Seb to drive around the block and pull in the driveway casually when I go around the block and pull in driveway casually wait out of sight around the corner, and while maintaining a low profile, Sebastian gets in the car at the corner.

We do this and Kyle doesn't seem to notice. Shortly after getting to the theater and parking, we both decide to go home because we worry about the house. We'll go to movies later, only once we're home, we didn't want to leave. This is very exhausting to have to feel so apprehensive.

June 26, 9:00 am Broken bottles on sidewalk in front of Barrington Hall. Kids must be back to old behavior.

June 27: We spend 1-1/2 hours making a plan for dealing with problem if we continue to get threatening messages. We feel very apprehensive.
June 28, 9:30 am Large bag of trash thrown into the backyard garden. Box of beer bottles thrown onto the patio-bottles broken around the area. From tilt the box and loca-

666
OB

tion, must have come from BH roof or 3rd floor. Must have made a deliberate effort to throw onto our yard, otherwise it would have gone into the alley.

Call beeper and Rob D answered. He said a problem person has been setting off the fire alarm. Stole fire hose etc. They are trying to kick out some troublemakers and are angry at everyone. He said he's send someone over for the garbage.

You are going to die!

10:30 pm: Return home to find message on 644 line that began with tackling witchy type laugh then said, "You are going to die." *(Male voice). Message renewed our anxiety.*

Wine Dinner

In September of 1987, Barrington threw a wine dinner with a bowl of punch laced with LSD served freely to party attendees. Several people were hospitalized after consuming the punch, one with spinal injuries after jumping off the three-story roof of a neighboring building.

A Barringtonian named Ron wrote a song to the music of the Beatle's Help! *Help! I drank some punch! Help! Not just any punch. Help! You know it was spiked with Acid!* HELLPP!

The news media picked up and ran with the story. Community members, including the City Council and University officials, were again alerted to a drug-related incident at Barrington. They pressured the U.S.C.A. to do more.

OH.
TAB

THE DAILY CALIFORNIAN
Berkeley's Independent Daily; Established 1871
VOLUME FRIDAY, OCTOBER 16, 1987 BERKELEY, CALIFORNIA

Barrington Bash

October 16, 1987

Seven Hospitalized After "Acid Punch" Party, House Chief Quits

By John Hawley

As a result of a party which lead to the hositalization of seven people, the house manager of Barrington Hall resigned.

Robert Dick announced his decision yesterday to a meeting of the University Students Cooperative Association's Board of Directors.

Dick, a former UC Berkeley student who lived at Barrington from 1881-85, was hired as house manager last year in an effort to save the House. The house was in danger of being sold because of continuing problems with alcohol, drugs, and neighbors' complaints.

The USCA board decided not to sell Barrington and created a strict probationary agreement giving the central directors and Dick unprecedented control of the coop.

As house manager, Dick directed the three floor managers and had the power to ban any person form the house who he felt will be detrimental to the hall's well-being.

According to USCA General Manager, George Proper, the Barrington situation has been notably improved. The rooms were filled last spring and there were very few complaints. But a wine dinner on Sept. 25 was the beginning of a chain of event that culminated in Dick's resignation.

Cara Vaughn, public information officer and manager of student health services, said four people who had been at the party were hospitalized at Herrick Hospital and she said thought three others were sent to Alta Bates.

"All of them seemed have been there for the same reason," she said. They were "suffering from adverse drug reaction."

Only the one student "who fell off the building on Channing and suffered back injuries" required more than a short hospital stay," Dick said.

Another person was "tripping heavily on Hallucinogens and had to be strapped to a gurney at the hospital," Dick said.

Dick said that only one of the hospitalized people was a Barrington residents.

An anonymous guest of the part said that "acid punch" was being served there, which she said was not an uncommon occurrence.

As a matter of routine, Herrick officials notified Cowell Hospital that they were treating several students for drug-related injuries, Vaughn said. Cowell then notified Dean of Students Don Billingsley who said he called Proper into his office and asked him what was being done about the incident.

"Given Barrington's checkered past, I thought the situation was quite serious. I suggested to Mr. Proper that he do whatever is necessary to make Barrington a safe hospitable place to live," Billingsley said.

Representing management team at the central office, Proper asked Dick to resign.

"I regretted the activity that has happened and I am sorry Robert has to resign. Although I do believe he did have to resign. He should have kept the party under control," Proper said.

Dick said he regretted leaving Barrington but he felt "somewhat relieved,"

"It's hard to be a signal man occupation force. The house and I were fundamentally uncomfortable about the situation," he said.

Dick said he notified house leaders of his concerns about the party but no precautions were taken.

"I had some bad Omens. I knew there was not guest list, the band had been advertising, and the security measures weren't tight enough. The whole thing just got out of hand."

The band, a popular local group called, The Sea Hags, did not know until too late they were not suppose to advertise and "half of Berkeley showed up," Dick said.

House president Mellissa Marshall admitted there was confusion in Barrington staff as to who should deal with these problems.

"There was a lot of finger pointing going on," she said.

Dick did admit, however, that as house manager he was ultimately accountable. "In that sense I exercised poor judgment," he said.

Proper, however, said the party was essentially a collective mistake.

"Barrington did not take the responsibility for its own actions and chose to delegate responsibility to Robert," he said.

UNIVERSITY OF CALIFORNIA, BERKELEY

BERKELEY • DAVIS • IRVINE • LOS ANGELES • RIVERSIDE • SAN DIEGO • SAN FRANCISCO

SANTA BARBARA • SANTA CRUZ

OFFICE OF THE CHANCELLOR

BERKELEY, CALIFORNIA 94720

October 16, 1987

Mr. George Proper, Director
University Students' Coop Association
2424 Ridge Road Berkeley, CA 94705

Dear Mr. Proper:

Re: LSD-Laced Punch Incident at Barrington

You should be aware that Barrington Hall falls under the student conduct jurisdiction of the campus so that, if identifiable students are alleged to have violated specific sections of the Berkeley Campus Regulations, they would be subject to student conduct proceedings and appropriate disciplinary action.

The above incident involving the LSD-laced punch could involve violation of section 420(7) of the regulations proscribing any act constituting "[p]hysical abuse, threats of violence, or f conduct that threatens the health or safety of any person..." Accordingly, if you have information concerning the identity of any students responsible for the above incident, please contact Student Conduct Officer Alan Rolling at 643-9069. Your attention in this matter is greatly appreciated.

Sincerely,

Donald Biiiingsley
Dean of Student Life

DB/awk

cc: Student Conduct Officer Alan Rolling
Chief Derry Bowles, UCPD

New Member Disorientation Party

At the start of each semester, usually on the second weekend, Barrington Hall held a New Member Disorientation Party. It was the Social Ed's job to organize parties, book the bands, get the tank, and so forth. The party was held in the Alternative Kitchen (AK), which was bedecked in advance with mattresses covering the floors. Because of N_2O's combustibility a "No Smoking" policy was put into in effect. There was always a long line to get into the party—until the tank ran out.

In the room, on the mats, under dark mood lighting, Each partier was given a large plastic garbage bag filled with nitrous oxide gas, from which they inhaled. Many passed out on the waiting mattresses. Barringtonians sat laughing until their bag of gas ran out. Going in and out of the nitrous oxide, a hallucinogenic experience, everyone rolled around on the mattresses laughing, while losing their minds.

When the bag was done, everybody got back in line for a refill until the tank was empty. Then they went off to Shitty's market, while dozens more drank and partied all over the house.

THE TRIBUNE

Acid Party Tosses Troubled UC Hall into Hot Seat Again

By Eric Newton

BERKELEY — An "acid punch" party that sent seven people to the hospital has lead to another look at closing Barrington Hall, the troubled student-run co-op that barely survived a "hell summer" of heroin use in 1985.

The latest incident, in which hallucinogenic LSD was popped into party punch on Sept. 25, led to forced resignation of Barrington's manager, according to George Proper, General Manager of the University Students Cooperative Association.

In addition, *The Tribune* has obtained documents showing that Berkeley City officials were considering suing to close Barrington last year after a confidential police report said that the Hall's problems will never be solved.

The punch party sent seven people to two Berkeley hospitals with what University of California at Berkeley health officials called "adverse reactions" to the LSD.

Robert Dick, Barrington manager for three months, admitted knowing about the LSD-laced punch, and his resignation was accepted by the co-op's all- student board of directors at a meeting that lasted until nearly 3 a.m. yesterday. Dick did not return The Tribune's phone calls yesterday.

At the co-op meeting, the 30-student board "decided to give Barrington one more chance," Proper said, even though the co-op violated the "no drugs" portion of its 1986 probation agreement.

"The board is looking for a solution that does not throw the residents out in the street," he said.

The decision infuriated neighbors of the graffiti-lined, 182-resident stack of stucco units at 2315 Dwight Way, which they say is the worst of the 18 student cooperatives that house 1,400 students around UC-Berkeley.

"It's a student ghetto," said Beverly Potter, a management psychologist who bought a house next to Barrington four years ago.

"We call this the combat zone," she said. "The noise … the mess … It's dangerous over there. Someone is going to get hurt."

In the spring of 1986 the co-op board voted to close and sell Barrington after two dozen frequent visitors and residents, including some in the Hall hierarchy, admitted using heroin. The confessions came after two non-fatal overdoses were reported in as many weeks.

But the Board later reversed itself, allowing the Hall to remain open under a three-year probation pact that barred everything from runaways to bad publicity.

Since then, Proper said, most of Barrington's residents are new and it has been "a model neighbor for nearly 18 months … an incident-free house."

Berkeley police Lt. Phil Doran disagreed.

Through arrests are down, he said, "Barrington remains a very busy site of police activity … We're there about every day, for noise or similar complaints. There's always something."

To neighbor Potter, the probation worked for about two months. That's how long it took the 4-foot-tall letters "LSD," so carefully painted over when the House was in danger, to be repainted on both Dwight Way and Haste Street, she said.

Proper, who said that the Barrington manager who quit, was a "scapegoat," noted that further co-op sanctions against the Hall will force residents to take some responsibility for the party.

Those include: having residents do five hours of community service each, requiring a new party policy to be drawn up, and giving the Hall four "floor managers" more responsibility.

He said the Sept. 25 party become a problem because one of the bands playing had advertised it publically, drawing non-Barrington residents. Future parties will be closed.

Proper said the student co-op Board on Oct. 29 will consider more sanctions. But he, for one, does not want to see the House closed.

"We call this the combat zone ... It's dangerous over there."

— Neighbor Beverly Potter

"We could replace all the residents, instead, and not lose any income," he said. "If it happens again, we could move all of them (the residents) out and start over."

Potter disagreed. "The building is nothing but a slum . . . a money machine that was paid off 40 years ago . . They should build a decent structure."

A confidential Berkeley police report, compiled on May 2, 1986, said Barrington Hall had been a drug not spot for more than six years and quoted one inspector as saying, "it is my belief that they will not be able to change the patterns in that building without selling it."

On May 7, 1986, City Environmental Health Chief Glenn Lynch wrote a memo setting up the rationale for a civil lawsuit that could be brought against Barrington Hall, declaring the Hall to be a public hazard under noise abatement laws."

Council Member Nancy Skinner, part of the council's 1986 Barrington Task Force, said she had not seen the memos, but that they may have been early ideas from a Task Force subcommittee that were dropped later.

The problem at Barrington, said Skinner, herself a former Hall resident in the 1970s, is that everyone says it's someone else's problem.

"The (Co-op Board) should take responsibility for what happened, and settle it," she said.

The Tribune
October 17, 1987

LETTERS TO THE EDITOR

Barrington Bash or Barrington Bashing?

Regarding your historic coverage of the situation at Barrington Hall:

While we realize that writing about our home in general is "good copy" for sensationalist publications, we could never have imaged a blaring inaccurate headline, such as the one appearing on last Friday's front page.

No wonder. Barrington is a sexy story.

Robert Dick, our former house manager is quoted correctly (thank God) towards the end of Monday's subdued follow up when he speaks of the sensationalist press "hampering our efforts to improve our situation." Subtle omission and blatant rehashing of old–truths abound whenever the press decides to talk about us.

One of the most basic journalistic tenets is never to print anonymous pejorative quotes. But for *The Daily Cal* it's OK when the quote is about Barrington.

Well, it's not OK. It's not OK to malign our home. It's not OK to print that some nameless person who came into our home serves as some voice of authority by claiming that "acid punch is a common occurrence at Barrington parties." This behavior is not, as your kicker suggests, reporting on a "Barrington bash," but rather, common another exercise in "Barrington bashing." And it is simply untrue.

When the press deals with Barrington, rumor and fantasy seem to take precedence over reality.And we have come to expect reality to be skewed by the media. Sadly, you have not let us down in this expectation.

None of us is claiming total innocence as to the events of Sept. 25. Our house was over-run by half of Berkeley looking for a wild party, and after a while, the party began to feed on itself. The entire house has accepted responsibility for letting it happen; immediately following the party, we met to take measures to prevent these events from ever occurring again.

The fact that we went to great lengths to deal with the situation was never really expressed in your (or anyone else's) coverage, giving the impression that we are a bunch of wild, irresponsible adolescent, "Unwilling and unable to police ourselves."

We are not Throwback Hippies from Hell. We are honor students, actors, artists, writers, scientists, anti-Apartheid activists and even fresh-faced kids next door. And the innuendo for a more creative venture. It doesn't belong in a "newspaper."

The Barrington Hall House Council

Letters to the Editor
October 22, 1987
The Daily Californian

My Barrington Gig

The band I was in – ***Special Forces*** – was asked to play a party at Barrington Hall. I had grown up in the area and heard the stories about what kinds of things went on there, but I had never been inside. This was probably in 1987. I knew this was going to be an experience like no other.

We arrived and I stashed my bass and amp off to the side before wandering around a bit, knowing we had some time before we were set to play. Hallucinogenics played a large role in my teenage years, and I had spent many nights in strange places, but Barrington was a strange place like no other. The walls were covered with spray paint and black light paint, made more noticeable by the black lights hanging from the ceiling. The place seemed to be designed to enhance your trip if you happened to be on something, which didn't take long to happen.

It was about an hour before we were set to play when a couple of the residents approached and informed me that anybody who played there had to dose up. I was handed a couple of tabs of LSD and some mushrooms and they watched expectantly as I gobbled them down. As it turns out, I think I was the only member of the band that took any that night, but that was ok with me. I knew the songs backward and forward and playing while dosed on LSD wasn't an issue for me.

As the drugs began to take effect, I wandered the rooms, amazed that they could get away with painting their walls and being such an obvious party house. Everything about that place screamed LSD, which is probably why I turned down the free punch they were offering. I could deal with a couple of tabs of LSD and some 'shrooms, but punch of unknown origin? Not from Barrington! Even I knew my limits, although it appeared many people didn't. The party was awesome, the show went off without a hitch (or so I seem to recall), and the night went down as one of the most awesome experiences in my life.

Barrington was an icon of teenage rebellion, a giant "screw you" to the other frat houses, and just plain awesome. R.I.P. Barrington Hall

Steven Whitacre Musican - Bass
author: *My Father's Prostitute*

BEVERLY A. POTTER, PHD.

Shirley Dean
City Council
City of Berkeley
Berkeley, Ca

October 18, 1987

Dear Shirley:

Late into the night, 2 or 3 am, I was awaken by chanting like screaming from Barrington. It sounded like they were yelling a name but I could not make it out. You can not imagine the profound sense of helplessness I experienced. Who do I call? The manager is gone. Should I call the police and then sit up for an hour or more until the officer's arrival. From experience I know that that gets little result. Do I call Proper and leave a message on his answering machine? Do I call my District Councilman Jelnick (sp?), who had ignored my past pleas for help and then asserted that he had heard of no problems? I feel that I cannot live peaceable in my own home.

Your call was a ray of hope! Thank you for your conscientiousness and concern for the larger Berkeley community and for the students.

I feel that the community, the Task Force and the media has been repeatedly sidetracked into blaming the students in Barrington. While each individual is responsible for his or her own actions, I do not believe that they can manage themselves as a group effectively within the current USCA structure. The USCA is responsible and George Proper, as general manager, is ultimately responsible - not the students in Barrington, many of whom are minors.

There was not one word of remorse over the plight of the injured students. It is rumored that the one that fell is crippled!

If something is not done to stop this decadent, ill-managed and irresponsible organization, I am convinced that eventually someone or several someones will be killed. To what extreme must things go before the USCA is forced to be accountable for their policies and actions in housing 1400 young people?

I am happy to help you in whatever way I can in this matter.

Regards,

Beverly A. Potter

Fast Forward: On the night of 3/10/90 Juan Mendoza was found at 3:05 a.m.with his head smashed in the parking lot, 25 feet from the building. Barrington was boarded up two days later and sold soon afterwards.

Don Biliingsley
Dean of Students
UC Berkeley
Berkeley, California 9470-

October 18, 1987

Dear Dean Biliingsley:

I and other Barrington Hall neighbors are concerned about the USCA's handling of the recent incident involving injuries sustained by seven students after consuming LSD in a wine punch during the party on September 25. According to Minutes of the USCA Cabinet meeting October 12, 1987:

> The USCA does not intend to replace the Central Office employed manager, Robert Dick, instead, "Barrington will restructure its manager organization itself." This is highly inappropriate, especially considering that such external management was specifically required by the Task Force as a condition of the "probation."
>
> That the USCA Central Office is investigating ways to get "release forms signed by those injured." Presumably, the injured students will be asked to signed the releases without benefit of council, which is unethical and irresponsible.

Robert Dick was employed by the Central Office (CO) and was, thereby, accountable to them and they, thereby, responsible for his performance. George Proper, general manager of the USCA, implicitly excused Dick's failure to act responsibility when he knew about the LSD in the punch beforehand, when he told *The Tribune* reporter that Dick was "a scapegoat." Dick's stated reason for resigning, as recorded in the Cabinet Minutes, as "it would be satisfying to the press, and allow him to go on to other things." in short, the CO has in no way assumed responsibility.

Further, Proper made false statements to the *Oakland Tribune* and TV Channels 2 and 5 when he was quoted as saying that Barrington has been "a model neighbor for nearly 18 months" and "an incident-free house."

The truth is that there was a serious nuisance problem throughout the Spring of this year. 1 personally was repeatedly harassed including having dozens of bottles smashed upon my front stairs, parking area and back patio, my name in sexually demeaning graffiti was painted twice across the front of the building, and I was subjected to group tauntings, spitings and threats. Additionally, bottles were repeatedly thrown at passing cars and pedestrians and bags of garbage were regularly dumped from a window overlooking my front door. There was considerable indication of vandalism inside the house, i.e., screaming, load breaking sounds, false fire alarms, as well as broken doors, radiators and other items thrown from the roof.

The matter became so oppressive and alarming that it lead to renewed meetings with City Council members and numerous police complaints as well as at least one written complaint to Berkeley Environmental Health. Carlos Cabana, CO House Manager at that time, was sympathetic and made several attempts to curtail the problem. I frequently observed him picking up the mess himself. But due to the USCA structure and policies and the lack of CO support, he was unable to control the uncivilized behavior. I was told that they could "do nothing#,"because student contracts could not be broken due to tenant laws - even though one of the offenders was no longer a student. (It should be noted that the USCA is exempt from the Berkeley Rent Control Ordinance).

After months of in vain attempts, the problem did stop abruptly, however, when I obtained the services of an attorney, Don Driscoll, and let it be known that 1 intended to sue the Co-op for $3 million, the estimated value of the building, because I was unable to live peaceably and safely in my own home. Within a few days, the CO determined that one offender was mentally "disturbed and potentially violent. They then removed him and the former student from the building, leaving empty the room in which much of the unacceptable activity occurred.

As a Stanford trained PhD in human behavior, with 13 years experience as an organizational management psychologist, 10 years direct experience in housing groups of students, and as an active member of the Berkeley Task Force on Barrington problems, I am qualified to set forth an opinion of the chronic behavioral problems at Barrington Hall.

I believe that it is a mistake to continue to point the finger of blame and responsibility at the Barringtonians. The Health Department documented ten years of nuisance and the Police Department has similar records of chronic criminal activity, especially drug dealing. The problem has been constant (sometimes better, sometimes worse) even though the students have turned over. Neither a building nor a reputation, in and of themselves, are powerful enough to perpetuate the problems, especially against the strong community pressures for change. The constant is the USCA structure and the personnel in charge; the CO.

It is my opinion that the students residing in Barrington, as well as in the other 17 USCA houses, are victims of a decadent, ill-managed and irresponsible organization. The CO actively promotes ill-will between the Barringtonians and the neighbors. When incidents occur Proper encourages the media and the community to blame the USCA's victims: the students and/or the neighbors. In fact, Barringtonians and neighbors actually have a common problem, the CO and Proper, in particular, who through inability or unwillingness has failed to correct the problems or to assume his rightful responsibility as dictated by being General Manager for more than 15 years.

The USCA, which houses 1400 students, alleges to be a "co-op." Yet, co-opers, are not allowed to select which house they live in or who lives in their houses - a basic principle of cooperative living. While the majority of Barringtonians are "good kids," because of its reputations and substandard conditions, the CO uses Barrington as a dumping ground for anarchists, dead-beats and other undesirables. Co-opers, do not control their money - a second principle of cooperative living, Barrington is a cash cow that brings in more money than the other houses, but their fair share of the money is not spent on Barrington. Without these two measures of control, it is unlikely that Barrington can ever manage itself effectively.

The USCA is exempt from Berkeley Rent Control and its registration fees, as Berkeley's second largest landlord, it pays no property tax on its $ 16 million dollars in real estate and pays no income tax on its rents or on its $25,000 a month (calculated at minimum wage) in unpaid required student labor. Like any slumlord, the housing and conditions the USCA provides is ghetto-like. When subjected to ghetto conditions, students would be expected to exhibit ghetto-like behavior. That is what I have observed in my 4 years of residence next to Barrington. There is apathy, tolerance of uncivilized behavior and filth, drug abuse, drug dealing, vandalism of their own community, nuisance, and so forth.

Students do not come to UC Berkeley to live in a place like Barrington, to room with dead-beats, to be exposed to unwholesome conditions, including rats and hepatitis, to have to resist heroin or risk exposure to AIDs if they fail, or to risk drinking LSD punch at an institutional function. Yet, the University implicitly supports such exposure by listing the USCA in the Housing Office so that many parents believe the USCA is appropriately supervised by the University. And the University financially supports the USCA, i.e., by leasing the property where Roachdale is built to the USCA for $1 a year!

With that stated, please be informed that if I must take legal action to protect my right to peaceable enjoyment in my own home, UC Berkeley will be cited as a co-defendent if it has failed to take assertive action in this matter against the USCA Central Office.

Regards,

Beverly A. Potter, PhD
Barrington Neighbor

cc: Editor: The Berkeley Voice
Eric Newton, Oakland Tribune
Shirley Dean, Berkeley City Council
Chancellor Hayman
File/other

Beverly A. Potter, PhD.

October 23.1987

Mayor Loni Hancock
City of Berkeley
& Barrington-Gate
2180 MilviaSt
Berkeley, Ca

Re: USCA

Dear Mayor Hancock:

Based upon my experience as a neighbor, as a Task Force participant, as a student group landlord, and as an organizational management psychologist, I believe that it is a mistake to continue to blame Barringtonians for the chronic problems associated with Barrington Hall

Managing a group of 182 people of any age **under the conditions existing within Barrington** is a master feat. It is folly to expect a group of inexperienced minors to do so. Focus should be shifted to the one constant over the past ten years and the actual source of responsibility: the USCA Central Office and George Proper, the employed General Manager.

Berkeley has traditionally mistrusted landlords. Yet, Berkeley's second biggest landlord, USCA is unregulated and collects more than $4 million a year in rent. Its tenants do not enjoy the benefits of Berkeley's Rent Control Ordinance. And Berkeley does not enjoy the approximately $90,000 in rental registration fees it could receive under the Ordinance.

Berkeley has traditionally mistrusted big business. Yet, the USCA is one of Berkeley's biggest businesses with $ 16 million in real estate, upon which it pays no property tax. And the USCA pays no income tax on its rentals or on the $25,000+ a month (calculated at minimum wage) in unpaid student labor.

Everyday more people are asking why the USCA and its big money is an exception. And people are wondering why the report and recommendation from Glenn Lynch, formerly the Head of Environmental Health, was not acted upon but was suppressed instead.

The enclosed documents will give you insight into the manner in which the USCA handles problems. A simple nuisance problem was allowed to grow to the point where we could not live peaceable and safely in our own home. How did that happen under the probation and the good neighbor policy?

Berkeley students deserve better treatment. The community deserves better treatment. When will the USCA be required to be accountable and to pay its fair share for its excessive use of City services?

Regards,

The City Council Reacts

Shirley Dean, proclaimed that the Co-op could not manage Barrington. She wanted the University to take control of Barrington and run it. This solution would strip Barrington of its independence. Dean ignored the important of democratic control of the co-op is to the members. She only saw Barrington as a political pawn and example that illegal behavior would not be tolerated. The University did not seriously consider her demand.

Don Jelnik, announced that he wanted to create yet another committee to investigate the charges. He thought the City Council should get the facts before condemning the place.

Other council members said Jelnik and Dean were overreacting. "Drug use is an endemic problem of student life regardless of whether you live in the dorms, the co-ops, or the Greek system. I don't condone the situation at Barrington Hall, but we have to realize that this is a student wide phenomenon and I don't see why the city should get involved in the affairs of the U.S.C.A. any more than it should in that of the frats or the dorms," said Councilwoman Nancy Skinner.

Don Billingsley, University's Dean of Students, sent a letter to Proper urging the U.S.C.A. to act to prevent such incidents from occurring in the future, threatening to remove all University recommendations of the U.S.C.A. as a viable housing option if effective measures were not taken.

Field Trip

In fall 1987, the House Managers organized a field trip, chartered a bus, and took a bunch of Barringtonians to the Exploratorium in San Francisco. They rented The Tactile Gallery—a pitch black, feel your way through maze—for an hour just for Barringtonians. Being clothing optional, most of the Barringtonians stripped down to their underwear and a few went buck naked. There was a slide that opened into a pool of dry macaroni with air blowing that kept it soft to land into.

Oct 25, 1987

THE TRIBUNE

UC Neighbors Edgy About Housing Co-op

Barrington Hall seeks another chance.

By Eric Newton
The Tribune

BERKELEY—Everyone's talking about Barrington Hall again and everyone wants something.

Neighbors of the student-run cooperative say it is unsafe and loud.

They want peace and quiet.

Barringtonians, as they call themselves, admit they allowed a party to get out of control..

They want another chance.

The students on the Board that run the student cooperatives clustered around the University of California at Berkeley say they can handle Barrington.

They want to be left alone.

City council members worry that a Sept. 25 party which sent seven people with bad LSD reactions to doctors, is a signal that the 182-resident house is turning back into the place that was almost closed early last year, a place where anything goes including heroin, runaways, crime and disease.

They want different thing: pressure on the University Students Cooperative Association board, a study of the "acid punch" party, and current housing conditions and a call for UC-Berkeley to take over the building

On Tuesday night the City Council, is expected to debate a proposal by Don Jelinek of District 7, which includes Barrington. It would create a subcommittee—made up of members from the City Council, the community, city staff, and the cooperatives — to meet within two weeks and to make, in Jelinek's words, "A fact-finding report, that will lead to quick action."

The wheels of government are turning again, which is why everyone is talking about Barrington.

And what they say — that the debate means nothing; or it means nourishment, or it means the death of the half-century-old student cooperative— depends, of course, on who you talk to.

■ ■ ■

"Cannery Row," John Steinbeck wrote, "is a poem, a stink, a grating noise, a quality of light, a tone, a habit, a nostalgia, a dream."

You could can say all that about Barrington— on one of the hallways, actually, if you had a spray can.

Or you could write a letter as the House Council did in defense of itself.

"We are not Throwback Hippies from Hell. We are honor students, actors, artists, writers, scientists, anti-apartheid activists, even fresh-faced kids next door."

"Then someone will write a letter, like Beverly Potter, south-of-campus, next-door neighbor to the 2315 Dwight Way building.

"Students do not come to the University of California at Berkeley to live in a place like Barrington, to room with deadbeats, to be exposed to unwholesome conditions, including rats and hepatitis, to have to resist heroin, or risk exposure to AIDS, if they fail, or to risk drinking LSD at an institutional function."

"We are not Throwback Hippies from Hell."

And then someone else would check the co-op's Board's minutes and find a report saying: "eats up more of our capital funds than any other house."

Through all the debate, what Barrington has given the city, the university, and the press is the dream of every parent or sociologist— a window into a new world, a way to pounce upon college students where they live, to examine them, poke at them, ask them to explain themselves.

■ ■ ■

As fast a graffiti grew, murals filled other Barrington walls, and some students scraped, sanded, and polished hardwood floors, built lofts, and painted their walls solid colors.

"Most of us are from regular middle-class American families," says Keenon McCloy, a history sophomore. "My parents hate it, but for me, it's a positive environment. There's an energy in there."

"It brings out the best in a person . .. or it can bring out something destructive ... it's the epitome of freedom of choice."

"We're responsible people," says Greg Sorel, a junior majoring in art. "Things were running smoothly. We made a mistake and then the media took it out of our hands. bThings here are nothing like they were two years

ago … Look, we get the message. We govern ourselves or die. This is our last chance to do it."

Adds Fritz Roth, who works the Barrington switchboard; "Even kids with mohawks stay up late to write papers."

"Barrington has always been a wild, free-loving house, even by Berkeley standards. And this attracts great numbers of creative, progressive and, sometimes, degenerate people.

Robert Dick, engineer-to-be and the house manager who was asked to resign will tell you:

"The people who ingested LSD knew what they were taking. It was upstairs in a room not part of the party. The party did get out of hand, but it was after 18 months of good behavior and we were walking around afterwards, saying, "Hey, we're never going to do that again."

And Jelinek, a lawyer:

"I'm trying to arrange for a trial before the hanging. We owe it to everyone to examine this. Once we get the information, it is warranted, there will be quick action. We have total power over that place, the city's power of public safety.

And Potter, a psychologist: "If Jelinek wants to do something, that's great. He has done nothing in the past, even though he has known about the problems of last year and the year before."

■ ■ ■

To some the discussion may seem excessive, since it is over whether students or residents or anyone else takes LSD in the City of Berkeley.

But it's just the latest twist in the tale of Barrington, a story that started back during the Depression, when student cooperatives were created to provide inexpensive, independent housing.

Barrington, at its current location since 1939, is now one of 18 student-run cooperatives housing 1,400 students around UC-Berkeley.

The building, at 2315 Dwight Way, stretching to Haste Street, is worth at least $2 million.

The students each pay $300 a month, roughly 40 percent less than they would pay to live in a university-run dormitory. They also provide their own labor.

Barrington is governed by the. University Students Cooperative Association, which is run by an elected student board.

That self-rule—students who make their own rules, separate from the university, or a national fraternity or sorority office, even separate from city rent control—is the pride of the co-op system.

But somewhere through the years, Barrington became the cooperative where self-rule meant little or no rule.

Like ivy, the slogans crept up the walls. The common areas got dirty. The building absorbed two major rehabs without turning into a Home and Garden centerfold.

In the spring of 1986, two dozen frequent visitors and

residents, including some of the Hall's hierarchy, admitted shooting heroin. The confessions came after two non-fatal overdoses were reported in as many weeks.

The co-op Board voted to close and sell the Hall, but later reversed itself, allowing the hall to remain open under a three-year probation pact that barred everything from runaways to bad publicity.

"At times, anarchy has taken over the building," as one student reported to the co-op Board in early 1987, "and some will argue that is good, and hundreds of thousands of dollars have been invested to restore order."

The co-op's hired General Manager, George Proper, says his office has spent "more time on Barrington than all the other buildings combined in the last 18 months . . . examining everything, looking at every little problem."

Neighbors strongly disagree, saying that rooms in Barrington have burned, bottles have flown from the building, harassing graffiti have been written outside the building and noise has continued to be a problem.

Even if everything else can be overlooked,, the "acid punch" party, they agree was a definite violation of the "no drugs" part of the probation.

There are more contrasts:

■ Police say they are at the Hall nearly every day; Barringtonians say police come every other week or so, only when called by students to solve an outsider's problem.

■ Students say outsiders who attended the Sept. 25 party by a band that advertised caused the event to get out of control; if the students can't even run a party, neighbors argue, how can they enforce their own rules everyday?

■ UC-Berkeley should take over Barirington argue Council members Shirley Dean, Mary Wainwright and Frederick Weeks; the university has the same kind of powers over its dorm residents that the co-op board has over its residents, says UC housing specialist Steve Barclay.

"Clearly what happened is a serious incident," says Barclay. "The question is: is it a one-time incident? The university would like to wait to see what the co-op Board is doing."

■ The house is a "money-making student slum," according to neighbor Potter.

"Students do not come to the University of California at Berkeley to live in a place like Barrington, to room with deadbeats, to be exposed to unwholesome conditions, including rats and hepatitis, to have to resist heroin, or risk exposure to AIDS, if they fail, or to risk drinking LSD at an institutional function."

—Beverly Potter, Neighbor

i,

October 26 Grading, loud music from the window over the solar heater with window open. I went out and threw pebbles at the window. Between records I called during the silence, as I've done before. *"Close your window. I don't like listening to your music."* The boy inside stood behind the curtain and said, *"Well, I don't like you calling This place a slum."* I said, *"If you want to talk, then come out here and we'll have a debate, otherwise, close your window."* The boy paced around while talking angrily and I heard the phrase, *"You call yourself a psychologist?"* I said, *"I can't hear what you're saying. If you have something to say, come out and say it. Otherwise close your window."* I went inside for a time I could hear muffled loud music, then silence.

I realize that I am a target if I speak up but then dismissed as "vocal minority" and thusly dismissed, which gives implicit permission to act out. Alternatively, I can say nothing and just take it

10

PERSONALS

USCA Members

We'll meet to talk with co-opers who *think for themselves.*

No attorneys. No recordings.

Sincere members only.

Beverly & Sebastian - 540-6278

[illegible]

We started up we strategize a way to defuse the tension and create safety. We think of talking to the house counsel I prepare a note for the house president Melissa M. We decides to get information on how to send them a note by calling the beeper and call at 8:20 pm.

We never get any reply to our request.

A BACK TO SCHOOL PARTY WITH

THIS SATURDAY NIGHT!

JANUARY 6 9PM

BARRINGTON HALL
2315 DWIGHT WAY

BERKELEY

$2.50

$3.

& PSYCOTIC PINEAPPLE

One of San Francisco's iconic early wave bands.

Psycotic Pineapple was formed in 1974 by Jon Rubin, Tommy Dunbar, John C. Berry and Henricus Holtman. Alexi Karlinski and Dave C. Berry joined in 1976

BEVERLY A. POTTER,

copy

October 26, 1987

To: **Melissa Marshall**
House President
Room 313
Barrinqton Hall
2315 Dwight Way
Berkeley 94704

From:
Beverly Potter
Sebastian Orfali
Haste Street Neighbors
644-2319

SInce Barringtonians may be drawing their opinions from the media -- and its rowdy students vs irate neighbors sensationalism.

With our right to disagress as well as our right to agree -- out in front -- we request an opportunity to talk with the Barrington House Council and any Barringtonians who want to participate.

BARRINGTON HALL MEETING
MINUTES
November 11, 1987
Ad Hoc Council Committee on Barrington Hall

PRESENT: Council members Don Jelinek, Ann Chandler and Fred Lynch (Acting Assistant City Manager for Health and vices), George Proper (USCA General Manager), Evan Steele (USCA Board President), Carlos Cabana (USCA Staff), Jule Archuleta (Barrington President and interim House Manager), Peter Spencer (Barrington), David Koistenen (Chateau), Ed. Gillan Eric Gran (Chateau House Manager), Don Driscoll,Beverly Potter, Sebastian Orfali, John Harmon, Adele Belinski, Marianne Pittman, Katherine Pittman, David Linderman, Larry Duga, Fredrick Hobson, Bill Taylor (Jelinek's Office) and Jim Goldstein (Jelinek's Office).

Council member Jelinek opened the meeting explaining the Committee was a fact-finding body that would eventually make recommendations to the City Council. The Council's options range from the City filing a civil lawsuit to close Barrington to making direct recommendations to the USCA Board of Directors about Barrington to taking no action.

USCA Background

George Proper, USCA General Manager, informed the committee about the creation of USCA and the events leading up to the current probation of Barrington Hall:

The USCA was started during the depression when a few students gathered $500 to buy some property. During the 60's and 70's, USCA acquired a lot of property. Coyne Court is leased from the University, while the buildings at Fenwick and Rochdale are owned by USCA and the land leased from the University. The USCA is a public benefit corporation and is exempt from property tax. There are 1,400 student members, and of those members, 33 serve on the Board of Directors. Barrington Hall, the largest USCA room and board facility with 183 residents, its students are subject to the jurisdiction of the University of Callfornia.

In the early 80's, the residents in the next-door Elsmere Apartments were having problems with Barrington over noise, debris and drugs. The City Attorney, at that time, recommended both groups go to Community Dispute Arbitration to resolve the dispute. An agreement was arrived at and was successful during the first semester but collapsed in the second semester. Three successive and inexperienced House Managers contributed to the troubles. During the summer of 1985 — called "Hell Summer" — there were approximately 50 legal residents and 75 illegal residents living in Barrington. Effectively it was "Animal House"

A heroin problem spread among 20-30 residents. By December 1985, the City Council established a Task Force on Barrington Hall, composed of 3 Council members — Vice Mayor Veronika Fukson, Nancy Skinner, and Wesley Hester — USCA & Barrington Representatives, neighbors, and City staff. By Spring of 1986 a Barrington manager ended up having a heroin problem and resigned.

This precipitated USCA staff recommendation to sell Barrington, which was approved by the USCA Board of Directors but overturned by the USCA membership. (The Barrington voters were decisive in overturning the Board decision.) The resultant Board decision was to place Barrington on a strict 3-year probation: For the first time in the 54-year history of the USCA, a full-time outside House Manager was assigned direct responsibility to the Central Office.

A major condition to the probation was not condoning drug dealing or use; violation would result in closing down Barrington.

The "Acid" Party: September 25, 1987

Jule Archuelta, Barringotn House Manager, discussed the night of the party.

The band that was playing had circulated fliers around town in violation of the House Rules. The result was "half of Berkeley showed up." Someone had prepared and passed out the "acid" LSD punch. People "knowingly" took the punch. She felt the whole' group was responsible for the activity. No individual has come forth to accept responsibility.

Normally when Barrington has a "wine" party*, it is controlled. Barrington residents, specific guests, former Barringtonians and other Co-op members can participate. There is security at the door, but on the evening of the event, people were coming in, saying they were with the band. Robert Dick, the House Manager, closed the doors for a half-hour when capacity was exceeded. In reaction to the drug, one person (a non-resident) jogged off the roof of a 3-story building and miraculously was not seriously injured. Overall, two Barrington residents and five visitors were hospitalized.

Resident Peter Spencer said there had been very few problems since the probation. The "acid" party became a bad "acid" party because non-residents were involved. When an event becomes public, the nature and interactions of people change.

* Note: it is well-known that "wine dinner" at Barrington is code word for acid punch party.

Neighbors Concerns

Beverly Potter felt that the USCA management style permits anarchy. She called Roxanne Neal, USCA Operations Manager, one time and was told by her that USCA can't tell the students what to do since she (Ms. Neal) works for them, that it is difficult to negotiate with anybody when no one is in control in dealing with situations like sewer overflows and people tossing things off the roof.

Sebastian Orfali felt that the students are the real victims of the situation. A lot of the stuff has been going on for years — mutilated dead rats, drug dealing, a child gang-banged and shot up with heroin, Satanic rituals, goat head symbols, witches, etc. The problem is the organization — USCA, not the students.

Daniel Linderman felt there is a lack of * immediate accountability. There is no system setup so that neighbors can talk to managers about house activities.

Student Concerns

Eric Gran mentioned that within each co-op there is a place for everyone. Each house has its own flavor and style. The houses are efficiently-run and serve students well. The main reason that students live in the co-op is democratically run. We define our autonomy on the house level. Co-opers want the right to control their own living area and they rebel when threatened.

Peter Spencer felt Barrington should be given more independence and control over its internal affairs. Solutions which aren't amenable to the residents won't work. People should collectively be in control of their own space. Neighbors are welcome to attend house meetings. There has to be a better attitude from community members in dealing with these issues.

Ed' Gillan felt Barrington has improved. Probation by the USCA Board should continue with the outside manager. The interim housing management solution should not be continued in the next semester.

City Staff Position

Glenn Lynch, Acting Assistant City Manager for HHS, mentioned that the original Task Force, was formed in December 1985 and met several times up to May 1986 but the meetings were hectic. Very few decisions and agreements were made about the problems. The Task Force didn't go anywhere. He still stands on his original recommendation to close down Barrington as a public nuisance, accomplished by the City Attorney filing a civil suit. An alternative is to have as an agreed, court-supervised probation that would have Barrington closed down immediately if there was a future violation of its terms.

Council-member Comments

Council member Fred Weekes felt that Barrington is a management problem. The Board of Charter should be changed. There are too many students and not enough longevity. The organization is ineffective. He wasn't sympathetic to giving Barrington another chance.

Council member Ann Chandler said that drug use is intolerable in a group living situation. We have a responsibility to our student community. Barrington has made some extraordinary efforts to deal with the situation. Noise is an issue. She recommended that a joint committee or ombudsperson be established and the University be involved in the process. The University shares the same responsibility as the City.

Councilmember Don Jelinek closed the meeting stating that Barrington has failed probation. Now the USCA has to take dramatic action. Autonomy for Barrington is out of the quesiton. Barrington is a peril to the young people living there. If the person, who had jogged off the roof, had died, Barrington would have been closed down the next day. If USCA does not act — and the University will not act — the City of Berkeley must do what is necessary to protect the Barrington students and the community.

If the person, who had jogged off the roof, had died, Barrington would have been closed down the next day.

—Don Jelinek
Berkeley City Council

FAST FORWARD: Barrington was boarded up three days after Juan Mendoza died on March 10, 1990, a little after 3 a.m. when he "flew" off the Barrington's roof. Some claim he was "on acid" thinking he was a bird. He "landed" face first 25 feet from the building. So he certainly must have been flying. But we're getting ahead of the story.

BEVERLY A. POTTER, PHD.

George Proper
General Manager
USCA
2424 Ridge Road
Berkeley, 94705

November 22, 1987

MAILED VIA CERTIFIED US MAIL

Dear George:
Since the decision to turnover the occupancy of Barrington Hall by 100% in May, nuisance problems have increased. Last night an electronic guitar was playing loudly at 1 a.m. Sometime after 2 a.m. I and several other neighbors were awaken by loud screaming. Today I learned that a group of students were in the Dwight Way parking lot yelling to John Harmon to wake up and taunting him.

This morning I spoke with House President, Jule A., about the incident, but her response was not satisfactory. She gave me the impression that nuisance activity aimed at John Harmon is acceptable and indicated that she did not intend to take any proactive steps to prevent such activity in the future.

I and other neighbors are very concerned. Please inform me as to what specific measures you and the USCA plan to take throughout the next six months to insure that the disgruntled Barringtonians will not create nuisance and waste in the neighborhood. Since my home borders upon Barrington and I have been outspoken about the problems, I feel particularly vulnerable. Please inform me as to what specific means you and the co-op intend to take to insulate us from your behavioral problems and to insure that we will not be made a target for angry acting out.

I am particularly concerned about Robert Dick. I've been told that he was a floor manager during "Hell Summer" when the USCA admittedly lost control of the Hall and the heroin problems were severe. While Dick did resign as the CO hired House Manager because he knew about the LSD laced punch, he continues to reside in the Hall. It appears that Dick has become the ring leader. He has been observed leading mock satanic rituals on the roof and he was the leader of the screaming event last night.

The USCA should not allow Dick to continue residing in Barrington Hall. He is older than the other students and is setting a poor example. That a former Central Office Manager acts as he has been sends an Implicit message to the Barringtonian inner circle.

Please inform me as to whether or not Robert Dick is now a UC student so that, if he is involved in future disturbances; I -may request that Student Conduct Officer Kolling advise him of his civil and criminal exposure. I look forward to hearing from you at your earliest convenience.

Regards,

Beverly A. Potter
Barrington Neighbor

CC: Dean Billingsley
Don Jelinek
Shirley Dean

PRIMUS

FRIZZLE FRY

"Frizzle Fry" is without a doubt, the BEST PRIMUS ALBUM EVER!
—amazon review

It is said that the lyrics of Primus' song Frizzle Fry tell of that infamous wine dinner in 1987 when four people were hospitalized.

When I finally sat down to listen to Frizzle Fry, I soon discovered that musically it was everything I had ever anticipated to hear from Primus. However, I'll admit that from the beginning I never expected to enjoy it. Then, to my surprise, with each listening I slowly uncovered the unique awesomeness that for so long I had been told this eclectic band possessed. I just didn't expect to find it within the lyrics.

Usually dark music like this, that seeps into your skin with forceful double bass drum pedaling, heavy bass and winding electric guitar riffs, doesn't do it for me. It's usually just too angry or aggressive for me to really enjoy. But somehow, Primus tapped into some uncharted territory (which subsequently made them famous) where they roam aimlessly through a futuristic desert landscape whilst mashing up funk, rock, metal and alternative music into one giant bundle of fun.

—Allison Franks
Band Reviewer

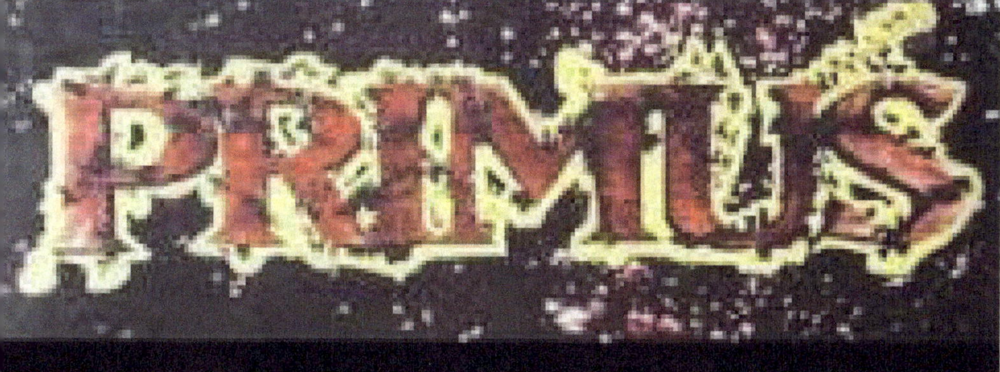

THE DAILY CALIFORNIAN
Berkeley's Independent Daily; Established 1871
VOLUME MONDAY, NOVEMBER 23, 1987 BERKELEY, CALIFORNIA

Co-ops Evict All Residents of Barrington

By Carolyn Jones
Staff Writer,

After a highly tense and emotional meeting, the Univer sity Students' Cooperative As sociation voted Thursday to evict residents of Barrington Hall.

In a 2-1 vote, the USCA Board of Directors, which is composed entirely of students, voted to require a 100 percent residency turnover for the 1988 fall semester.

The turnover plan will allow current Barrington residents to move to one of the 17 other houses owned by the USCA. Next fall, Barrington's new residents will be drawn from the first 182 people on the USCA's 800-person waiting list, with the exception of veteran co-op managers.

The USCA took the action in response to an investigation launched by the Berkeley City Council into alleged drug use after a Sept. 25 "wine dinner" that left four people hospitalized with LSD-related injuries.

The City Council will "vote 9-0 to close Barrington down if the USCA doesn't do something drastic first," Jim Goldstein, an aide to City Council-member Don Jelinek and member of Chateau House co-op, told the 30-member board.

USCA General Manager George Proper acknowledged that the turnover decision was "the lesser of two evils."

Barrington residents pleaded with the Board for four hours to consider other options, with several members bursting into tears.

Following the meeting, the dejected students crossed town carrying lighted candles to their home at 2315 Dwight Way.

"Barrington Hall was sentenced to death by its own representatives," said Peter Spencer, one of Barrington's four representatives on the Board, all of whom voted against the turnover plan.

"We were strapped to the tracks and the train was coming—it was a no-way-out situation," he said.

Although Proper said he supports the decision, he "wasn't pleased" with the Board's meeting because so many Barrington members appeared to be "alienated" and "angered."

"I'm unhappy that some members felt disenfranchised from the cooperative, but I still support the turnover decision, mostly for lack of better alternatives," Proper said.

But Council member Don Jelinek, who is spearheading the Council Subcommittee investigating the co-op, called the USCA's decision "encouraging and courageous."

"I think it's a good first step," Jelinek said. "I'm very pleased with the decision."

Many Barrington members say they still think other options should be considered, such as an occupancy reduction, or a partial turnover, and they have vowed to fight the decision.

"I think the Board acted very harshly," Spencer said. "They made their decision in a manner that was absolutely unjustified."

Bill Heidbroder, a resident of the Rochdale co-op at 2424 Haste St., charged that requiring a Barrington residency turnover "is not a solution. They're trying to make Barrington another version of Cloyne Court or Ridge Project, and it's not going to work."

"It is a hard decision. I can see why they're angry," admitted Council-member Frederic Weekes, who serves on the city's Barrington investigation committee.

Major changes, such as a new name or painting over Barrington's historic murals, will not be decided for a "few months," Proper said.

"The staff is in a very difficult position," Proper said. "We have to disband a co-op house in a peaceful and non-destructive manner, plus create a viable new entity that can survive in a totally new climate."

Spencer, however, said that any such action by the Board, especially erasing the murals, would send "creeping alienation throughout the entire co-op system."

"The Board is turning into a landlord, which is exactly the opposite of what it's supposed to be," Spencer said. "I think the whole co-op system will feel the effects of this three years down the line."

Some members of Barrington have threatened to overrule the Board's vote by filing a referendum, which would require a petition signed by 10 percent of the membership of every co-op house, Spencer said.

Jelinek said that if a referendum succeeded, "we'll just have to start from scratch."

NOW U.C. IT . . .

by Stew Huntington

IT'S THE U.C. BERKELEY BUREAUCRAT DOLL!

WHINE HIM UP AND HE SAYS:

- "TAKE IT UPSTAIRS AND GET IT STAMPED BY THE CASHIER."
- "I CAN'T FIND YOUR NAME ON THE COMPUTER."

NOTE—INOPERABLE BETWEEN 12 NOON AND 1 PM!

UCB Bureaucrat Doll

Frat Boy Doll

Barrington Hall Doll

THE DAILY CALIFORNIAN
Berkeley's Independent Daily; Established 1871
VOLUME
BERKELEY, CALIFORNIA

Co-op Represents Civil Liberties

By Jeff Kravitz

Jeff Kravitz is a former house manager of Barrington Hall.

NEWS FLASH: Student co-op well known for its history of political dissidence, social experimentation and artistic expression is being harassed by government officials and threatened with closure because of a rock and roll party held there.

If this news were from Poland or Chile people in the City of Berkeley would certainly be among the first to protest this infringement on personal and cultural freedom. Unfortunately it is right here in Berkeley that the rights of students are being threatened, and the Berkeley City Council is leading the pack of wolves.

The City Council, which decries U.S. intervention in Central America, is itself intervening in and urging the UC administration to intervene in the internal affairs of Barrington Hall, a democratically-run student co-op. The irony of the situation is magnified by the fact that Barrington represents to the City of Berkeley what Berkeley represents to the United States — an iconoclast that refuses to reform, a refuge from the mainstream of American life.

The latest attack on Barrington grows out of a party held there some months ago. One of the rock 'n' roll bands playing there advertised their appearance, lots of people came to the party, lots of people took LSD, the party got out of hand and four people went to the hospital. They were all released the next day.

The people of Barrington and the University Students Cooperative Association, which oversees Barrington and the other co-ops, were upset at the situation and the manager of Barrington resigned.

Adults living in a private home, and the residents of it are perfectly capable of government their own lives.

The recent situation in Barrington is not an isolated event, and that is why so much publicity has surrounded the co-op recently. From the day Barrington opened in the 1930s to the present, it has been a center for political, social and cultural experimentation. This experimentation was rarely applauded by the establishment. In the '30s, Barrington was one of the few integrated housing situations near campus and in the '60s and 70s it served as a center in the free speech, anti-war and Peoples Park movements. In the 70s, Barrington has been involved in almost every political movement on campus.

Along with political expression, Barrington has been a haven for artists and musicians. The walls are covered with murals, and rock groups from X to Vicious Hippies have played there. At times Barrington has allowed homeless people to eat and sleep there. Like everywhere in the world, Barrington's social experiments have included the use of drugs.

It is the use of drugs in Barrington that is today making headlines. The drug situation in Barrington is really no different from anywhere in the Bay Area. From Jerry Garcia to Carlos Castaneda Tim Leary, proponents of drug use have found an audience here. The hills of Berkeley are filled with people who have turned on and tuned in but then dropped back into society. As the recent case of Supreme Court nominee Douglas Ginsburg shows, the drug laws in the United States make no sense and are an invasion of privacy.

Two years ago the drug situation in Barrington reached a crisis point when some people began using heroin with the usual ill results. Eventually the USCA central level to step in and a manager appointed by the USCA's central level was appointed, in addition, Barrington was put on a strict probation; if any thing unseemly happened, the house could be shut down.

The probation proved somewhat successful at first. Complaints from neighbors decreased and more people living in Barrington chose to stay here. The vacancy rate decreased and Barrington operated at a break-even level. However, all was not well as far s Barrington's critics were concerned. The house continued to behave in a counter-culture manner, people with drug problems were dealt with internally instead of being handed over to the police.

The real problem was the intense scrutiny and lack of self government that the probation put Barrington under. It was only a matter of time until something happened that would cause the house of cards to collapse.

That incident occurred at the recent wine party when hundreds of uninvited guests showed up and some people decided to have an LSD punch. The mix proved too potent and a few people freaked out. Immediately following the party Barringtonians assured that the problem would not happen again. The house manager resigned, self-rule was restored and it was decided to not have any more parties for the rest of the year.

For a while it seemed that all was settled. Unfortunately, opportunistic forces in the City Council and the media jumped on the chance to turn Barrington

into a pariah. The USCA has now buckled under pressure and plans to evict all current residents of Barrington at the end of spring semester. Even that drastic draconian act may not satisfy the Barrington bashers in the City Council who want the building shut down.

There seems to be nothing that the people inside of Barrington can do to placate their enemies. At this time those who lived there deserve privacy. What's needed is an examination of the larger forces at work to suppress Barrington,

First of all, there is a nationwide media campaign to prove that today's youth are conservative. Barrington stands out by showing that some people still are radical. The City Council, by joining in on the clamp-down of Barrington, is only building its own gallows. The rest of the United States still sees the City of Berkeley as a left-wing iconoclast that should be suppressed. It would not be surprising if soon some state or federal agency decided to investigate Berkeley because of its leftist politics and its attitude toward drugs.

Second, there is a growing trend in Berkeley to try to quiet and control student life. One of the first complaints a number of years ago was that, the Hall served as a punk rock club on many weekend nights. These concerts were abandoned in favor of occasional house-only parties such as the one that caused the recent crisis. Last year the City sought to close down Telegraph Avenue and recently the fraternities have also come under attack for loud parties.

Despite what some might say, there is no point in urging the City Council to investigate frats instead of co-ops or vice versa. Students and civil libertarians should see that an injury to one is an injury to all.

Some people on the City Council believe that the university can act in loco parents regarding Barrington. However, that concept clearly does not apply as Barrington is not associated with the university and the people who live there are adults. The nonsense spewing forth that the university is to blame for allowing students to live in a place like Barrington ignores the fact that many people like to live there.

The City Council should leave the people of Barrington in peace.

Former residents of Barrington, now lawyers, doctors,City Council members,teachers, accountants, newspaper publishers, Republicans, cops, drug addicts, editors, business people, musicians, artists, shopkeepers, archaeologists, and all of the other things that people do after graduating from and living in Berkeley, the most eclectic place in the United States.

The City Council should leave the people of Barrington in peace. The USCA should rescind its absurd eviction notice and let Barrington govern itself. When the government starts to tell people how and where they should live, the sun begins to set on personal liberty. Hopefully, if Barrington is allowed to live, it will come to be seen not as a burnt-out remnant of the past but as a harbinger of a more free and tolerant society.

December 3, 1987

BEVERLY A. POTTER, PHD.

Don Jelinek
City Council
City of Berkeley
2180 Milvia ST
Berkeley, CA 94704

December 3, 1987

Dear Mr. Jelinek:

Listening to the defenses of George Proper and the latest group of "Presidents" and "Vice-Presidents" representing the USCA and Barrington made it evident that the Co-op is not proposing any substantive change. And worse, that change, without intervention from the outside, is all but impossible.

Again, we were reminded that the Co-op is owned, and ruled, by the students. Mr. Proper, as always, emphasized that he can do nothing because he's merely an employee who reports to the Board. So, he is not responsible and he can not be expected to exert leadership. The Board, on the other hand, is composed of a revolving door of students with little knowledge of business or corporate functioning, little long-term commitment to the Co-op and no investment on the bottomline. Such a transient, ill-skill Board could hardly be expected to re-invent the Co-op. There's no continuity, except for Mr. Proper. He explained that Co-op corporate functions, no matter how critical, must fit into the schedule of finals and semester break. Presumably, dealing with crisis, also, must wait.

Mr. Proper described losing control of Barrington and the repetition of events, despite the turn-over of kids. He chastised the City for not helping. The latest President of Barrington explained that large groups of party crashers, such as those attending the September 25th party that featured the LSD punch, were inevitable because in the first several weeks of school the managers simply don't know who does or doesn't live in the building. Presumably, we can expect future disturbances.

I am reminded of Hannah Arendt's *The Orgins of Totalitarianism* , (as discussed in *The Oppressed Middle*, Shorris) in which she says,

> *"...bureaucracy or the rule of an intricate system of bureaus in which no men ... can be held responsible, and which could be properly called* ***Rule by Nobody.***

*"...**Rule by Nobody** is clearly the most tyrannical of all since there is no one left who could even be asked to answer for what is being done.*

*"...for the **Rule by Nobody** is not no-rule, and where all are equally powerless we have a tyranny without a tyrant."*

About that, Shorris says, *"a leader (either one person or an oligarchy) rules over a bureaucracy, making society answer to a despot in the person of Nobody, leaving the people utterly helpless and hopeless, without the possibility of appeal..."*

Our community is tyrannized by a despot in the name of Nobody. We are awaken in the night by screaming. Bottles are thrown and smashed, again and again. Who did it? Nobody knows. Nobody is responsible. Nobody can be asked to answer for what goes on at Barrington - least of all the USCA. Nobody is responsible for the pain Barrington has caused countless students and their parents. Nobody is responsible for lives injured by drugs, or Aids, in Barrington. And Nobody can be expected to correct it.

As long as Nobody is in control at the USCA and Barrington, there will be drugs, there will be nuisance and there will be City expense. The USCA is a hazard - most of all to the students living there. I urge the City to demand reform. There must be responsibility. There must be continuity. There must be guidance from mature persons with long term commitment to the Co-op as well as the community - persons with professional expertise and wisdom. Without this we will continue to be tyrannized.

Sincerely,

Beverly A. Potter
Neighbor

cc:
Shirley Dean, Councilmember
Fred Weeks, Councilmember
Ann Chandler, Councilmember
Glenn Lynch, Health Department
Dean Billingsley, UCB, Student Affiars

City of Berkeley

Fire Department
2121 McKinley Avenue
Berkeley, California 94703

(415) 644-6665
TTY (415) 644-6915

V.C. Porter
Assistant City Manager for
Public Safety Fire Chief

December 23, 1987

Mr. George Proper
2424 Ridge Road
Berkeley, California 94709

RE: Barrington Hall Incident
12-12-87, 0038 hours

Dear Mr. Proper:

On December 12, at 0038 hours the Berkeley Police and Fire Departments received a call from a citizen stating that there were flames coming from the roof of Barrington Hall. The Police and Fire Departments responded.

Apparently, the residents started a fire on the roof in some kind of make-shift container. They were burning books and papers celebrating the end of finals. The resulting fire burned vigorously carrying sparks and burning papers into the air.

The Fire Department feels that this fire endangered lives and property which is a violation of the Berkeley Fire Code BMC 19.48, Section 11.116. Citation #F30595 is enclosed. No fires of any kind will be allowed upon any part of the roof of Barrington Hall.

Sincerely,

Ronald J. Littley

Ronald J. Littley
Captain/Acting Fire Marshal

RJL:mh

Enclosure

Animal House on Acid

Tradition of Protest

Barrington had a tradition of protest. In 1983, Barringtonians established "SAFE"— Students Against Fee Extortion, which organized a statewide boycott of classes—the first in Berkeley in ovcr ten years—to protest the UC Regents fee increase and cut¬backs in humanities and minority studies.

Barringtonians dropped a banner that measured the length of the Barrington dining room off of the campanile that read, *"Boycott at Noon"*. Thousands of students took part.

Throughout the 1980s Barringtonians participated in liberal causes, including the Animal Liberation Movement, housing for the homeless, the anti-Apartheid movement, recycling to save the environment, and movements to end war and US involvement in Central America and the Middle East.

January 1988

Who is going to stand up for Barrington?

Who is going to stand up for Barrington? Anyone who thought CO. was going to do it can put those mistaken thoughts to rest. The USCA is a bureaucracy that at best, as George Proper's "lesser of two evils," has been scared into submission. Only an independent grassroots political mobilization can save Barrington.

What Barrington stands for was not created by and cannot be defended through Bourgeois parliamentary politics. It is a culture of resistance born out of the socio-political rebellions of the 1960's. It wasn't by chance that the counter-culture surfaced at the same moment in history as the anti-war movement, Black Liberation, Women's Liberation, and etc. It wasn't by chance that the Biko Plaza News came out of Barrington during the anti-apartheid movement or that Barrington served meals out on the steps. Every political outburst throughout history, every organized threat to the established socioeconomic base of a society, has brought with it an antagonistic culture that represents, fosters, and intellectually justifies a new social order.

The War on Barrington must be seen in this broader social context. The current leaders of this country, those making policies and setting the tone for this society are a reactionary force in relation to the uprisings of the 60's. Their political position arose as a reaction to the revolutionary movements of that era. Ronald Reagan and Ed Meese got their start right here in California, right here in Berkeley beating, jailing, and tear-gassing the flowering of a new cultural/political/economic society—a society that stood against imperialist genocide in Southeast Asia, that stood against racism, sexism, capitalism,

Animal House on Acid

and the entire materialist bourgeois television culture that reinforces his exploitative social structure. The changes those movements achieved were fought for. Rights that we now take for granted like just being allowed to put up a table in Sproul Plaza had to be fought for--fought not in debate against the official representatives of the ruling class, but fought in the streets against the armed and trained representatives of the ruling class.

Have no illusions. If they can take Barrington, they're going to take People's Park. They'll build ten more Miller's Outposts on Telegraph. How do you spell Chateau in Greek? Their cultural counter-insurgency won't stop here. What happened to Stoney Burke? They even want your drugs. City Councilman Don Jellodick concludes that Barrington is a peril to young people because of the availability of drugs. But there are hundreds of thousands of heroin junkies and millions of coke addicts in this country. Meaningless American commercial culture is the peril to young people. Barrington is, if anything, a refuge of significance for some of the disillusioned, one small alternative to corporate hell.

Yes it's true, after Barrington, Chateau is next. But the way to save Chateau is not by running and hiding, not by canceling parties and postponing special snacks. If we want Chateau to be just an apartment building or a mindless dormitory, if we want Chateau to be just a cheap place to live while we go to school, then these defeatist tactics are fine. But if we want Chateau to be a <u>cooperative</u>, a different kind of living arrangement with a vision towards social change and a more humane existence for ourselves and for others, then we must fight, The fight doesn't start here. It starts with the defense of Barrington.

Chateauvia Underground Barrington Action Network

(We do not represent an official Chateau position)

November 5, 5:30 PM, Sebastian
Fire truck and ambulance in front of Barrington. The crowd is gathering around the entrance. Firemen and medics administering to a young black man collapsed by the front door. The medics are trying to revive him. The man's eyes keep rolling up so that only the white shows. I asked Joule (Barrington President) what happened. She said, "This person has passed out. I could not get him up so we called an ambulance." *A student in the crowd said,* "looks like an overdose to me."

November 15
Returned from out-of-town weekend to find broken bottles in the backyard, on the sidewalk under the living room window. This is approximately 25+ feet from the fence on bearings inside and the same distance from the yellow building.

From the way the models are broken, it is clear that they came from Barrington. The distance from the yard edge and the building means that they had to be thrown from an upper window or the roof.

This is no accident or simple dropping a bottle out of the window. The bottles were very close to house and just under the living room window. Not only is this a harassment but a danger to us and our property. Now we have more broken glass where we and our pets walk.

When cleaning up bottles I noticed that they had wax in opening and neck. Looks as if candles were in the bottle, but it was melted on the side, as if it laid in the ground and burned. I wondered if the candles were burning in the bottles when thrown and if it was attempt to set our house on fire. One bottle with candle was approximately 1 foot from the house!!!

November 21 Saturday night

2 a.m. Awaken by loud screaming. Yelling: "John! John! John!" *I think they were taunting John Harmon. Guess they have no reason to behave now that USCA is going to have 100% turnover.*

Informed by Ruth Oscar that this is the 2nd illegal party planned for night before Thanksgiving.

December 8 John Harmon said, "big bag" *who was calling at him from the driveway on November 21, stopped him in the little store and told him he was* "going to die."

December 12 Saturday night; 1 a.m. 12/13
Large group of Barringtonians on roof at the Dwight side built fire with newspapers. Very windy. Papers on fire were blowing off the roof onto the nearby trees. The fire department was called to put out the fire. Also very noisy party.

December 15 10 p.m.
Loud screaming. Can't tell what they are saying in the backyard

10:20 p.m. Loud screaming from the parking lot on Haste. "We are bad" *I see couple in punk-like garb, carrying bedding, screaming, appeared to go into Barrington*

January 3, 1988
Harmon called police. Ofc G H Kim #49 regarding Joel R. A "415" – harassment Joel R. threatened John (Was ring leader of bottle-throwing sprees from Rm 208, last April) and said he'd "pull a piece on you."

January 12 Ofc. Silas BPD,
Harmon reported kids in lot yelling at John, saying "going to hack him to pieces"

January 14 8:45 pm
Loud, bloodcurdling screams of anguish, as if someone were being seriously injured, accompanied by hysterical laughter.

Boy - tall, blond, semi-mohican hair cut – Tom – reluctant to talk, said police were coming. Someone "freaked out" and indicated that several people were trying to control him until police arrived. Haste entrance had several students at the door milling around. Seemed like a drug related incident.

January 14 (SEB)
Police took a long time to arrive. A large group of Barringtonians came out onto the street. Dwight and Ellsworth Police squad cars start arriving. A young man screaming. He runs north on Ellsworth. Police take chase. Crowd of Barringtonians followed.

On the corner of Ellsworth and Channing young man screaming obsenities and is restrained by the police. Four squad cars and paddy wagon with lights flashing and 10 or more patrolmen. Young man being taken to Highland Hospital. Barringtonian says he took acid and a lot of alcohol. His name is Max. Students said it was lots of alcohol and acid but his behavior more resembles PCP.

January 17 Midnight
Loud music. Yelling and wild pounding sounds, like someone beating on the walls. Call beeper line 3 times but no one called back. Finally found the number for Susan, House President. She said no one called beeper and she couldn't hear the noise. Then she called back and said they had made them be quiet she did have the beeper message. Minutes after she hung up, loud yelling like a child playing, "Indian" with hand beating on mouth. Yelling very loud. Lasted a few minutes.

January 18 1 AM
Woman screaming outside by dumpster in Barrington lot. Hippie-looking guy and punk-looking woman. Man is hitting her. She

John Harmon

I lived next door to Barrington Hall for a few years. very interesting experience... impolite, insensitive, pretentious, uncivilized, arrogant savages for the most part. I was instrumental in closing it down. They called me Red.

**Do not annoy people at home.
Do not pester them at work.
Leave them alone, or they will curse you.**

--Lao-Tsu

Barringtonians were a mellow sort, and people high on acid generally don't look to violence as a solution. Acceptance of all cultures—while some may seem foreign, may even freak people out—was the unspoken, unwritten rule at Barrington Hall.

Living in Barrington made you grow socially and accept differing opinions, whether you wanted to or not.

January 15,1988

Sebastian Orfali
PO Box 522
Berkeley CA 94701

Glenn Lynch, Health Dept
City of Berkeley
2180MilviaSt.
Berkeley, CA 94704

Dear Mr. Lynch,

A distressing incident that occurred on the night of January 14,1988. At about 8:45 pm loud, blood curdling screams emanated from Barrington Hall. It sounded like someone was being seriously injured. Beverly Potter and I went to investigate and found a tall, blond young man with a Mohican's haircut, looking distressed, in front of Barrington Hall. He identified himself as Tom (no last name), and said that he was waiting for the police. Someone inside Barrington had "tweaked out," several people inside were trying to control him until the police arrived. A number of students were mlling around at both entrances to Barrington.

After a long time, police squad cars began to arrive. A young man screaming loudly ran north on Ellsworth with several officers chasing him. A group of Barringtonians followed.

A couple of minutes later, on the corner of Channing and Ellsworth, there were about twelve officers, four squad cars and a paddy wagon and a crowd had gathered. The young man was screaming obscenities and struggling with tremendous strength. It took six officers to restrain him; he kicked and screamed as they put him in the rear of a squad car. We overheard that his name is Max, that he was being taken to Highland Hospital. We were told that he was a Barrington resident who had taken LSD and alcohol.

The young man's behavior (loudness, tremendous physical strength, violence) seemed more characteristic of PCP than LSD. We are concerned that students at Barrington are taking LSD that has PCP or some other dangerous adulterant. Can you request that Barringtonians provide you with a sample of the LSD that they are taking so that it can be tested for adulterants? In light of the circumstances there, young people taking unknown drugs, it is important to find out what exactly the purported LSD consists of.

Please find out what you can about this unfortunate incident and include the information in your files on Barrington Hall.

Yours Truly,
Sebastian Orfali
Concerned Neighbor

Acid Rain

Acid Rain was highly theatrical and indigenous to Barrington Hall in the 1985. They changed their name to Idiot Flesh prior to the release of their first LP. Members were Nils Frykdahl, Dan Rathbun, and Wes Anderson.

In 1980s the Dead Kennedys and Primus and many other Bay Area local bands played at Barrington Hall, at the Wine Dinner acid parties. The Primus song Frizzle Fry tells of that Acid Punch party in 1987. During this time, Nils, a Barringtonian Music major, composed Stravinski's Rite of Spring for guitar, bass, drums, violin, and flute.

Acid Rain performed Stravinsky's Rite of Spring on the grassy lawn in front of the Music Building on the UC Berkeley campus that spring afternoon. Acid Rain finished their show, closing with the RnR classic Free Bird.

Idiot Flesh was an American experimental rock band formed in Oakland, California in 1985, initially under the name Acid Rain. Their work was characterized by its "rock against rock" attitude and defied classification with its incorporation of marching band routines, puppet shows, and the playing of household items as tuned instruments. Adopting the **Idiot Flesh** moniker in 1987, they went on to release three full-length albums before disbanding in 1998. Founding members Nils Frykdahl and Dan Rathbun later played in Sleepytime Gorilla Museum, while Gene Jun later joined the Sun and Moon Ensemble.

was probably hitting him, too. Then went in front of Barrington. Police came with several cars. Man yelling obscenities at the police. 3 cops trying to hold him. Then woman says to leave them alone. They're not Barringtonians.

Go to sleep
Loud screaming. Can' t tell what they are saying in the backyard

10:20 PM loud screaming from the parks the <<check>> Wake up

January 18 Seb Midnight
Woman screaming in Barrington Man outside yelling back □shut the fuck up you bitch" 3 police squad cars arrive and cuff the man□□he yelled obscenities at them After while police leave and release the men

1/21 Call: "Hi. This is Bev Potter. Lick my plate, you dog dick!" to Harmon, saying it was BP. Harmon makes Police Complaint #88-4369, Ofc Torrence Badge # 63 I send Proper letter about obscene calls.

January 22
Saw Kyle going into Barrington yesterday. He's the redhead "anarchic" who lived in the room last spring and threw the bottles and garbage. It's the 2nd time I've seen him in the last one to 2 months.

January 23 12:15 a.m.
Carpet thrown earlier in the day, on the front yard area. Now bedding and broken bottles and beer cans on the public sidewalk and walkway to Haste St door at the walk going to a street.

2 girls come out of Barrington. They look like freshman. They run across the street laughing loudly. One pretends to drop a bottle, says, " Oh! I dropped it" as a bottle is thrown across the street. Then grabs it and smashes it somewhat timidly and then

says, "Oh, can you believe it? I broke that bottle!" She then throws it up in the air and let the smash in the middle of Haste. Both girls run to the glass stop on it boldly.

It was as if they were practicing anarchy and being Barringtonians. And as we walked by with Kuku, I called to the girls and ask, "Are you going to pick up that glass?" The girl says, "There isn't any glass." I say, "I saw what you did." The girls had not seen us watching them and seemed somewhat embarrassed that they were observed

1 AM When we returned from the walk 3 high school looking kids were loitering in front of BH. I asked and they said they were not Barringtonians. We could see 6 or more boys pacing and roaming about in the driveway near Elsmere. Loud guitar, live music could be heard from the Haste Street door.

January 23 6: 30 p.m.
Came home and as drove up, saw 4 Barringtonians on Haste Street steps with the fire on the step. I went over and asked what they were doing and they said they were burning a book. I insist they put the fire out. They didn't want to, but finally did so

15 min. later, 4 Barringtonians – girls – came over to explain what they were burning sexist porno book demeaning to women. Debby from third-floor, former manager, said she wants to talk to us and hear our opinion directly. I said we were not against Barrington, but the USCA, which has gotten derailed from its mission and is decadent and victimizing the students. They agreed.

January 26 2 PM
Meeting the City Hall, Jelineck. Hear tape.

January 27 9:15 PM
Get message from Dave, BH floor manager. Follow-up from January 27 meeting. He leaves no number. I called beeper. No reply to the beeper I called 3 times. No replied by 10:35 PM

Witches Sabbath – June 23

Satan was present at the Sabbath, often as a goat or satyr, and many more demons were often present. Sometimes a person could offer his or her own body to be possessed by a demon serving as a medium. The Sabbath commenced at midnight and ended at dawn, beginning with a procession, continuing with a banquet, then a Black Mass, and culminating with an orgy in which uninhibited sexual intercourse with demons in male or female form was practiced while consuming hallucinogens and alcohol.

BERKELEY FIRE DEPARTMENT

M E M O R A N D U M

January 26, 1988

To: GLEN LYNCH, Acting Assistant City Manager for Health and Human Services

FROM: RONALD LITTLEY, Captain, Deputy Fire Marshal

SUBJECT: BUILDING HEALTH AND SAFETY COMMITTEE INSPECTION REPORT FOR THE MONTH OF JANUARY

BARRINGTON HALL 2315 DWIGHT WAY

FIRE: Inspect and repair all fire doors on a regular basis. Several fire doors were found to need minor repairs.

CODES AND INSPECTIONS

BASEMENT: Provide electrical cover plate for outlet on north wall, repair west exit door. KITCHEN: Repair electrical outlet (detached and loose from wall). FIRST FLOOR: Repair broken lock, room 114, repair broken window south side exit door, repair broken window north exit door. SECOND FLOOR: Repair self closer on south side fire door. THIRD FLOOR: Repair self closer on east center corridor door (loose), repair east center stairwell light fixture (wiring exposed). Remove combustible material stored in private hall outside room 305. Repair broken glass panel and adjust north exit door for proper closing. Repair painted wall and ceiling finish northeast stairwell. SECOND FLOOR KITCHEN: Investigate cause of gas odor and repair smoke and heat detectors.

HEALTH

KITCHEN: Repaint kitchen, provide pest control service immediately (spray now), respray in two weeks and continue on a monthly basis. Cockroach infestation throughout. Please provide the Health Department with receipts for the above work, repair tile under two-compartment sink next . to stove, affix floor drain seal under dishwasher, cove bottom of storage room floor to prevent rodent entry (suggest steel cove). Repair broken tile next to stove, thoroughly clean kitchen area including floors, walls and equipment.

POLICE

During the inspection, two non-tenant persons were found sleeping on the roof. They were ordered to leave the building. Take necessary action to prevent a recurrence of unauthorized use.

THE DAILY CALIFORNIAN
Berkeley's Independent Daily; Established 1871
VOLUME BERKELEY, CALIFORNIA

Suit Filed Against Co-op Association

Neighbors charge management with permitting drug sales at Barrington

By Carolyn Jones
Staff Writer

The neighbors of Barrington Hall filed a law suit against the University Students' Cooperative Association yesterday, charging that the central management of the 1,400 member coop organization " intentionally permitted" illegal drug sales at Barrington.

The suit, which demands $375,000 in actual and punitive damages, also states that the USCA distributed wine laced with LSD at the Sept. 25 Barrington "wine dinner" party. The party, which lead to the hospitalization of four people for injuries they allegedly incurred because they ingested LSD at Barrington, has resulted in a Berkeley City Council investigation of the 2315 Dwight Way coop. "We're convinced legal action is the only way to get anything done," Sebastian Orfali, one of the plaintiffs said yesterday.

Orfali and Beverly Potter, who live next door to the 170-member coop said they filed the suit partially because the City's Barrington Task Force, which was established last October by Council member Don Jelinek failed to accomplish any change in the USCA management.

"The students who live in Barrington are, for the most part, innocent victims," Potter said yesterday. "The co-op system has become decadent and has strayed from its mission — it needs to be revamped."

USCA officials said Barrington President Susan Miles refrained from common yesterday because the suit had not been to them. USCA general manager George Proper was not available for comment.

However, Board of Directors President Elaine McCormick denied that the USCA was complicit in illegal drug dealing, and that the accusations were "far fetched."

The suit urges the USCA management, which consists of a 30-member student Board of Directors and a full-time staff, to "dissolve and be replaced by University of California trustees."

The suit was filed at the Alameda County courthouse one day after Jelinek reverse his original recommendation for a 100 percent residency turn over at Barrington Hall. Jelinek said Wednesday that he changed his mind after a visit to the co-op on Feb. 4 convinced him that he was previous mislead about a majority of co-op residents.

Councilmember Shirley Dean, who serves on he Barrington Task Force, admitted yesterday that the suit "reflects terribly on the city."

February 12, 1988

"The whole purpose the Task Force is to bring these forces together and it's done exactly the opposite," Dean said.

Although she was unable to determine how the suit would affect further progress of the Task Force, which meets again on Feb. 18, Dean said she was worried about the reaction from other unsatisfied citizens.

"We've gotten a whole rash of complaints from frustrated neighbors who think the City never accomplishes anything," she said. "This suit is positive proof that there are some unhappy people."

The suit seeks damages for nuisance, listing 22 charges including noise, garbage and graffiti, such as "Beverly gives good head!" (spray painted) on the side of Barrington Hall which faces Haste Street.

Potter, who lives on Haste Street and her attorney, Don Driscoll, said that they will "keep going with this until the problem is solved."

"The decision to file suit is serious," Driscoll said. "When we make that decision, we don't walk away from it."

Jelinek reverses his position on Barrington. Now he says it was an "isolated incident."

Bev & Seb's Attorny, Don Driscoll

John Harmon calls. Said George Proper threatened him directly. He ran into George at store. Harmon bought George a six-pack of beer. George already seemed drunk. They drank beer by the dumpster. Harmon asked that Proper make them stop bothering him. George Proper said he would make them stop for February! John said he referred anonymously to lawsuit. George said, "you will regret this for the rest of your life." Apparently, he indicated very loudly that he would "sic" Barringtonians on John. Only it is not John who's on the verge of action. We feel it's actually a covert threat to us. John seemed really scared telling me the story.

Later we look up the number of Elaine, new president of USCA. We told her no one answered the beeper and we wanted to talk to Dave. She said all Barrington managers were in a meeting. They must be discussing 100% solution, referendum, and our lawsuit. George must be there, too. He doesn't hang out here at the little store! Running into John was not an accident. We feel personally threatened for even contemplating exercising our rights

Tribune Reporter called about the Referendum.

January 27 11:45 PM
Someone in the 2nd and 3rd floor playing electric guitar

January 27 12:15 AM
Music–guitar and drums–still playing. Sounds like it's over the parking lot. Also room over gazebo with several boys talking very loudly. Must be from same room that the boy was talking very loudly last night and the night before. Last night I was awakened at 4 AM by boys talking loud. Clock said 4 AM. Awaken by same voice on Monday night, about same time, kept me awake. Had to get up at 6 am. Very sleepy all day.

January 27 noise continues. I called the beeper again. Susan Miles finally calls. Gives meaningless excuse for not answering. SM said she checked on it. Then would turn off the beeper because John Harmon had gotten the number (only John's had the number for a year and a half years). Then she said something about

George talking about John calling him. Got the impression she had never gotten call on beeper from John. Yet, she made reference to expected harassment calls from John "now that he has the beeper". And that George had given her that idea

January 28 Morning
Realize we got two strange messages, one on 540, and one on 548, both were Morse code-like taping, identical pattern.

Evening–John Harmon called–last night he got 5 calls–4 were nearly identical tapping to those we got, one was heavy breathing, left on his machine

John Harmon's report: Ofc Torrance #63, case number 884639; our report: Case number 885784

Spoke with Charles Spinoza. He said he saw a drug deal in front of Elsmere two weeks ago – white powder – was connected with Barrington. John Harmon suggested John Johnson as a witness who is the VP at Fenwick. He is anti-Proper but devoted to the USCA he was Deep Throat during Hell Summer.

January 29 midnight
Very loud music, screaming, from back step–sounds like it's coming from the alley and Dwight end of Barrington. Call beeper. No response. At 12:30 call Susan M number and get tape. Tell her big bird not responding and "it's a drag." About 1:15 or so Susan calls. She was angry. Said there was no noise in Barrington. As she talked I could hear screaming. She said she was in San Francisco. We argued over whether or not the beeper response had deteriorated. I told her if she's in SF, someone else should have the deeper. She had all excuses as usual. They were in class, they were in meetings, no one else is authorized, etc.

I could still hear the screaming. She said there had been 3 strangers in Barrington who threw firebombs but denied any other noise. Just as in the past, she did not investigate. Each time I spoke to her attitude is very adversarial. It's not appropriate to the house president. She's the worst president since Hell Summer

PRESS RELEASE
RICO Suit Filed Against Student Co-op

Neighbors Orfali and Potter filed a suit for nuisance in February, 1988 following an LSD "acid" party at Barrington Hall that sent seven students to the hospital. The suit was amended December 19, 1988, adding Plaintiffs Oscar and Spinoza and asserting nuisance, intentional tort, negligence, racketeering and drug activity, filed in Alameda County Superior Court (No. 635475-0) by neighbors against the University Students Cooperative Association for Racketeering and drug activity.

Neighbors' RICO complaint asserts:

2. "*...the USCA has unlawfully distributed drugs, including LSD and nitrous oxide at Barrington Hall. Further, the USCA has ... unlawfully sold alcohol and unlawfully distributed alcohol to persons under 21.*"

14. "*...sold, distributed, and used unlawful drugs including LSD, nitrous oxide, methamphetamine, and heroin within Barrington Hall.*"

22. "*...the USCA maintained a policy that emergency police services (i.e., 911) and other emergency services could not be called in the event of a drug overdose....the USCA has routinely dragged the victims of drug overdoses out of Barrington Hall before calling 911.*"

39. "*...Barrington Hall was, as a result of distribution of drugs by the USCA itself, a major center for the unlawful distribution of alcohol and drugs in the Berkeley South-Campus area.*"

55. "*By falsely representing the wrongful conduct to be less common than it in fact was, the USCA intentionally limited private and government investigations that would have terminated the conduct.*"

69. "*...the USCA would threaten injury to any USCA member who sought to disclose information about drug use to who sought to disclose any of the conduct alleged in this complaint.*"

The 50 year old student coop is a non-profit and tax-exempt 501 c.3 corporation (Exempt from property and income tax like a church.) It owns and operates 18 residential buildings in Berkeley assessed at over $16 million and is Berkeley's second largest landlord. (University of California is the largest landlord in Berkeley.)

Since 1983, Barrington Hall, its largest building which houses approximately 180 students (mostly freshmen and sophomores) has been the subject of intense neighborhood pressure in response to nuisance and drug activities: Elsmere, a neighboring apartment building, took Barrington Hall to **Arbitration** (1983-84); a **City Task Force** investigated heroin activities (1985-86) and a **City Subcommittee** investigated LSD and other drug activity (1987-88).

Use Immunity Order Granted

Attorney Don Driscoll obtained an Order, without objection from the United States Attorney or the Alameda County District Attorney, granting use immunity for 29 Barrington residents and employees of the USCA from the use of testimony concerning "drug use" and alcohol use in Barrington Hall. A "Use Immunity Order" deprives a witness of his or her right to claim the privilege under the Fifth Amendment against self-incrimination because the testimony cannot be used against him or her.

BEVERLY A. POTTER, PHD.

Council member Don Jelinek
City of Berkeley
23180 Milvia St
Berkeley, CA 94704

February 15, 1988

Dear Don:

We are confused by your announcement reversing your position vis-a-vis the 100% turnover and closing of Barrington for the Summer. You were quoted in *the Tribune* saying that before you would drop your campaign to close the hall "we must have a monitoring mechanism so that these things don't happen again." *The Daily Cal* reports that you now believe the acid party was an isolated incident.

What you were told at the meeting in Barrington should be suspect. Barringtonians subscribe to the "Onngh Yanngh," a code of silence regarding drug activity that says, *"Those who know don't tell and those who tell don't know."* There a documented record spanning more than ten years of drug activity, including dealing and overdoses. Many parents, whose children have been seriously damaged by drug-usage in Barrington, have protested.

The September 25 "acid punch" bash was an institutional event, endorsed by Robert Dick who reported directly to the Central Office. How many acid parties are acceptable? The 3-year probation specified that any drug incident constituted a violation of probation. The acid bash was no isolated incident. Evan Steele, (then) President of the USCA reported that he had remained silent about another acid party last summer (see enclosed). On November 5, 1987 a non-student over-dosed and was removed unconscious by paramedics. On January 14, 1988, a Barringtonian was arrested for acting violently in a drug-related incident,

City staff professionals, including those in the Building, Health, Fire and Police Departments, have worked hard (and at great expense to the City) to correct the situation. Yet, it is on the record that you and other Council members have had private meetings with USCA officials and promised to help fight efforts to curb the problems at Barrington. We are quite concerned about such Council support against the neighborhood's efforts to get a lasting solution to the problems. We can't understand the motive for protecting this unwholesome activity. We are hoping that you and the City will be friends of the Court, or be at least neutral and not run interference with our constitutional right to seek recourse through the Courts. And we request that you actively dissuade attempts to harass us,

A number of meetings have been held without notice to all interested parties to discuss the problems at Barrington. We are interested parties. Please inform us of all meetings.

Sincerely.

cc: All interested parties

Dildo in the Door

We found a large black dildo pushed into the front door mail slot. We figured it was from Barriington. Who else?

Later when I walking home from Cody's Bookstore on corner of Telegraph and Haste, I noticed a squad car parked on Haste just a few feet from the sidewalk. As I got closer I saw that the cop was in the car.
"Ah, an opportunity," I thought.

So I tapped on the car widow and the Officer lowered the window. *"Officer, my house was subjected to vandalism earlier today."* I began. *"Oh?"* The Officer replied. *"What happened?"*

Pointing down Haste I said, *"Officer my house is just drown the street next to Barrington Hall. When I came out about an hour ago I found a black dildo stuck in the mail slot in my door. I think someone from Barrington did it to harass me."*

While looking up at me, the Officer held up his hands, with the palms facing about a twelve to fifteen inches apart—as if indicating a length. He asked, *"Was is about **this big**?"*

The Officer recommended that we make a Police Report:
3/3/1988 # 88-13308
Ofc Bachman #12.

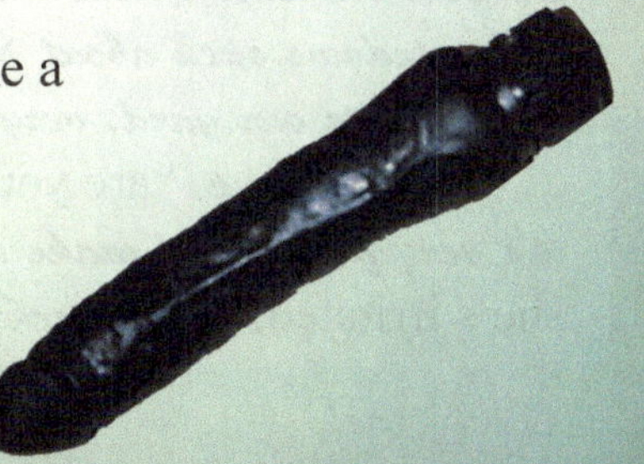

After call, I can still hear noise. I go out. The noise is still coming from the alley. Finally determine it's coming from the back of the yellow building. In lull of noise, I call the kids to be quiet and close the door. They are immediately quiet.

It's one of the few times noises not from BH. Problem could have been handled much more quickly had the beeper responded and had a Barringtonian investigated. Instead I was up and down and walking around in almost 2 AM in the bathrobe. Once in the past about a year and half ago was a Barrington and Carlos called back when the noise was identified

January 30 carpet is still in front yard

February 5
Talking to Eddie, he says his frat is new and they had to go before the Board of Adjustment and the City Council for a use permit. The City Manager said there should be no more frats because they are racist. And he said their attorney said that's illegal. They are allowed to "associate". City, especially Jelinek, said frat must learn to be good neighbors. City imposed limits (reduced occupancy, apparently some kids had to move). "Party papers" must meet with neighbors and they MUST have a live-in, non-student manager! They got one-year conditional permit. His frat has no complaints

Why not the same contracts controls for the Co-op? Why the contradiction? Why shouldn't Co-op have to be a good neighbor? Why shouldn't they have to get the use permit, especially with the 10-year bad record?

February 5 8:30 PM
Weird screaming, heckling noises in the back. Finally go out. Several students on the 2nd floor window over the solar heater. The windows open about 8 inches. Have mouths in open space and calling into our yard, very loud.

I call up, "are you deliberately bothering us?" They think it's very funny and make more noise. Girl yells to friend, "I think she's irritated." I go back in

DEAD SOULS

Little while later, 8:50 PM, much louder. I go out in the yard. They laughed when seeing me and yell louder. Girl says, "I'll do the machine gun sound." *I hold up a tape recorder. She immediately stopped. I tell her to keep on that I'm recording and I find out whom they are and they'll "pay". They are immediately quiet for the remainder of the evening*

February 6 1:08 PM
False alarm at Barrington. 2 fire trucks responded to Dwight Way entrance

February 6 11 PM Kuku's loud barking brought our attention to a person in a car parked in front of the house. Sebastian said he kept coming back to the car and rummaging around. Seb asked me to check him out. He was extremely furtive, all in black, frightening looking with strong muscular arms, very demonic looking. Taking things out of paper bag and putting them into another bag. He took out a sickle and put it in his belt, like a weapon. Then he took out a bag—black plastic—and slung it over his shoulder and went into Barrington. He was extremely frightening

Sebastian thought he was very stoned because he seemed to be undirected and repetitive. The sickle was frightening because he put in his belt like a weapon and because of the association with satanic rituals, etc.

February 7
Car still there in the morning. Person was not a Barringtonian, stayed overnight

Monday: suddenly the places cleaned up. Quiet. No carpet- graffiti and Satan symbols painted over.

>>> Missing here - get<<<

Begin 2/8 Carolyn Jones to 2/21

2/8/88 Carolyn Jones from Daily Cal – says there was a

meeting with City Councilman Jelnick, Susan Miles, Proper and others. Carolyn Jones was excluded.

2/9 2pm Bill Taylor, aid to Jelinick called, Very angry, defending Barrington. Tried to explain the beeper problem. Bill called them "charges" and was very hostile. I tried to explain it wasn't necessary to defend them. I said Don (Jelinick) was conflicted and couldn't act. BT agreed that he was conflicted. Kept emphasizing that Jelinick was sincere and perhaps hadn't been thorough enough to see the repetitive pattern. There's a hazard there that must be correct. I emphasized repeatedly that we weren't trying to discredit Jelineck.

Taylor was insistent to get our log. I said I had to talk to attorney. He brought up Harmon and the potato incident. I explained how Harmon is constantly provoked. That USCA doesn't tell the story accurately.

Mentioned that Proper said he couldn't act due to Berkeley's rent laws. Taylor said that was bullshit. I agreed and pointed out how USCA not helping kids to get the bad ones out. Preventing it.

Emphasized that our action can be used by Jelineck. Unwholesomeness, not good for students. Wrong to defend.

Taylor very attackingly said, "So you want to shut the USCA down?" I wouldn't tell him the contents of the suit but said that he'd be the first one to know.

Seems like Jelineck is actively defending and protecting USCA – giving them legal advice etc. Why?

2/9 Eric R's father said from his contact with the kids he suspected that management at high levels were involved, especially since they would discuss and create agreed upon stories.

Father said he had made mathetical projection based on his knowledge of drug business of how much money was going through Barrington each month. He's a mathematician. He said he's concerned and will cooperate and will make a statement to the attorney.

2/10 Ruth Oscar said twice in last week to week and ½ she has seen a fire in a Barrington room. She can see into the boy's room and he is burning papers in there. She is afraid he's becoming a "pyro". She says she's afraid if Barrington goes up, the whole block will go. I told her I was concerned and she should keep a log or call and log with me.

2/10 Late afternoon. Carolyn Jones of Daily Cal called and said she was not calling about the lawsuit but to ask me of what I thought of Don Jelineck's decisions. (Wasn't clear if it was formally announced.)

He told Jones he had gone into Barrington and meet with 50 Barringtonians (must have been Wed night meeting) and had decided that eviction – 100% turnover and closing Barrington was a bad idea and had decided against it. What did I think?

I was very surprised. I wondered under what authority could he do this. Is he running the USCA? I said I thought the "100% solution" was a bad idea, but what was the alternative or was it that nothing would happen –again??!!

I am very confused by this. It feels like Jelineck is protecting himself and overstepping his bounds, being over-reaching. I don't understand why the Coop gets such leeway and not the same contract as the Frats.

2/16 Ruth Oscar reported calling beeper on Saturday afternoon (2/14) because of loud music. Took 25 minutes to respond. Susan M called and said she wasn't at Barrington and was in an important meeting and couldn't do anything. Ruth was told to call the main switchboard. This is the same kind of response I've gotten when calling the beeper. Susan is usually extremely rude and snippy, makes little or no effort to correct the problem.

2/17 George F on Dwight Way called at 10:30 pm very angry, attacking. Said Barrington is an addition to neighborhood. "Why are you doing this?" "Don't you know how much pressure they've been under?" Kept saying how angry he was. When hanging up he said, "Go back to Marin!"

2/19/88 6:45 pm Oscar R called. He got a threatening call from nervous person who said, "We are going to fuck up your car and burn your house."

2/21 missing<<<<

—

2/25/88 J Harmon said he went out for a while and got 5 hang up call.

2/26 8:30ish A fire engine at Barrington. Seb asked driver and he said, "It seems to be a false alarm."

3/2 We found a large black dildo pushed into the front door mail slot. We believe it was from Barriington. On recommendation of Lt Phelps, we made a police report.

3/3/88 # 88-13308 Ofc Bachman #12
Lt Phelps gave info re: Oscar Romano's harassing calls. Case # 653M, Radio Rm 644-6743

3-4 Referendum Passes. 1 am and 2:40 am Barringtonians yell to J Harmon from rood "We won john and you're stuck with us for another year!"

3/5 8 pm Three fire trucks at Barrington for false alarm.

3/5 Harmon reported that at 11:15 pm Party on lower roof – "Stump-dance". In black & white robes – including Peter S. Harmon called Susan M – she closed party down. The police came.

3/6 Harmon reported Matt R – recycle person –breaking wooden boxes for dumpster. Harmon told him to be quiet – then threw two apples at the kid. Called Susan M at 11:16 pm – she said he woke them up too. So what?

Student who walked off roof on acid Scott Hewett – lives in CZ.

3/6 8 pm Very loud banging noises from Barrington – like slamming a metal door or banging the metal fire escape. We looked and saw nothing. Noise several more items. We go out-see nothing. Then old Barringtonian from 1985 – tall, lanky, maybe glasses & mustache & brown shoulder length hair in page boy – walked by and said, "Do you keep your lawyers number on your rolodex?" and continued laughing as he walked to Ellsworth and around the corner. Then I saw 2 guys younger looking up at the front of Barrington. I asked them what the noise was. They said they didn't know. Another guy was holding the door open. I asked him what the noise was. He said he was there to find out also. I told all 3 that the guy said about the lawyer. They said he must have been demented. I said, "No, he was an old Barringtonian."

Saying sexual things -⊠ sex unit 644-6062
Case #88-14288, Ofc Dew #106

Old call cases:
#88-5784 #88—4369

Disturbance #88-6274
#87-23946 Advice Ofc Latrell

3/18 2 pm Extremely loud music – heavy metal.

3/18 10:57 loud drumming from Barrington. I worry that Mr. H – tenant – will get upset and move out.

3/20 1:15 am A lot of laughing, talking and music room 3rd floor over alley.

3/22 CASE #88-17576, OFC BLACKWELL #122

Around 4:30-5p, Sebastian & I were going out front door when a pipe landed about 5 feet in front of Seb on sidewalk betw/car and house. It had to have come from Barrington. We looked up and could see no one in the windows, which were all closed. I picked up the pipe, which had been smoked a lot but had nothing in it and smelled like tobacco. We looked up to roof and down alley but saw no one. We decided it was nothing and I tossed the pipe up against Barrington wall behind bush.

About 45 minutes later a call on 644 came. Seb answered. Caller, a male, said, "I heard a pipe was thrown into your yard." Seb asked, "How did you know about the pipe. We didn't tell anyone." He gave the phone to me and the caller said, "Are you Beverly Potter, PhD or Beverly Potter?" (Those are my phone book listings.) I said, "Who is this?" Caller said, "I want you to know that I'm not a resident of Barrington --unintelligible – but a member of the USCA and I hate you. You cunt! And hung up.

About 10-15 minutes later I went out to get the pipe but it was gone. We looked and we could not see BH roof when leaving because of our roof overhang. Someone on roof could see us come down stairs by our feet. Seb was just about in the place where person on roof could see him when pipe landed. The pipe was substantially into our yard – about even with bathroom window. So it just didn't fall.

Also due to tree, we can't see if someone is hiding on roof watching us or about to throw something. They can all see us.

John Harman mentioned pipe bombs and how easy they are to make. That is extremely frightening, considering the work shifters threats in the USCA Referendum packet and their rhetoric that sounds so similar to the IRA/Ireland. They are constantly throwing bombs at people. We are very afraid and feel scared going in and out of our house.

3/26 Night. Very noisy, music, loud voices.

3/27 1:30 am Loud drumming from Dwight Way end. Lay in bed. So tired – too tired to call beeper. Very grading.
4/11 Loud drumming. 12:15 pm

4/12 Stereo and talking. So tired just listen. Too tired to call.

4/14 11:48 pm Party-type talking.

5/7 Saturday. Barrington Party. Weird screams, very loud music. (Prior to party saw 6-8 high school kids – ghetto looking – coming out of BH) Electric guitars coming from Dwight Way. Still very loud after 2 am when finally fell asleep.

5/9 Barrington Task Force
Last 2 meetings no USCA people attended. One prior was attended by G Proper only. Unexpectedly 14 USCA people showed up at meeting, including G Proper, Attorney Felix S., Roxanne Neil, Neil Houston all form the Central Office plus student USCA officials. They seemed to walk in concert as if by a plan. They questioned the purpose of the committee, objected to being asked for documents, tried to change the name of the committee. John Harmon repeated the high salaries of each and accused them of obfuscations. Shirley Dean repeatedly asked for a written statement specifying the USCA relationship with Barrington. E. McCormick said it was stated in the Probation and it was still in effect unchanged. They repeatedly insisted that the probation was in effect unchanged but would be acted upon by committee on June 2.

However, when it was pointed out that en external manager was a provision of the probation, the kid who was recoding who said he was the VP of BH said, "Oh, they forgot to mention this one small change." It became clear to everyone that they were bullshitting. Shirley Dean continued to press for a statement of policy – in writing.

Neil, Houston and Proper all made strong statements discounting us. We were defaming; we couldn't really tell high school kids, we were lining our pockets, etc.

Roxanne Neil and George Proper both agreed that BH has exhibited a cyclic pattern. Proper in the closing statement spoke of the extreme problem at BH "Probation is not a light switch" The message as always was that they had taken great action and made great strides and improvement. Proper talked of "failures" vs. "a failure".

Beverly emphasized being tormented and not knowing whom to turn to correct the problems, esp. with maintenance and nuisance.

After, Sebastian asked Proper whom do we go to with

problems, i.e., the gate. He said, "Legally I'm not responsible." Seb pushed to how to deal with problems. He said if Barrington "blows you off" then you can come to me. He said Susan, the house mgr, is leaving in 2 weeks. When we asked WHO was replacing her, he said that he wasn't legally required to tell us that.

Beverly overheard B Taylor, Jelineck's aid, admonishing Emmitt Jones, the City Mgr, replacing Glen Lynch, for taping the meeting and telling him "It'll be subponed" and Jones said defensively, "I only did it for my notes. It'll be destroyed in the morning."

Shirley Dean asked us to call her later. She said on the phone, "They're out for blood" She indicated that the BCA was extremely pressuring.

We were very apprehensive all night.

The USCA repeatedly expressed concern over notes requested by the City – especially the minutes of the executive Committee. Roxanne Neil seemed to over do it in her repeated assertions that NO minutes were ever taken.

6/4 1:30 AM
BANJO PLAYING WAKES ME UP. I GET UP AND TURN OFF ALARM. GO OUT IN BACK TO CONFIRM IT IS FROM BARRINGTON. I'VE GOT TO GET UP AT 6:30 AM FOR NSA WORKSHOP. I CALL BEEPER. POLITE BOY NAME TONY ANSWERS. HE PROMISES TO HANDLE IT. IT'S QUIET IMMEDIATELY UPON MY DIALING AGAIN. I WONDER IF THEY HAVE A SCANNER? 2ND BEEPER? It's the old shooting gallery

Susan M must be gone. Who's the new president? What's the system? There's been no response to our request to fix the fence.

6/4 9:45 pm A lot of yelling from Dwight Way. We stand in

the yard to check. There's a large group on the roof. Later noise increases with yelling and loud music.

6/14 Tuesday
Returned from Vancouver exhausted. As we drove up we saw security gate wide open. Made us feel insecure since our house was empty and alley gives access to our yard. Then noticed that the mechanism to make it close automatically had been vandalized. Totally broken apart. Can't help thinking it's in response to our letters requesting that it be repaired.

After 10pm Very loud electric guitar player practicing in BH. We call beeper at 10:20 pm No reply to beeper. How can we sleep? Things are getting worse. Who do we turn to?

6/14 11 pm Noise is louder. We call police. Now we can't go to sleep because we must wait for police to arrive. Another room facing Haste St is also making very loud noise. Live drumming. Seems evident that there are no behavior standards in force.

6/15 12:20 am Police still have not arrived. Finally we cancel the call so that we can go to sleep and not be awaken by police. Also the noise in back – had quieted. I called the beeper and there was no reply. Finally I call Roxanne Neil's beeper and she replied. She couldn't do anything then but agreed to talk with Tony and Joyce to find out why beeper isn't working.

7/2 3 am Extremely loud electric guitar. Called Barrington beeper 3 times - no reply. Call Roxanne Neil's beeper. No reply. Went out to Haste St door in bathrobe and knocked and knocked. Finally someone yelled at me. I told them to stop the noise and they told me to "fuck off" I kept knocking. Finally a guy came. Wouldn't open door. He said it was not the 1st time he'd stayed over in BH. I kept asking him to get a floor manager. Finally he said that if I'd go away, he'd "act as a manage" and make them quiet. I left. And noise had stopped anyway. Next afternoon Tony called and said he was sick so didn't answer the beeper.

7/7 Awaken at 3:20 am by loud yelling and laughing. Called beeper. It answered. Girl said she would quiet them.

7/12 11pm Again loud electric guitar starting around 11 pm and went on and on. I called police about mid-night. Noise went on. Called beeper at 1:10 am. No reply. Noise went on until about 2 am.

8/24 Extremely loud noise though out Barrington Yelling, several music sources, electric guitar unrelenting until about 1:45 am. It was intolerable. I finally called beeper and noise coincidently stopped just at that time. No one responded to beeper call.

8/26 1:32 am A sleep and suddenly awaken by what sounded like someone using a garbage can lid as a drum. Called the beeper and again no response to it.

8/27 7:30 am Awaken by screaming and hooting. Someone yelled "Wake up, God damn it!" After about 15-20 minutes they were quiet. I am beginning to thing Barringtonians are deliberately trying to bug us and the other neighbors.

9/23 Loud music in room above back doo after 12:30 called beeper. No answer. Beeper continues to be ineffective.

10/14 Wake up at approx. 2:30 am, 2:45 am, 3 am. Finally around 3 am get up and call beeper. Sporadic high-pitched almost hysterical giggle laugh then strange screaming laughing sounds. Beeper does not respond. Then hear laugh screaming and crying. Then silence.

10/15 After midnight. Return from walking Haiku. Group of 4-5 young (under 20ish) ran out of fire escape. Saw Sebastian and ran back into bldg. Then he noticed 2 5 gal kitchen buckets filled with dirt. Looked as if they had been thrown from roof or fire escape. One was in middle of the street, on the sidewalk. Returned with camera. Then saw broken glass in street and several broken boards. While taking pictures several girls came out of bldg. They asked if we saw anyone and said someone – not Barringtonian had taken their fire extinguisher. Said they were high school kids. Then they saw dirt buckets and substantial dent in a brown VW Rabbit. It looked pretty certain that the car had been hit. When they noticed who I was and that I was taking pictures one 17 yr ish girl challenged me. Wanted to know why I wanted to search their rooms and asserted that they owned the bldg. I made several remarks about the USCA being a slumlord. Then out came several old time Barringtonians including Ged, David S and another guy I've seen at meetings. The 1st group rapidly disappeared. Some exhibited concern over the dented car. Others said forget the car. One asserted it was not a "house authorized event" and brushed all the dirt aside. Everyone left. In the morning we notice the dirt had been swept up. The board removed and no evidence of the event.

10/16 10 pm Heather Jones of The Daily Cal called. Pretty challenging about inspection of BH. I urged her to call Don Driscoll.

2/25/89 About mid-night something hit the side roof next to BH. It had come from BH. I went out back to check. As I stood on the deck I saw live cigarettes come off roof – flashing in the dark. I was very upset, recalling the burning object that fell a couple of weeks ago.

2/28/89 While putting in skylight Sebastian found a hole. A fresh looking hole in the roof about where the noise came from. It was a gash. Sebastian patched it We feel assaulted by fire and objects thrown from BH roof.

Beverly A. Potter, PhD `
PO Box 1035
Berkeley, Ca 94701

November 17, 1988

George Proper
General Manager
USCA,
1414 Ridge Road
Berkeley, Ca

Dear George:

Perhaps you are aware that last Saturday night John S, who seemed to be under the influence of speed or some other strong stimulant, arrested me for loitering when I stopped for a few minutes in the driveway near Elsmere. When I attempted to leave with Sebastian, J.S. assaulted him. The only reason we were not injured is because we did not fight back. Sebastian was repeatedly and forcefully pushed into the wall, bumped and shoved. We were forcefully detained until the police arrived.

There is no City ordinance prohibiting "loitering." Even if J.S. meant "trespassing," trespassing is not a criminal offense. One cannot be arrested for it. Further, even if the "arrest" were a legitimate action, it was improper for J.S. to physically assault Sebastian in order to prevent my departure. In short, J.S. unlawfully arrested me, assaulted Sebastian and imprisoned us.

J.S. seemed to be acting both as an individual and as an official of the co-op. All of the Barrington floor managers and party bouncers acquiesced to his demand to detain us. And no one stopped his physical abuse of Sebastian.

J.S. as an official of the coop and the coop's responsibility will be handled in the lawsuit. I wish to address J.S's responsibility as an individual separately through the Student Conduct Office at UC Berkeley. However, I have been informed that J.S. is not enrolled at the University. He dropped out in the Spring semester, over 6 months ago.

Please inform me at what educational institution John S. is enrolled. If he is no longer a student, and the facts suggest that he isn't, then inform me as to when the USCA intends to terminate his residency and remove him from the premises. I believe that J.S. poses a threat to our safety. If he continues living in the coop, which under its 501c3 status is allowed to house students only, I will ask Mr. Moy in the Country Assessor's Office to investigate the matter.

Regards,

Beverly A. Potter, PhD
Sebastian Orfali
2310 Haste Street
Berkeley, Ca 94704

November 17, 1988

Internal Affairs
Berkeley Police Department

Dear Internal Affairs Officer:

Enclosed is a complaint that we prepared for the Police Review Commission. We feel that the actions of Officer Thornton, #108, significantly diminished our safety. We spoke with the Watch Commander shortly after the incident. However, since that time we have discussed the matter with our attorney with neighbors, with Shirley Dean's Aid, and Captain Jenkins and come to the conclusion that a formal complaint is in order.

We are bringing the matter to the attention of your office first because the Police can most effectively act to correct the dangerous impression created by Officer Thornton.

We feel it is essential that the Police Department issue a written statement to the USCA and to John Scully who committed the unlawful acts against us .

We look forward to hearing from you in the near future.

Sincerely,

Beverly A. Potter
Sebastian Orfali

cc: Captain Jenkins
Barrington Subcommittee
Don Driscoll, Attny.

Complaint: #88-68831 Police Review Commission

There was a loud party on Saturday night, November 12, 1988, at Barrington Hall which is next to our home. There were many fire crackers being set off and numerous people milling around the front of our house. We are members of a City Subcommittee investigating activities at Barrington. Another member of the Committee, who lives in the Elsmere Apartments on Dwight Way next to Barrington called and told us that she had been informed by the Barrington person who answered the phone beeper that the fire crackers were being set off by high school students. In response we decided to walk over to Elsmere. At about 11:30 pm we walked down the driveway/ally connecting Haste Street and Dwight Way. Elsmere holds an easement on the ally, which is used regularly by the neighborhood as a pass-through. There are no private property signs posted. Twelve or more other people were walking through the alley at the same time.

Just below the stairs midway down the alley, a Barringtonian was guarding the side door and a stranger was asking to enter and being rebuffed. John Scully, a Barrington resident who is known to us, was loudly calling to the door guard, telling her to let the stranger in. She was insisting that she was not supposed to do so. Several people were watching the incident. Beverly stopped for 2 to 3 minutes to observe whether or not the stranger would be allowed to enter. She said nothing, while standing on the far side of a parked vehicle. She was not conspicuous and did nothing to attract attention to herself. She was facing away from Scully and approximately 8 to 12 inches from the Elsmere building.

Apparently, one of the several people who squeezed between her and the building recognized her as a member of the Committee and party to a civil suit against the USCA, which owns and operates Barrington Hall. Suddenly, John Scully began loudly calling out her name. At that point, Beverly moved a few feet to a step behind the building on Elsmere property. And stood facing Scully. The truck was between them.

Scully made dramatic gestures as he accused her of "loitering" and ordered her to leave. He seemed to be trying to provoke an incident. She said quietly, *"Come on, John."* He continued to accuse her of loitering and said he would call the police and threatened to "arrest" her. Beverly pointed to some strangers standing several feet away and asked, *"What about them?"* Scully said, *"They're invited and they're not suing us."*

Scully's behavior was like that of someone under the influence of speed or some other strong stimulant. Beverly remained on the spot briefly, watching Scully and trying to determine if he was under the influence. The encounter up to this point was no more than 3 minutes. As Scully continued to order Beverly to leave, Sebastian, who had walked ahead, returned. Scully said, "*I'm leaving now and if you're here when I return I'm going to call the police.*" At that point, with Sebastian in the lead, we began moving down the narrow passage between the truck and the building to leave.

Suddenly Scully ran around the front of the truck and attempted to block us from leaving. He yelled, *"I've arrested her. You can't leave."* When we moved to walk past him, he grabbed Sebastian and pushed him violently against the building and held him there. He seemed to have extraordinary strength for his size. When Sebastian attempted to break away, Scully repeatedly banged Sebastian into the building while yelling, "*I've arrested her*" over and over. Scully's hands were rapidly moving around Sebastian's shoulders, neck and head as he grabbed and pushed him.

Several Barrington door guards ran up and began yelling at us. We were quickly surrounded by several yelling people, all who seemed to be dressed in black. Beverly keep pleading with Sebastian to stand still and begged Scully to stopping putting his hands on him. She said over and over, *"John, this is not smart. Don't do this."* Scully continued to grab and shove Sebastian as we slowly pushed our way toward Dwight Way. He kept yelling, *"I know my rights. I've arrested you and I can stop you from leaving."* We moved about 30 feet while surrounded. Many more people came. We stopped moving. Barrington floor managers came and asked Scully what he was doing. Scully seemed in charge and no one stopped Scully from detaining us. We had made it to Dwight Way when the police arrived - approximately 10 minutes. Apparently there had been two 911 calls.

Just before the police arrived we noticed that Ruth Oscar, the Elsmere resident who had phoned us earlier was standing there. She said she had heard a lot of yelling, looked out of the window and saw Sebastian being pushed around

18. Describe incident in full. Give specific times, dates and locations of Police conversation and directions, nature and extent of abuse. Be sure to state how the incident concluded.

Two officers arrived. One took Scully and other Barringtonians aside. The other, Officer Thronton #108, asked us to follow him to a spot about 20 feet from the others. Ofc. Thornton asked us what happened. Each time Sebastian tried to tell him, the Officer interrupted, telling him to calm down. The most Sebastian was able to say was *"He arrested Beverly for loitering and assaulted me when we tried to leave."* Officer Thornton asked Beverly no questions and wouldn't allow her to talk.

After about 2 minutes, Officer Thornton went over to the Officer questioning Scully and then returned in about a minutes. He said, *"The man says you were on his property. He was acting within his rights."* Sebastian said, *"He assaulted me!"* Officer Thornton said, *"He said he didn't hit you."*

The Officer then took out his small pad and asked first for Sebastian's name and then for Beverly's name, which he wrote on the pad. He would not allow Beverly to make any statement, even though she repeatedly asked to tell her side. The Officer walked over to the other Officer again and then returned again. This time Officer Thornton seemed angry. He called the incident "ridiculous" and chastised us at length for "wasting police time" and *"calling the police for ridiculous reasons."* *(See footnote) We protested that we had not called the police. Sebastian asked, *"What about his assaulting me?"* Officer Thornton snapped back, *"I don't want to hear any more about this."*

Beverly asked Officer Thornton, *"Won't you please talk to our witness,"* and pointed at Ruth Oscar who as standing about ten feet away. Officer Thornton said he would not. Beverly said, *"Please take her name down."* Officer Thornton turned and as he walked away said, *"I"m not talking to any witness and I'm not taking any witness's name. Go home. This is a waste of time and we're leaving."*

Officer Thornton seemed angry and walked quickly to his car, got in and drove way. He did not disperse the crowd which had grown to over 25 people. Instead, we were left standing there within five feet of Scully who was loudly bragging to the crowd about his actions. We quickly walked away before he saw us.

Distressed and feeling that we had not been able to tell our side of the story we called the Watch Commander, Lt. Borders at about 12:30 am. Sebastian relayed our concerns. Lt Borders called back at about 1:15 am, saying that he had spoken to Officer Thornton. We repeated our concerns about Officer Thornton's handling of the incident and our fear that the police report would not reflect our side of the story. We told the story again to Lt. Borders who assured us it would be included in the report. He gave us the case number, which Officer Thornton had failed to do.

** Later Beverly recalled John Harmon, another neighbor, telling her of his frustration with an Officer Thornton's responses when he called for police intervention in altercations with some Barrington Hall residents. He said the Officer was "out to get him."*

28. Summary Allegations) of Primary Complaint(s) against police personnel.

a. Officer Thornton and/or the other officer put words into Scully's mouth. When Scully said Beverly was "loitering" they reinterpreted it as "trespassing."

b. The Officer said that Scully was "acting within his rights" instead of chastising him for making an illegal arrest and for wrongfully using physical force to detain us. From Scully's bragging to the crowd, it appeared that the Officers had given him the impression that his behavior was appropriate.

The Officers have increased the risk to our physical safety. We can only assume that Scully and/or other individuals will take similar action in the future against us or other neighbors. Officer Thornton clearly gave the . impression that it is okay to arrest neighbors and to use physical force in the process.

c. Officer Thornton refused to take any statement from Beverly, the arrested individual. He discounted Sebastian's account of being assaulted.

d. Officer Thornton refused to take a statement from our witness or to take her name.

e. Officer Thornton wrongfully concluded that we had called the police. He chastised us for wasting police time when Sebastian had just been assaulted.

f. Officer Thornton did not disperse the crowd or escort us to safety. Instead, exhibiting visible irritation with us, he left us in a hazardous situation. A brawl could have ensued and we could have been injured. The situation was hot.

g. Officer Thornton was extremely rude and would not listen. He gave every indication of accepting Scully's story wholesale. Officer Thornton has no knowledge of the property lines or of the easement. He asked no questions about where the incident took place. Instead, he told us that Scully claimed we were on his property and that he was "acting within his rights."

h. There is no indicaiton that Officer Thorton informed Scully of the unlawfulness of his actions;

i. Officer Thorton let a personal beef with another neighbor affect his handling of this incident;

SLINGSHOT

The public perception of Barrington as a drug haven is nurtured by the fact that Barrington is an alternative living environment. Most of Barrington is a huge mural and many residents are punks, hippies or weirdos. It is a highly creative environment. Some bourgeois

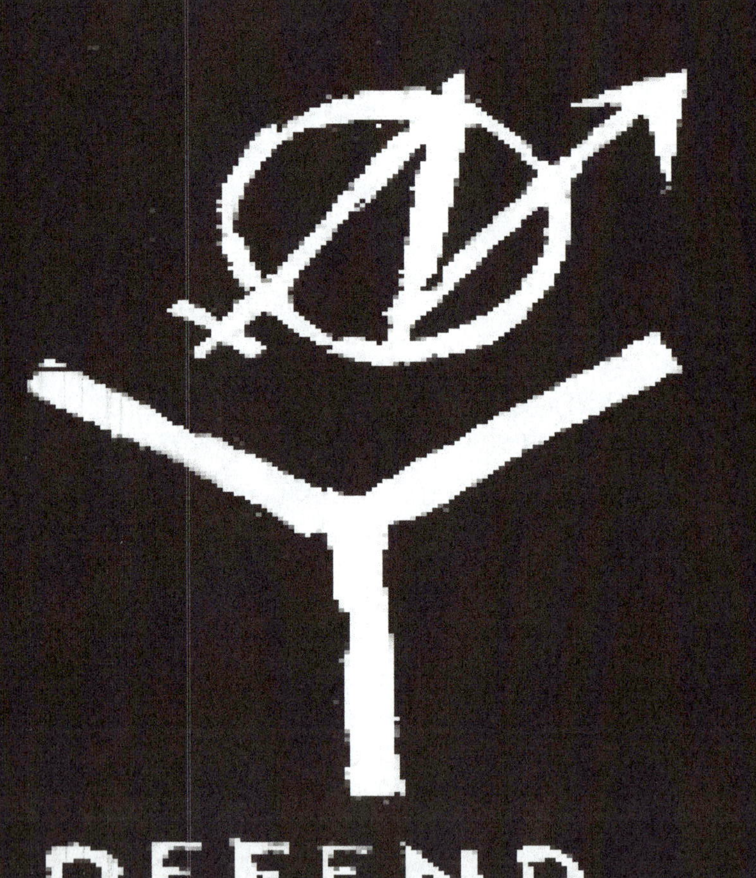

standards of behavior are questioned (this is really the definition of a creative, alternative environment) and this questioning makes outsiders very uncomfortable. Barrington represents a positive and necessary dissenting and creative space within that larger, often oppressive society.

Negative perceptions of Barrington growing from its history are kept alive by people uncomfortable with its current role as a creativc space, and as a space that nurtures political activism.

The first issue of *Slingshot* was published at Barrington. We are not the only radical group to get a good start there. *Biko Plaza News*, Berkeley's newspaper of the anti-apartheid movement of 1985–86, was produced at Barrington. Recently, the pro-choice, *Retain Our Productive Rights,* was established that Barrington. These are only a few examples of political groups to come out of Barrington. Barrington has been one of the few places radicals are accepted. It offers a place where people can think and be temporarily free.

Attempts to close and destroy Barrington must be interpreted as being attempts to smash the alternative and critical culture that exists there. Barrington opponents have used the drug argument to justify attacks on Barrington. Hard drug problems of several years ago are constantly reemphasized even as these problems have been dealt with and solved by Barrington residents. It becomes clear that what hasn't changed about Barringotn is that members of the outside world are a little disquieting to the residents of Barrington. While outsiders criticize the wealth of artwork on the walls, the graffiti, the nose rings, the incense, residents of Barrington criticize the outside world's enthusiasm for Reagan, McDonald's, television and Pine–Sol.

As the ultra–boring and conservative 80s finally (finally!) come to a close, attacks on all of the gains we fought for 20 - 30 years ago are increasing. Attacks on Barrington are merely part of the total attack.

Other fronts include the "War on Drugs" and urine testing; attacks on reproductive rights and women's control over their own bodies (which is the foundation of many other gender–related gains); the cooptation of People's Park; the chipping away of free speech rights in campaigns against flag burning and fighting words; attacks against economic gains made during the New Deal; and on and on. Why is Barrington under attack? Our competitive society trains everybody to be a consumer first and human beings later. Barrington trains and contradicts social bounds by allowing people not to be robots all their lives. The machine is scared that such a placement not only exists, but prospers and offers an alternative to the rat–race.

Animal House on Acid B

The attackers of Barrington feel very uncomfortable about the fact that someone in your community has a lifestyle different from their own. A community of alternative lifestyles make you question your socially assigned duty.

Barrington represents a small liberated zone where people can escape the competitive hell that their society enforces on us. But it represents more than merely an escape. Barrington is an active agent for change. For example, it has inspired the creation of groups that fight the oppression of women in apartheid in South Africa. Like People's Park, Barrington is seen by the Establishment is a pain in the ass that they need to get rid of in order to make way for squeaky clean student yuppie mall on Berkeley's Southside.

The "good neighbors" of Barrington complain of high levels of noise and find free expression hindering the privacy that they paid for. (All but two United States presidents belonged to fraternities.) It is clear that the struggle over Barrington is part of a series of attacks on our freedom of choice and our rights to self–determination. Now is the time to fight back against this rising-repression.

Taking Acid

There's something about taking acid that reminds me of an episode of the Twilight Zone, the one where the astronauts come back from space and disappear one by one. No one remembers the last one except the guy who's next to go. Since you're in the middle of all of time while your dosed, it seems like the stuff that's in your mind is how the world will be when you come down. I was often worried that I would forget something, like a friend, and that when I got up the next day he'd be gone, with only a glimmer of a recollection. It could happen to anything, your family, your house, your life; if you forgot it, it would no longer exist. And I was never quite sure the next day that I hadn't forgotten something. My hope was that if I could forget my paranoia, forget who I had become, I could somehow come back to who I really was, and I had to test this theory on my own.

Barrington used to have wine dinner once every quarter. I think it started in the more innocent days, when drinking cases of wine constituted a party. As Barrington became a stronghold of psychedelia, electric Kool-Aid supplanted the wine as the beverage of choice. I don't recall the theme of that dinner, but acid was budgeted, and I sold them a bottle for the punch, which Luigi made from Tang. He told me it was exactly 100 cups, into which he dumped the whole bottle. Veterans, we each had a couple cups to start things off. It was only about fifteen minutes before I started coming on,

hard. I looked around for Luigi, but couldn't find him. I went upstairs and finally tracked him down, but my body was already vibrating like electric jello.

"Duuude." "Duuude," he mirrored back.

"This acid is more than 100 mics. I think it might be 250," I sputtered, against the stream of synaptic firings.

"I'm frying," he concurred.

"I think we'd better warn everybody." We nodded jerkily in mutual concern, since it was an effort to control our neck muscles. Our eyes were blown open black holes, both from coming on and worry that anyone else had drunk more than one cup. We worked our way down the stairs but it was already too late. The ritual had begun. The room was a pounding cacophony. Every plate, pan, bowl and tray in the building was being beaten in a primal thunder. We went to the punchbowl but it was less than a quarter full, which meant that more than half the room was on the way out. Nothing to do but join the fray.

I grabbed a pot and started beating, despite the dark overtones my psyche was painting on the scene. My now hypersensitive nervous system was being assaulted by an atonal dish ware gamelan. It crescendoed and decrescendoed a few times before finally breaking down, after which milling about commenced. I went back to Eileen's room, 107, to get some bud and clear my head, but I was swimming. I really wanted to hang out with Luigi, but I could hardly walk. Eileen found me there, looked at me once and laughed, "You're trippin, huh?" She could read me. She wanted to go upstairs to Mina and Terry's room, but I was too blown away to move. When I finally gathered enough resolve to head upstairs I walked past a group of punks on the stairs. They had obviously dosed, and were having their catharsis.

"I became a punk so I could be myself, and not belong to some fucked up clique," a scrawny, spike-haired, chain wrapped girl cried. "I don't want people to hate me just because I look different." It really struck me, in that moment, that everyone was crying for acceptance, no matter how bizarre and frightening they may look, everybody just wanted to fit in. I ascended the stairs, in my favorite purple velvet shirt, my fuzzy safety blanket. I found the girls chatting away delightedly,

MARIHUANA
You'd Lov
If It W
Great Ente
CAUTION
ACID
PLAYING TOGETHER:
FRED FRITH
HANS REICHE
SAT. NOV. 7th, 8 PM
HELLER GALLERY
UC BERKELEY STUDENT UNION
APISTS FOUND
CING ON TV!

none of them having imbibed the punch. They decided that I needed decorative accessorization, which came in the form of a tinsel garland wrapped around my head. Looking at myself in the mirror, my dreads and beard melted through the centuries until I saw myself reflected, Jesus, being crowned with thorns.

I guess I wasn't crying blood, so the girls took no notice of my inner panic, as I staggered out into the hall to be scourged. Martyred for the sins of Barrington, how epic! I wandered down to Ruth's room. Rachel's younger sister, who I had fantasized about years before, now lived here too. She wasn't in, but her roommate Derek was. The champion Lothario of Barrington, he enjoyed seducing whoever came through its doors, male or female. I think his sexual certainty scared me as much as his gender blurring, since I was often lost behind my haze of fear. To my abject horror, he was lying in bed and watching TV with none other than my brother Dave. They invited me to join them, which was probably harmless, but to my trip it was one more grievous perversion for me to atone for. Luigi's door was locked and there was no response, perhaps because he was being molested by Lina Hosenman, the fright of which he recounted to me the next day.

I spent some time on the roof, but it was too populated, so I went back down to the AK. The Alternative Kitchen, which was where vegetarian meals were prepared every night, had the most beautiful mural in Barrington. It was The Last Supper, with each of the character's heads a vegetable. Jesus was a carrot, Judas was a beet, the colors were so rich you could just have an epiphany and die there. I spent a long time looking at that mural the first time I took acid, and now it was finally realized, certainly I would be crucified that night.

I went downstairs to see the band, Spacely Sprockets, playing to a sparse crowd. They weren't very good, and everyone had pretty much left. When they started packing up the lead singer complained, "I've taken plenty of acid, and these people can't handle it."
He drank a Dixie cup and before the band could pack up he was crawling on the floor, "I'm looking for my keys," he moaned, and there he spent the rest of the night.

Sheldon Norberg, Author
Confessions of a Dope Dealer
Healing Houses

The Suicidal Iguana

In 1989, I accepted an offer from my friend Ged to housesit her room at Barrington Hall while she was away. I rode my bike, with a bulging backpack strapped to my shoulders and my clothes in a cardboard box bungie-corded to the rack over the rear wheel. As I chained my bicycle in the alley alongside Barrington, I heard screams coming from one end of the building and the sound of loud orgasms emanating from a window above my head. "Seems like an interesting place," I thought.

Ged worked for a reptile store called the Vivarium and had amassed an extensive collection of exotic reptiles, amphibians, and arachnids. Most of these weird critters solemnly sat imprisoned in their aquariums, requiring little care other than being fed crickets or mice. The only animal I was supposed to play with was the iguana. "You have to soak him in water to prevent his skin from drying out. The poor thing seems depressed. So it's good for you to take him out of his cage and carry him around. He doesn't mind being handled. Just make sure he doesn't escape."

So every few days, I placed the sad-looking lizard in a few inches of water in the bathtub, which covered most of his body—just his head stuck up. The first time I soaked him, he stared at me with a forlorn expression, then submerged his head, resting it on the bottom of the tub. Was it attempting to commit suicide? I lifted its head up, and it fell limply back underwater. Seriously worried it would drown, I peeked in every few minutes to see if it was still underwater. The iguana had lifted its nose up to breath, but it went back down as soon as it saw me. I realized that this was merely a cry for help rather than a genuine suicide attempt. So I picked up the lizard, which seemed so weak that I feared it was dying. I took it out for a walk along the hallway. Suddenly, it leapt out of my hands and scurried down the hall with surprising vigor. The crafty creature had me fooled into thinking that it was sick. I managed to recapture it.

Somehow, the suicidal iguana seemed a symbolic embodiment of the spirit of Barrington.

Reid Stuart
Author: *Triumph of the Green Man*

4/12/89

This evening Bebo, our favorite, cat, came in with a strong chemical smell on his back. At first we thought it was some kind of bug spray but finally determined that it was charcoal lighter fluid (we smelled our can). The cat was very upset and so were we. Was someone going to try to burn him? Would he be poisoned by licking it? We rinsed him in the shower but after drying the smell was still strong. It took two more washings with a lot of soap. By then the cat was freaked out, hissing, growly, clawing but we finally got him clean.

Beeboo, son of Alphie and Gerdy

W e can't help thinking it's related to Barrington especially since things have gotten so much worse in the last several days. It's getting harder and harder to exist here. We're under siege.

We moved and rented our house 6 weeks later. We immediately sold our fourplex rental next door—a big sacrifice—to buy a mix-up building on Shattuck near Ashby next to a liquor store that is now a Cannabis Dispensary. Seb died there.

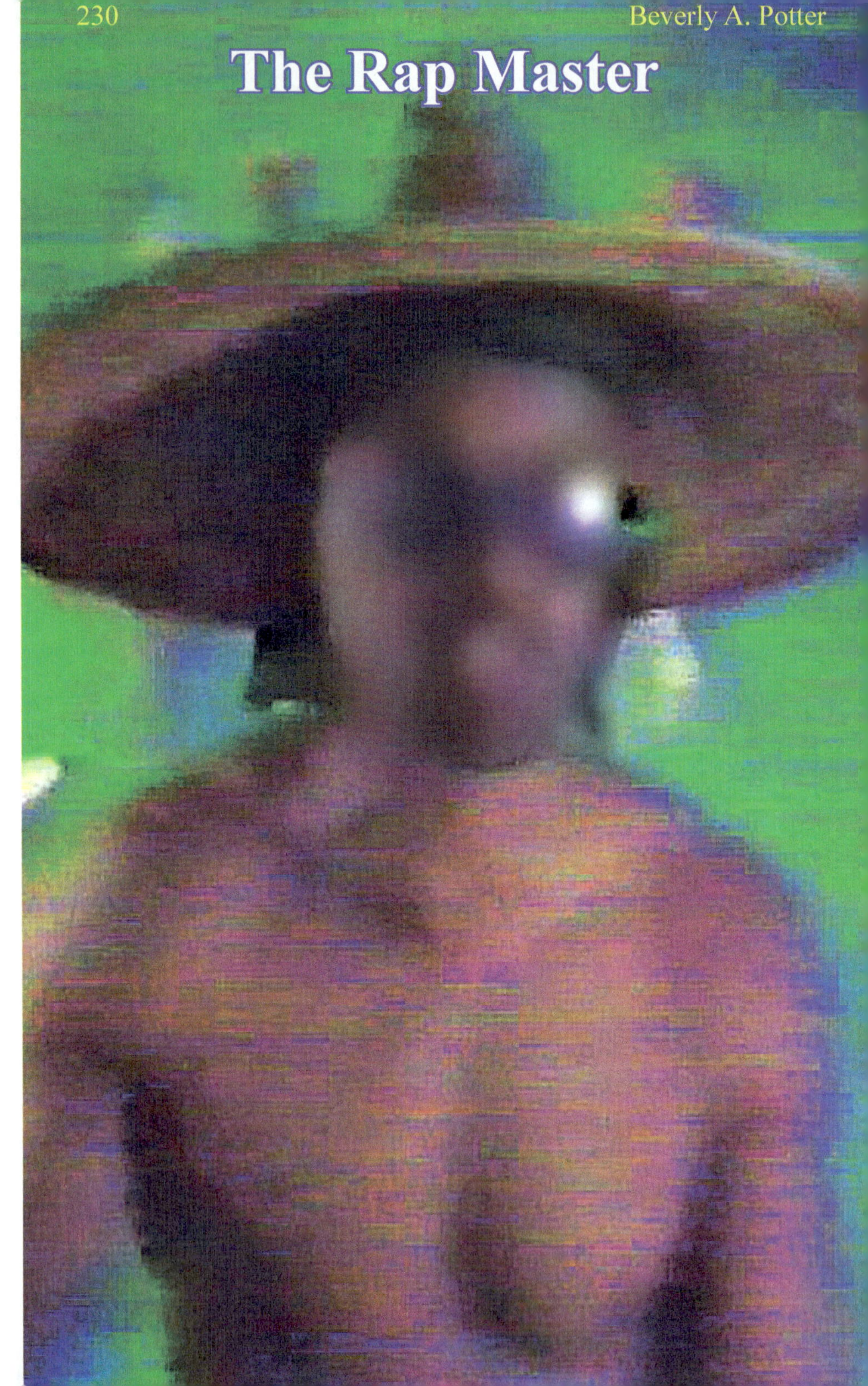
The Rap Master

Dun, De Dun, De Dun, Dun, Dun. Dun, De Dun, De Dun, Dun, Dun. Dun, De Dun, De Dun, Dun, Dun

Well, gather around people because I'm gonna tell ya all about the pushers and junkies in Barrington Hall.

They come here stoney to get a debriefing and everytime I hear a fire truck I know itsa O.D.

If some people fucking up they are home sick . . . . .
I'm a dick.

I'm from Chicago, what else can I say, I'm getting my diploma on the 21st of May.

from Christian Soto video.

Satan's Village
Wine Dinner
666 &
Cartoon
Experience
Special Guest

Saturday, December 2, 1989
Party Begins at 3PM. Dinner at 7PM

Sunday 11/26/89 2 messages on my answering machine, saying my name in extremely threatening manner, promising to put a hunting knife in my ear, will put a pitch fork in my face, smash my skull, etc. Guttural noises, laughing. Sounded like young, white male, with another in the background. Later hang up calls. Made police report.

Police report #89-67304 Ofc Fred Eihl #55 Threatening calls.

11/30/89 Ruth reports invitations passed out at Elsmere by two Barringtonians. One is Ali W. Two pushed under her door. "Satan's Village Invited

Barrington's last Wine Dinner

You to a Wine Dinner. With many satanic symbols on the red cards.

Dec/2/89 Party. Brian McCracken goes with our invitation and is drafted into Barrington security. We drive by to drop him off. We see a studio couch on side walk in front of Haste St door. Appeared to have been thrown from bldg.

Brian returned at about 6 am. He reported bottles thrown from roof. Boys urinating onto the motorcycles in driveway from roof. Beer freely disseminated from vegetarian kitchen and $$ collected at the door. He was offered acid.

We dropped Brian off at the Dwight Way door where he was drafted on to the Security Crew - our spy!!!

Many volunteered to him that they were on acid or speed or both. Dozens of mattress in the halls and under stove in the kitchen. Extreme filth in kitchen. Boy was hit on side of head with 32 oz. beer can. He had convulsions and was taken out on a stretcher. Fire alarms when off about 8 times and each time security immediately disconnected alarm before checking for fire. Extremely large crown, many seemingly underage kids.

In the early morning, someone tapped Brian on the shoulder and handed him a folded note, which contained a black dot with, "You die" under it. They followed him to the door.

Dec 3 89
Seb called and said a washing machine and bottle throw on property. I went there and washing machine was approx 1 foot from kitchen. Also 50-gal steel drum and dozens of bottles. Called out boy named Mark and showed him and asked him to remove it. He said no one in the house did it. He told me about boy being hit in head at party.

Our tenant (we moved and rented the house) David G said they got red invitation too! "Bev gives good head" painted in front of bldg. on Haste side in 2 places.

Dec 3 89 (Seb notes)

I went over to Barrington with Brian McCracken at about 3 pm I took some pictures of the after effects of the rowdy "wine dinner" party at "Satan's Village" the night before There were several freshly broken bottles in the back yard of 2310

Haste and driveway between 2310 and 2308-6 Haste. The bottles must have been thrown with some force, as they landed 25-50 feet away from BH. I was very worried that one of the students living at 2310 or 2308--6 could come out to see what all the nose off the party was about and get hit in the head with a bottle.

When I went to the alleyway between 2310 and BH I noticed a washing machine or dryer had been thrown from the roof of BH and landed on our house. There were also a 50-gallon drum full of trash and dozens of broken liquor, beer and champagne bottles, which had been thrown from the roof at BH towards our house.

I decided to take some photo when I got out the ladder and climbed on to the porch roof at 2310 and noticed damage to the roof around the spot where the plumbing vent pipe was attached. As I climbed down the ladder a young Barringtonian resident named Brad began to speak with me. I pointed out the machine, barrel and numerous bottles thrown towards our house. He said that the party had been hard to control and he would try to get the machine, barrel and debris cleared. I told him I was worried about the damage of all this falling debris and he replied that it as probably thrown by guests.

I notice that graffiti saying, "'Bev gives good head" was written twice on the front of BH. Once in large red letters and once in dark blue on black. This really offended me and I took it as evidence that the objects were deliberately thrown to harass us.

Dec 5 89 12:30 pm Police report #89-68989

At 2310 Haste 50-gal drum removed. Washer and bottle still there I meet with Voice photographer. Boy with long dyed hair and all black clothes yells at me say if I step on his property he'll have me arrested. Extremely hostile. Another boy on bike is extremely hostile. A girl is responsive. We show the washer.

Call police. Ofc Larson makes report. Roger, manager from Yellow bldg., comes by and closes alley gate. He tells Ofc and us that someone broke neck in bldg.

Later talk to tenant John on phone. He says washer hit about 3 am. Ever since there's been a plumbing problem. Says he saw boy go out on stretcher.

We go to 2310 at approx. 9 am to check plumbing. Appears damaged by pipe having been hit. Leaking. It's clear that the washing machine hit the building *and bounced back. Broke bush and shingles. We were on deck. Brad in room 208 looked out window and said they were gong to help us with the lawsuit. Agreed about USCA. They had fined them the night before for "things we didn't do" He looked over at the machine and suddenly realized there was a second machine there. Said no one in the house did it. I said we weren't trying to hassle individuals but we didn't want washing machines thrown at our house.*

As leaving realized there was indeed a second machine thrown since the afternoon. Decided to return in morning to take picture.

Earlier approx. 2:30-3 pm called Coop 848-1936 # - after explained about wasing and graffiti with my name George Proper came on. He was friendly when I told him of the graffiti. He said, "Persistent bastards aren't they?" I told him of threatening calls. He said, "You're not alone. I have the 1:30 am caller, too" Someone has been assigned the job of calling me every morning at 1:30 am" then I told him we had offered to drop him as a plaintiff. He said he'd declined but was dropped on Friday. I was surprised. He said he'd get washer out today or tomorrow.

12/6

Went to take pictures at 9:15 am 2nd washer was gone and dirt still there. Three men from Coop Central Maintenance were there. Taking pictures and writing notes. We showed them the broken cables. They said they'd remove it and the bottles.

We showed them the "Bev" graffiti. And they said they'd remove it after the 20th when the bldg. would be emptied. We asked what if they don't leave? They said they'd be hauled out by Sheriff. I said that's not easy. They said, "We're getting better at it"

One man said, "We're closing it for a semester" (That's til summer).

12/19/89

Red paint thrown on house. Made police report #89-71663

1-10-90

Ruth says gas can has been under the stairs for several days. Today she noticed the can was moved and there is a large puddle of gas on the ground. There is a long cloth banner in the gas and up to the motorcycle almost like a wick. She is very afraid of fire.

1/17/90

Flying Appliances

Barrington's foremost foe was an annoying next-door neighbor named Beverly Potter. Dr. Potter was widely regarded as a laughable stick-in-the-mud who continuously complained about such irrelevancies as loud noise that kept the entire neighborhood awake all night and the incessant torrent of litter flowing out of the Co-op into the street. Apparently, Dr. Potter also disapproved of the fact that Barrington was at one point Berkeley's heroin-trafficking epicenter, with cafeteria trays full of the drug being openly divided up in the upstairs dining room for distribution to every junkie in town.

I knew many substance abuse therapists who often looked askance when they learned where I was living. Dr. Alex Stalcap, an eminent addiction-treatment specialist, once told me, "I cannot believe how many of my clients took their first shot of heroin at Barrington Hall." I replied, "Yeah, but the folks at Barrington really know how to throw a good party."

The Haste Street end of the roof had a laundry room, solar panels, and a small chamber decorated with mirror mosaics. This little structure had ceiling too low for standing, so people mainly used it to sit around smoking DMT or 5-meo-DMT.

A broken washer and a dryer were rusting away outside the laundry room. Some Barringtonians got inspired to tidy up by disposing of these decrepit appliances. First, they got together and carried the washer to the edge of the roof. Then they hurled it down onto Beverly Potter's house. The crowd roared with laughter as the washer crashed into Beverly's roof and bounced down into her yard. Next the dryer flew overboard, causing uproarious mirth as it smashed a giant dent into Beverley's home before resoundingly smashing down to the ground. —Reid Stuart

Animal House on Acid

This machine, or one of its cousins, was "air mailed" to Beverly Potter, by way of a gift, by Danny Tunick. I kept his secret for 15 years, but now I'm spilling the beans.

—Rob Griner

Above message found at the web-archives for Barrington Hall Mar 2014 – kinda kool. Mystery solved, eh?

In the morning after the last Wine Dinner—acid bash—at Satan's Village on December 2, 1989, we found this clothes dryer in our yard, having bounced off our roof when thrown from Barrington, which towered over our house. When we complained it was joined by a washing machine. In Court, Driscoll, our attorney, demanded an injunction from Barringtonians being on the roof. The Co-op's counsel argued that we had not proven that the drier came from Barrington's roof, where there was a laundry directly above our house. To which Judge Demetrius Agratetis loudly demanded, *"Where did it come from? The sky?!!* The injunction was initially denied, until a few days later when buckets of orange paint were thrown from Barrington's roof onto our skylight. To enforce our injunction, the Co-op hired Phoenix Security. Interestingly, the injunction enjoined the Barringtonians from being on the roof of their own property. Being a cooperative, presumably they were the owners. Phoenix Security cost the Co-op $1500 day—$45K month.

When I went to the alleyway between 2310 and BH I noticed a washing machine or dryer had been thrown from the roof of BH and landed on our house. There were also a 50-gallon drum full of trash and dozens of broken liquor, beer and champagne bottles, which had been thrown from the roof at BH towards our house. I decided to take some photo when I got out the ladder and climbed on to the porch roof at 2310 and noticed damage to the roof around the spot where the plumbing vent pipe was attached. As I climbed down the ladder a young Barringtonian resident named Brad began to speak with me. I pointed out the machine, barrel and numerous bottles thrown towards our house. He said that the party had been hard to control and he would try to get the machine, barrel and debris cleared. I told him I was worried about the damage of all this falling debris and he replied that it as probably thrown by guests.

I notice that graffiti saying "Bev gives good head" was written twice on the front of BH Once in large red letters and once in dark blue on black. This really offended me and I took it as evidence that the objects were deliberately thrown to harass us.

Dec 5 89 12:30 pm Police report #89-68989

At 2310 Haste 50-gal drum removed. Washer and bottle still there I meet with Voice photographer. Boy with long dyed hair and all black clothes yells at me say if I step on his property he'll have me arrested. Extremely hostile. Another boy on bike is extremely hostile. A girl is responsive. We show the washer.

Call police. Ofc Larson makes report. Roger, manager from Yellow bldg., comes y and closes alley gate. He tells Ofc and us that someone broke neck in bldg.

Later talk to tenant John on phone. He says washer hit about 3 am. Ever since there's been a plumbing problem. Says he saw boy go out on stretcher.

Barrington was famous for the Wine Dinner. These epic parties started with a special dinner and would feature music by local bands, like Primus. The most distinctive aspect of the Wine Dinner was the punch. "Was it spiked with booze?" Spiked, but not with booze."

The Wine punch was spiked with LSD, a well-known to the party-goers. The party officially started when the acid kicked in and people began peaking. Since acid typically lasts around eight hours, these parties were an ultra-marathon, with plenty of time for festivities.

Wine Dinners were fun. As people were peaking, they would beat on chairs, kitchen pots, cutlery as a group faster and louder into a crescendo. I really liked feeling complete freedom, destroying the furniture and throwing it out the window at Bev's house.

The Social Ed would prepare a punch bowl in the AK with a deliciously fruity concoction heavily dosed with LSD. Servers warned if you imbibed you could expect to trip for the ten ten hours. They made sure folks knew what they were getting before serving the punch..A lot of doses were served throughout the night.

We go to 2310 at approx. 9 am to check plumbing. Appears damaged by pipe having been hit. Leaking. It's clear that the washing machine hit the building and bounced back. Broke bush and shingles. We were on deck. Brad in room 208 looked out window and said they were gong to help us with the lawsuit. Agreed about USCA. They had fined them the night before for "things we didn't do" He looked over at the machine and suddenly realized there was a second machine there. Said no one in the house did it. I said we weren't trying to hassle individuals but we didn't want washing machines thrown at our house.

As leaving realized there was indeed a second machine thrown since the afternoon. Decided to return in morning to take picture.

Earlier approx. 2:30-3 pm called Coop 848-1936 # - after explained about washing and graffiti with my name George Proper came on. He was friendly when I told him of the graffiti. He said, "Persistent bastards aren't they?" I told him of threatening calls. He said, "You're not alone. I have the 1:30 am caller, too" Someone has been assigned the job of calling me every morning at 1:30 am" then I told him we had offered to drop him as a plaintiff. He said he'd declined but was dropped on Friday. I was surprised. He said he'd get washer out today or tomorrow.

12/6
Went to take pictures at 9:15 am 2nd washer was gone and dirt still there. Three men from Coop Central Maintenance were there. Taking pictures and writing notes. We showed them the broken cables. They said they'd remove it and the bottles.

We showed them the "Bev" graffiti. And they said they'd remove it after the 20th when the bldg. would be emptied. We asked what if they don't leave? They said they'd be hauled out by Sheriff. I said that's not easy. They said, "We're getting better at it"

Banjo Boy

You can see the magic on the roof, where people break free of social change and moved under the warm sun, or simply wash their clothes for $.25 and let them dry on the clothesline for free, while they read books or discuss philosophy and "Reaganomics". Many discuss many especially gather after classes all day long, to watch vibrant colors blaze across the bay and into the Berkeley hills. Lakota Indians, who guest lectured in Berkeley, said that after living in open plains, they could not understand how so many people could live in Berkeley and never see the sky. In a way everyone feels that–it is necessary to have a place where you can see life without the monstrous monuments to our capitalist system.

—*Slingshot*

From the roof, Barringtonians
look down into our yard.

Neighbors Skeptical of Barrington Closure

Residents may ignore Dec. 20 eviction deadline.

by Jim Christie
The Voice

Neighbors of Barrington Hall are skeptical that the controversial co-op will remain closed for long and are fearful that residents will act increasingly unruly as the December 20 eviction date approaches.

About 30 residents, according to one of the Hall's managers, are already planning to disregard the eviction and intend to "squat" during the semester break.

Barrington Hall is the student-managed cooperative the University Students Cooperative Association voted last month to shut down because of a long history of noise, health and narcotics violations. (Voice, November 16)

The USDA is a $16 million corporation that oversees UC Berkeley's 8 team student managed cooperatives.

Kyle Miller, a student and one of Barrington's three managers, said many residents may find themselves in

cooperatives not of their choosing if they comply with the US CPAs plans to relocate them—a scenario which has compelled many to defy the USDA.

According to USDA plans, residents of Barrington will be placed within the cooperative system at a house of their choice.

You are an evil person. Rot in hell— and tolerate music or God will kill you!

Found on front door

Miller said that many Barrington residents will be unable to find openings and cooperatives of their choosing and will then be placed in houses where they may not be welcome.

"What we're finding out more and more," said Miller, "is that the eviction is fraudulent."

The plan to squat has re-energized the halls reputed militancy. "The atmosphere (in Barrington)," Miller added, "is actually quite exciting."

But according to one of Barrington's most vocal critics, it's also quite unpredictable.

"I just don't know how hot-headed the hotheads are," said Scott Fritz, a student USDA official and leading closure advocate, the morning after residents broke a window at the USDA office in response to the 695–485 closure vote.

Since then, the co-op's future has been a lively question for all parties involved in the lawsuit against Barrington Hall and the USDA.

One of the plaintiffs in the unsettled $280,000 lawsuit, Beverly Potter, is convinced that when coverage dies down, the USDA will reopen Barrington Hall for economic reasons.

"They may open it up again in the fall—or even in the

summer," said Potter. "I don't see any indication that anything is going to change.

"We've heard all these plans before. I'm skeptical. I say, well, the co-op is going to have a hard time giving up their cash cow."

Barrington Hall is the oldest and largest of the USDA Cooperative. Established in 1939, the facility can house more than 180 residents. Right now, 165 students lived there.

All parties involved agree that not all Barrington residents are responsible for its reputation. Also, almost everyone agrees that the cooperative has improved in light of its history—especially what Potter describes as and "uncontrolled stage:" when garbage was thrown daily into her yard, fires on the Hall's steps and roof were commonplace, and when she witnessed an overdose victim being dragged out onto the front steps.

"The issue of drugs was, at one point, very legitimate," said Miller, "But now there are no hard drugs. You may occasionally see pot, but you see that walking down Telegraph."

Potter, however, fears the same element that gave the cooperative its reputation as a "shooting gallery" and a "pig free zone," will return. Right now, Potter is afraid some of its residents will vent their anger on her and other litigants.

Potter no longer lives next door to Barrington. She moved out last August because of threats and continued harassment. At one point, Potter found a note reading, "Learn to love loud music or God will kill you," on her back porch. "We were th focus of a lot of antagonism," said Potter. "We became very apprehensive coming and going form our house."

Located on Dwight Way between Dana and Ellsworth streets, Barrington is an impressive building decorated with graffiti of political slogans, Profanities and cryptic messages. "Really unnerving, horrible graffiti," according to Potter.

From the point of view of the people living next door there is fear," according to Don Driscoll, the neighbors' attorney. He said his clients have been asking, "Are the people in Barrington going to leave peacefully?" Driscoll confirmed a report from Potter that a neighbor in the suit who still lives in Elsmere apartments next to Barrington found "You Die" written on her car. "I know it sound absurd," added Potter, "but it's wonderful to go days on end without thinking about Barrington."

The conflict may be getting more personal because the lawsuit itself is becoming more personal. Driscol said a December 11 hearing in Alameda Country Superior Court in Oakland will decide if he and his clients can obtain files with names of know drug dealers and problem-causer from Barrington. "The neighbors aren't gong to walk away from two years of litigating . . The USCA has an obsession with the rights of its members, but not its neighbors," said Driscoll.

If the court rules to release those names, then Driscoll may pursue a Racketeer Influenced Corrupt Organizations Act (RICO) suit against persons listed in the files.

The racketeering charges on top of existing nuisance charges, could raise the value of the damages asked in the lawsuit to $975,000.

Meanwhile Miller said any fears the neighbors may now have are from reputation and rhetoric. "They judge us on history and on little incidents," said Miller. "We have a stigma attached to us that we are the bowels of the USCA. Once established, it's very difficult to get rid of."

East Bay

EXPRESS

A LONG STRANGE TRIP

By Paul Rauber

On the evening of November 9, crowds of UC Berkeley students milled about in the murky, candlelit dining room of Barrington Hall, its subterranean atmosphere accentuated by the low ceilings and graffiti-encrusted walls. The smell of incense was over powering. Many of the Barringtonians were naked. Some of the women had the symbol of Onngh Yanngh, the house cult, painted between their breasts, while some of the men had adorned their chests with painted messages: "CO [Central Office] sucks my..." read one, with an arrow pointing downward. It was, even by the liberal standards of the University Students' Cooperative Association, an extraordinary Board meeting.

That noon, at the USCA's more sedate Euclid House on the North side, the association announced the results of its system-wide referendum on whether to close Barrington: 695 in favor, 485 against. Unofficial results, however, had leaked out earlier; at about five-thirty that morning, a group of Barringtonians had taken to their roof, yelling, waking the neighbors and leading them to falsely conclude that Barrington had won. Another group of Barringtonians trashed the USCA's central office on Ridge Road, smashing a window and dripping Onngh Yanngh symbols in candle wax on the carpet.

Many of the Barringtonians were naked. Some of the women had the symbol of Onngh Yanngh, the house cult, painted between their breasts

By the purest chance, that evening's USCA Board meeting, which regularly rotates among the association's eighteen houses and residence halls, had been scheduled for Barrington. USCA officials decided to tough it out; "Better they should trash Barrington than someone else's house," one said.

The meeting could not be held in the customary meeting room because the fumes from newly painted graffiti were too strong and the paint was still sticky. "You betrayed us, you fucking smug bastards," read a vivid two-tone message on the floor. "Your houses will pay for what you've done." In the main hall, an angry group of Barringtonians surrounded me, demanding that I leave the building. While the Board voted on whether or not to allow the press to cover its public meeting, I waited outside with John Harmon, a one-time neighbor of Barrington whose early efforts to reform the house have changed over the years into a bitter vendetta against the USCA and its general manager, George Proper.

"There were kids up there, teenagers, shooting up with her-

oin," Harmon declaimed loudly. "George Proper knew it, and he didn't do a damn thing about it. He earns $60,000 a year off those kids—he's just protecting his ass." From the upstairs windows, Barringtonians proceeded to pelt us with eggs. I moved to the relative safety of the porch, while Harmon stood his ground, interrupting his rant with occasional target information for the egg-throwers. ("Got my leg that time. Just don't throw anything hard.") Eventually Derek Glass, the USCA's community relations coordinator, appeared at the door to tell me that the Board had voted to let me in. "But there are a lot of Barringtonians who are against it," he added. "You can make up your own mind whether you want to come in."

From the upstairs windows, Barringtonians proceeded to pelt us with eggs.

Inside, a debate was raging on whether to establish a committee to oversee the scheduled December 20 closure of Barrington.

"You're kicking me out of my house," screamed a naked young woman. "Don't fucking do it in a committee—do it right here so I can fucking hate you for it!"

Barrington house president Todd Siders rose to address the Board. "I would feel inappropriate speaking to you without pulling down my pants," he said, doing so to the cheers of his constituents. "This is not politics. This is our declaration of independence. We have lost our home. If you think we're going to be nice and considerate, think again." More cheers from the naked crowd.

Outside, after the meeting had dissolved into chaos, Scott Fitz, one of the leaders of the anti-Barrington referendum, was assaulted by an irate Barringtonian. "Do you think you can destroy this house and just walk away?" his attacker asked, throwing a punch. Dan Ban, another referendum leader, was chased for three blocks by angry Barringtonians.

"I would feel inappropriate speaking to you without pulling down my pants,"

—House President

Thus fell Berkeley's last outpost of the '60s. Barringtonians held fast to the culture of sex, drugs, and rock 'n" roll long after it had ceased to be fashionable, and clung to the sanctity of individual expression—even to the point of covering up not only illegal but genuinely harmful acts with a cloak of silence. Inside Barrington Hall, the youth rebellion never grew old, because each year it was replenished with a new crop of eighteen-year-olds, sorry to have missed the '60s and glad to find a small chunk of it still alive just down the street from People's Park on Dwight Way. Barrington became a victim of its own mythology: with a house culture dedicated to outrage, it eventually outraged all, even its natural allies.

For the last five years, Barrington has been a continuing disaster for the USCA. LSD parties, open drug use, heroin over-doses, crashers, raucous parties, and disputes with neighbors and other co-op houses have sapped the patience of everyone involved. A suit by Barrington's neighbors, charging the USCA with

SQUAT OR ROT

racketeering and drug dealing and asking for $1.5 million in damages, is awaiting a court date, and will proceed even after Barrington is closed. The suit has already cost the association $161,000 in legal fees. With assets of over $17 million (it's the second largest landowner in Berkeley), the USCA is not in danger of being bled dry by Barrington; nevertheless, this month it decided to stop the hemorrhaging—by amputation.

No one will admit to knowing much about the origins of the Onngh Yanngh cult: its slogan is "Those who know don't tell, those who tell don't know." The Onngh Yanngh symbol, an "O" in the crook of a "Y," is shared by City Lights Books in San Francisco, but no one seems to know where it comes from. "It might be a martini for all I know," suggested a harried clerk there. A more likely explanation is the logo of the Berkeley Co-op's old "Co-op Label," which divided the word "Co-op" with what looks like two hockey sticks and a puck—a short step away from the Onngh Yanngh symbol.

Where did Onngh Yanngh come from? George Proper (who lived in Barrington for four years in the mid-'60s, and who has worked for the USCA all his adult life) thinks the cult might have been founded by an entomologist who lived at Barrington in the mid-70s, who was famous for serving Bug Dinners: meal-worms and termites, things like that. Todd Siders, the long-haired current president of Barrington, thinks the name comes from a temple in Tibet. But according to the suit against Barrington filed by attorney Don Driscoll on behalf of former neighbors Sebastian Orfali and Beverly Potter, "'Onngh Yanngh' was and is an enterprise consisting of an association of persons (each known as an 'Onngh Yanngher') for the promotion of drug use at Barrington Hall. It is an enterprise which has distributed heroin, LSD, and methamphetamines in each year, January, 1985 to present."

Barrington Hall was Berkeley's last outpost of the '60s. Barringtonians held fast to the culture of sex, drugs, and rock 'an* roll long after it had ceased to be fashionable, and clung to the sanctity of individual expression-even to the point of covering up not only illegal but genuinely harmful acts with a cloak of silence.

"Complete and utter bullshit," responds Siders. Yet, he admits, it's hard to live down the legend, because the unfortunate slogan sounds so much like a code of silence. "We don't have any initiation process where people are told to be quiet," Siders insists. But members of the house are notoriously taciturn in speaking to the press, a trait shared to some extent by the rest of the USCA. In the course of researching this story, I was ejected from one USCA-board meeting, and allowed to stay at another only on the sufferance of USCA president Paige Wolverton, who cast the tie-breaking vote to allow me to stay.

"She was absolutely delightful," says S.D. wistfully, recalling the lost daughter whose photographs fill a wall of her tasteful, book-lined Berkeley Hills home. "A bright, pretty, talented, affectionate child who became a drug addict of the worst kind: filthy, with matted hair, a blanket around her and shoeless." In 1983, S.D.'s daughter dropped out of Berkeley High six weeks into the eleventh grade and ran away—to Barrington Hall.

In 1984, S.D. joined a Berkeley group called PACT, Parents and Children Together, a support group for parents of children with chemical dependencies. Every other Monday for the past five years, she has met with other PACT parents to talk, listen, and offer help when help is needed. The group has been active for years in efforts to close Barrington Hall.

"There were five or six parents who had verified stories that their kids ran away and stayed at Barrington," says S.D. "The girls were prostitutes there. The kids thought it was cool, getting invited to stay with these college kids. We found out that our daughter had been given LSD at Barrington when she was eleven."

A.R. listens, nodding. Three years ago, she says, her seventeen-year-old son was dealing drugs out of Barrington. One evening, after he told her he was going to the library, she saw his car in Barrington's parking lot. She stopped, and was able to slip into the locked building as another parent was coming out. "Are you looking for someone too?" he asked. "Yes, I am!" she said, and marched in. Once inside, A.R. was surprised to see her own phone number written above the house phone. She found her son in an upstairs suite ("Someone told me that's where they had the very wildest parties") and ordered him home. But he just went back again.

At Christmastime two years ago, A.R's son had been missing for weeks. Then, two days after Christmas, she heard him come back late at night, go up to the bathroom and turn on the water. Overjoyed to have him back and determined not to ask any prying questions, A.R. lay in bed, wondering if she should get up to say hello and welcome him home. The water kept on running and and running. Finally she called at the door, but there was no answer, so her husband broke it down. Inside, their son had overdosed on heroin. (After a trip to the Alta Bates emergency room and a stay at a psychiatric hospital, he has "more or less straightened out.")

Soon afterward, A.R. and S.D. went to a meeting at the North Berkeley Senior Center, held in response to neighbors' demands that Barrington Hall be closed and attended by representatives from the USCA, the university, and the city. "I was very emotional," says A.R. "I had seen the place; I didn't know how they could allow this place to be open. But the man from the health department didn't say anything. Don Jelinek [the Berkeley city council member whose district includes Barrington] did his famous dance of the veils, and didn't say anything either.. He made it very clear that a lot of his votes came from these kids, and he was playing it safe. It was obvious he wasn't going to help us."

Nor did they get any satisfaction from the USCA. "George Proper," says S.D., "can be very charming and accommodating, but he would never do anything.

Don Jelinek, the Berkeley city council member whose district includes Barrington, did his famous dance of the veils,

"They would always say they were going to have a task force, and they were going to have a committee, and they would write a report. We finally got fed up and stopped going to these meetings. They were just humoring us."

After A.R. and her husband got home from the meeting at the senior center, they got a threatening phone call. The callers said they were from Barrington. "They said, 'You were at that meeting, we know where you live, you're against Barrington, and we're going to burn your house down.' So my husband sat up all night" Both A.R. and S.D. say the only reason they won't let their full names be printed here is for fear of retribution from Barringtonians.

Like the recently failed Berkeley Co-op, the University Students' Cooperative Association was born in the progressive atmosphere of the 1930s, with the aim of providing low cost housing for UC students. It still meets that goal—a year's room and board at the USCA currently costs $2,675, only half the cost of similar accommodations in a dorm. This miracle is achieved by having each resident do a five-hour weekly workshift, cooking, cleaning, answering phones, or doing maintenance. As a co-op, the USCA is legally owned and operated by its student members, who govern their individual houses through house councils and the entire organization through a board of directors. A professional staff provides central management, technically at the pleasure of the board.

The USCA has grown through the years by playing Monopoly, mortgaging its existing property to buy new houses and rooming houses as they become available. (Hoyt Hall has now been mortgaged in order to finance the USCA's defense in the Barrington lawsuit) The association now houses over 1,400 students, in both group houses and apartment complexes like Rochdale Village. Barrington Hall, with 166 current members, is the co-op's largest house.

An important organizational change took place within the USCA in the late 70s. Prior to that time, the central office kept the books for all the individual houses, and sent out ready-prepared food to all the houses from a central kitchen. This required the centralized labor of a large number of members, and resulted in a lot of mixing among the various houses. (Interhouse intercourse was also spurred by the fact that until 1966, all USCA houses were segregated by sex.)

As a result of demands for autonomy and decentralization, however, by the late '70s each house was made responsible for handling its own finances and workshifts. Responsibility for food preparation was also shifted to individual house kitchens. Now, raw supplies are delivered to each house, to be prepared as the house sees fit

Not surprisingly, as a result of those reforms, houses became increasingly independent and self-sufficient. Distinct house cultures, passed on from one generation of students to the next, were accentuated. While some contact between houses continues, many current members have never even been to another USCA house. Although decentralization has brought its problems, it seems to be irreversible. "I think the cooking has improved too much for us to recentralize," says Scott Fitz of Stebbins Hall.

Barrington, which had been developing a counter-cultural reputation throughout the '60s and '70s, had its house culture reinforced by the Balkanization of the USCA—particularly as the house began to be looked on by the rest of the organization as a problem.

A 1983 complaint mentioned a "live boa constrictor, fire, dried blood on her door, food and burning matches thrown at dinner, person wandering through halls 'brandishing a whip and striking the walls with it.'"

As early as 1976, it was recognized that cavernous, dilapidated Barrington lacked the "physical amenities" of other houses; a price-differential was instituted, whereby Barringtonians would pay ten percent less than residents of other houses. (The differential was phased out in the mid-'80s.) In 1983, following a suit by a woman who fell down an air shaft, the USCA's insurance company inspected the building. Horrified by its condition, the company canceled Barrington's policy. Large sums of money have since been invested in attempts to renovate the building: $425,000 in 1983 and a further $150,000 in 1986, when many large suites were broken up into smaller units. In 1984, health inspectors from the city almost closed down the kitchen following reports of rats, roaches, and uncollected garbage; instead, they put the house on probation. (During one kitchen cleanup, S.D. says her daughter told her, Barrington officials distributed speed to those willing to do the dirty work.) Six months after the 1983 rehabilitation, general manager George Proper brought this unhappy report to the board:

"Barrington certainly does not look like a newly renovated building. The new paint, both interior and exterior, is covered with graffiti. Windows are broken and walls have holes in them. The new carpet is badly stained and covered with paint in many locations. Many of the newly remodeled bathrooms have been trashed. The common bathrooms are hardly usable."

The filth and general chaos within Barrington encouraged the highest turnover rate in the USCA system, ranging as high as 75 percent A not-untypical complaint from a disgruntled resident in 1983 mentioned a "live boa constrictor, fire, dried blood on her door, food and burning matches thrown at dinner, person wandering through halls 'brandishing a whip and striking the walls with it.'" by neighbors who lived in the adjacent Elsmere Apartments, mainly objecting to noise from all-night parties, asked the District Attorney to declare Barrington a "public nuisance." Because of its size, Barrington has traditionally been an "entry level" house: new ASUC members would spend their first semester or two at Barrington, escaping to quieter and smaller houses as soon as they had accumulated enough seniority points. According to operations manager Vicki Cucarola, only four percent of the current population of Barrington has lived there for two years or more, and one-third of members who sign contracts at Barrington stay there for one semester or less. As recently as this semester, two Barrington residents were released from their contracts because their living quarters were found to be uninhabitable. By this semester it was taking four offers to fill each spot at Barrington, with many of the refusals coming from outside California. Barrington's reputation had spread nationwide.

A "Barrington Lobby" has asserted a powerful influence on the Board.

Ironically, it is the rapid turnover at Barrington that has preserved its unique, anarchic culture. Of the large numbers of new students passing through the house each year, there were generally a handful who found the freedom and excitement exactly to their taste. "Those are the people who provided all of the continuity for the house," says Fitz. "The people who didn't like it didn't stay to change it, because they had this very easy option of moving to a pleasant, smaller house somewhere else. The easiest thing for them to do was just to leave the situation, and the easiest thing for the people who liked it was just to stay and keep it going."

In addition, while many people don't find the prospect of four or five years at Barrington appealing, hindsight often provides those who have moved on to other houses with rosy memories of good times and Onngh Yanngh. The fraternity of exBarringtonians in other houses has traditionally combined with Barrington's own sizable voting block to constitute a "Barrington lobby," which has asserted a powerful influence on the board. Barrington has what former USCA member Bob Bonneau calls "the advantage of interior lines... any threat from the organization against Barrington immediately rallies [the Barrington lobby] to the defense, but the other houses are left scattered and disorganized."

Barrington's legal battles are not about anti-authoritarianism, loud parties, or Barrington's history of political activity (notable examples of which include the "Biko Steps" anti-apartheid demonstrations in 1986 and the "Slingshot" anarchist group), but about drugs. Drugs are central to Barrington's "anything goes" ethos—as they were to Berkeley's, not so very long ago. But while the same Berkeley Citizens Action officials who once campaigned for the relaxation of marijuana laws now line up to sponsor the latest anti-crack programs, Barringtonians' attitudes have been slower to change.

In the '80s, the house's traditional hallucinogens—LSD, psilocybin mushrooms—began to give way to heavier stuff, cocaine and heroin. As early as 1983, the Potter/Orfali suit alleges, George Proper told the then-current USCA president that one Leo Sullivan was dealing heroin in Barrington. With the hard drugs came big-time dealers, guns, threats, physical intimidation, and overdoses.

Barrington had a policy at the time not to call 911 immediately in the event of drug overdoses, dragging the victims out in front of the building first so as not to have the incident associated with the house.

The heroin problem reached its peak in the "Hell Summer" of 1985. Proper admits that Barrington, then open at only 25 percent capacity to avoid the necessity of a cooking program, attracted scores of squatters and other nonmembers. Many people lodged alone in five-person suites and brought in friends to join them, or sublet rooms to people from the street; of the approximately 125 people living there that summer, Proper estimates that as many as 75 may have been without contracts. Vandalism and drug use were general; as many as 25 people were using heroin. Suite 306, the Potter/Orfali suit alleges, became a shooting gallery. Neighbors charge that Barrington had a policy at the time not to call 911 immediately in the event of drug overdoses, dragging the victims out in front of the building first so as not to have the incident associated with the house. That fall the USCA's second insurance company bailed out.

It was about this time that Barrington neighbor John Harmon began his feud with the USCA. Over the years, he has developed a kind of joking symbiotic relationship with Barrington. At one point, Harmon kept a large sack of potatoes next to his window, which he would hurl at Barringtonians taunting him from their roof, prompting the Barringtonians to paint a bull's-eye on their stair tower. Harmon sued the association for pain and suffering, eventually agreeing to a settlement of $6,000. The USCA thought that would be the end of him; however, Harmon has dogged the association ever since, as a self-proclaimed "dumpster-diver" coming up with many embarrassing interior documents. Harmon makes no secret that his aim is the destruction of George Proper, whom he loathes. According to USCA physical plant manager Neil Houston, however, Harmon is only interested in shaking down the USCA: "Eight out of ten calls from John end up with him asking for more money," Houston says.

The fall of '85 brought criticism of Barrington to a crescendo. Negative stories about Barrington appeared in every local paper. In September, Proper appeared before the board. "I told them that the building was out of control," he says. "I said, 'If they can't conduct themselves in a cooperative manner, we should kick 'em out.'" Proper suggested closing Barrington at the end of the next semester. Instead, the board formed a committee, during the course of whose deliberations "serious rumors and allegations regarding heroin and other drug usage surfaced," according to a USCA "Management Team Fact Sheet." Among these was a public declaration by Barrington's then-manager, a clean-cut professor's son, that he had tried heroin, and was afraid that if he stayed in Barrington he would become addicted. It was also during this time that the City Council formed its own committee, the Barrington Hall task force.

In February, 1986, the USCA held a poorly attended press conference to announce the presence of heroin in Barrington,' 'which makes it funny," says Proper, "when people like John Harmon accuse us of covering up." The next month, the board voted to sell the building at the end of that semester. Barrington organized a referendum drive to over-turn the decision, but it wasn't even necessary; the Barrington lobby brought pressure on the board, and the decision to sell was rescinded even before the members voted. The eventual membership vote was 565 to 419 to keep Barrington open.

Nonmember heroin deal and other undesirables would be "PNG'd," their pictures posted in the main hall.

There was a catch, however. As a condition to staying open, Barrington agreed to place itself on a three-year probation. Satisfied at this apparent progress, the city's task force folded its chairs and went home. The terms of this probation have been amended several times since, generally in the direction of softening them. The original agreement clearly set forth what was expected of Barrington, and what consequences would ensue from violations. "Barrington Hall shall not use house money to purchase drugs," it stated. '.'There will be no drugs at house sponsored events. There will be no drug dealing in the house. There' will be no widespread public usage of drugs in the house."

Probation also codified the notion of personae non grata, transforming it into an active verb. Nonmember heroin dealers Theoretically, should a PNG enter the house, the police could be called to arrest him or her for trespassing. Unfortunately, the system had little legal weight. According to Proper, "really awful" situations would develop' 'when a house PNGs someone, and that PNG arrives, is causing a problem; you call the police and say you want this person arrested for trespassing, and then some resident says, 'Hey, leave him alone, he's my guest,' and the cop says 'Goodbye.' That's catastrophic. Any officer who knows the law knows that as soon as you've been identified as a guest by a legal resident you're not a trespasser."

During the fall of 1985 and spring of 1986, Barrington voted to PNG fourteen people, among them the following:

Robert Caesar—Violence
Anthony—Sexual harassment of house members
Leo Sullivan—Dealing heroin
Sol Samuels—Clear and present danger, violent to house members
"Icepick Al"—Dealing heroin, destruction of house property
Manfred—Racism and sexual harassment
Marybeth—Dealing heroin
"Skateboard Kenny"—Dealing heroin

Resident dealers, Proper says, were evicted "once we've made a decision that the person's a dealer." House members who were heroin users, or who were known to harbor PNGs, were placed on "conditional contracts," which might require them, for instance, to seek drug treatment. In addition, the USCA hired a trusted member from another house, Carlos Cabana, to manage Barrington, rather than rely on a manager elected by the house.

The USCA was quick to claim success. In an article in these pages on December 5, 1986, Karen Laws wrote that "Proper now calls Barrington 'virtually an unqualified success.' Board Vice-President Kristen Cupps is 'ecstatic,' and residents describe Barrington as a 'different place now,' saying it's 'under control' and that heroin and other drug-related problems have completely disappeared."

The problem, however, was not so easily solved. In a legal declaration related to the Potter/Orfali lawsuit, longtime co-op member Bob Bonneau states that the events following the time that Barrington was placed on probation led him to conclude that there was "a cover-up on the part of the USCA and its management of a very serious drug problem that has been on-going in Barrington Hall for several years.... I believe that the management team of the USCA has furthered this cover-up in order to protect its own position in the USCA, and to protect the USCA from outside scrutiny."

During his long stint with the USCA. Bonneau held a large number of official positions, including serving as a board rep, chairing the administrative committee ("the co-op's version of the People's Court"), and acting as member advocate, a sort of devil's advocate for people who had run afoul of the co-op system. Bonneau, a hyper, thirtyish mathematics student, was evicted from the co-ops earlier this year, allegedly for failure to do his workshifts; he claims it was in retaliation for his attempts to organize information about Barrington. He sued the association and the case was tried before a jury, where Bonneau was forbidden to mention anything about drugs. He lost; he now manages the North side Theater.

Bonneau charges that Barrington's probation was regularly violated, with the full knowledge of co-op officials. Barrington manager Cabana, Bonneau says, admitted to the board that heroin dealer Leo Sullivan had been allowed to stay in the building, despite the fact that he had been PNG'd. Cabana also allegedly told the board "that a quantity of Quaaludes had been available in Barrington Hall, and that they had been distributed in the public areas of the building.'.' Bonneau's then-girlfriend, K.M., became addicted to heroin while living at Barrington; on one occasion she overdosed, he says, and was shot up with speed by her roommate, who went on to become a USCA officer. '

Bonneau once asked K.M. if she wasn't afraid of being arrested. "This is Berkeley," she replied. "I'm a white college co-ed; nobody's going to do anything to me."

When the USCA board tried to evict her in the fall of 1987, well into the probation period, Bonneau in his capacity as member advocate defended K.M., arguing that "Since heroin in Barrington was so ubiquitous, and the management team did not have the political nerve to declare the building in violation of probation, it was unfair to single out one person to be the scapegoat." She was even-

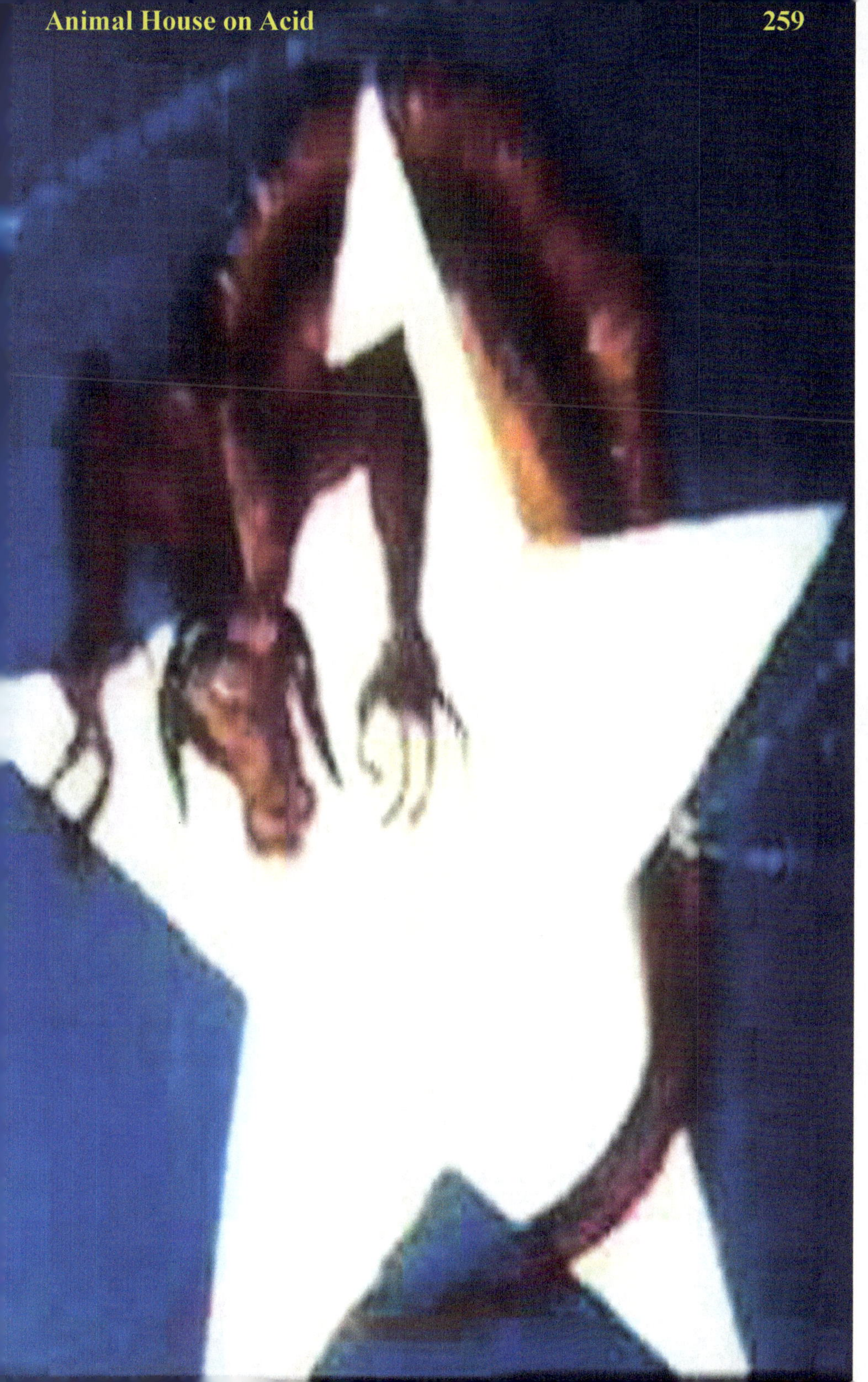

WELCOME

WINE DINNER

A GUIDE...

END OF IMAGINATION

RETURN TO GO AND...

tually allowed to move to the Rochdale Village co-op apartments.

In a similar case, Bonneau defended a woman who had been an Olympic athlete before she became hooked on heroin at Barrington and was being evicted for not being a student and non-payment of rent, "a natural end to people when they wind up down that road." Again Bonneau lost; the woman, he says, eventually became a prostitute in Oakland.

The most notorious violation of Barrington's probation came on September 25, 1987, the infamous "acid punch party." At a time when the house was supposedly" still under strict central office supervision, LSD-spiked punch was distributed at a large "wine dinner." At least four people required treatment for adverse drug reactions; a resident of another co-op house fell off a neighboring roof while tripping. Barrington house officials later argued that "the drugs at the wine dinner were not house approved, in any way. The acid punch represented the independent action of a few members. And each individual was made aware of the contents of the punch before being served."

A far different story emerged in October, when Reggie Clermont, a board rep for Casa Zimbabwe (formerly Ridge Project), revealed the minutes of an executive session of the USCA board at a meeting of his own house. According to the house minutes of October 19, "The house manager, Robert Dick [who succeeded Carlos Cabana] knew about it but did not make an effort to stop the punch from being served. Robert has resigned as of last Thursday.... In this case, the house voted to serve acid at the party and the house manager did not wield his power."

Clermont also disclosed other details of drug use at Barrington, including the information that "New people have become heroin addicts at Barrington this year, even under professional management." This information, Clermont said, was known to USCA president Evan Steele, but kept from the board. (Steele denies the allegation; his subsequent resignation as chair of the board, he says, was for entirely personal reasons.)

"George Proper and Roxane Neal [then-USCA member services director] threatened that Mr. Clermont could be sued for revealing this information," states Bonneau in his declaration, "and members of the board sought his removal." Bonneau, who at the time was Casa Zimbabwe's house manager, sought legal advice, and reported that "If the board of directors of a California corporation conspired to cover up a felonious act, then it would be acceptable for a member of the board (Reggie) to inform the stockholders (us) about what transpired at the meeting."

These developments were kept largely quiet from the USCA membership and the public at large. In fact, the story of. the acid punch party was successfully suppressed entirely for several weeks. "Since the press had not

the story of the acid punch party was successfully suppressed entirely for several weeks.

been informed," Proper told me, "we didn't think it wise to bring it to their attention."

An enormous uproar did ensue after news of the party became public. The university threatened to remove any reference to the USCA in all of its official housing literature unless something were done about Barrington. Yet again, the USCA had to find a new insurance company. The Berkeley City Council created another Barrington body, the Barrington Subcommittee, chaired by Council member Don Jelinek. Jelinek argued that Barrington had failed to meet the terms of its probation, and demanded drastic action. In November, at the urging of the City Council and USCA management, the board voted by a two-to-one margin to institute a one hundred percent turnover at the end of spring semester: that is, to kick all current residents out, and start afresh.

In the spring of 1988, Barrington residents once again mounted a referendum campaign to overturn the board's action. They brought out the familiar arguments: Barrington is improving, the house is cleaner, there were already 120 new members since the previous fall who shouldn't be punished for the actions of a few. "The house now has a perspective on heroin issues," Barrington's board members argued in a "pro/con packet" sent to all USCA members before the vote. "The drug is no longer considered 'cool.' There is no member currently living in Barrington Hall known to have a heroin addiction."

Just before the election, Barrington got a surprise boost—from Don Jelinek. "[A]fter a three-hour meeting with house members February 4," Barrington's board reps wrote in the pro/con packet, "Jelinek realized that one hundred percent turnover is entirely unjustified. Thus, while the board's November decision for turnover was based primarily on Jelinek's threats, Jelinek himself has revoked his support for

the plan, and has announced his mistake publicly in the Daily Cal."

Jelinek now says that his previous position on Barrington was based on misinformation received by the task force. He told me that he was very impressed by his meeting at Barrington: "They convinced me that what had happened had not been house endorsed, nor were people approving of what went on. I realized that I now had become the prime reason that Barrington was closing, and I thought it was my obligation to set the record straight."

Once again, Barrington had won the day. USCA members voted against a total turnover; subsequently, the board decided to continue the probationary period, although what if anything "probation" might mean had been put in serious doubt by the previous failures to enforce its terms. Barrington opponents were furious at Jelinek; at the March 22 City Council meeting, John Harmon delivered a vicious denunciation of his former ally. "Mr. Jelinek is a creep," shouted Harmon. "He is a political animal who is sacrificing the well-being of the community, the neighborhood, and the kids in Barrington to preserve his voting base.""If there ever was an unelectoral decision, it was supporting Barrington," counters Jelinek. "If there was a constituency I was appealing to, except for 160 Barringtonians, I don't know who it was—I antagonized just about everyone. in the community by that decision."

Since the USCA had failed to take action on Barrington, the fight moved to the courts. "If they'd closed down Barrington in 1985 when they first discovered a heroin shooting gallery there," says attorney Don Driscoll, "the neighbors probably wouldn't have sued." Beverly Potter and Sebastian Orfali filed their suit in February, 1988. (Other Barrington neighbors filed a nearly identical suit early this year in federal court.) The suit contends that Barrington was a nuisance to live next to, that the USCA has engaged in racketeering, that it covered up drug use, and that it has a "pro-drug corporate policy." "If you go out and say we've got the problem solved while there's still heroin dealing there," says Driscoll, "that tends to facilitate it—you're covering up the heroin dealing."

"I don't believe it will ever be shown that the USCA was liable, because the USCA did not take part in the alleged activities," says Proper. "There's a real difference between not taking action, and not taking the action that John Harmon would have taken, or that the university would have taken. We're living by different rules. I'm the employee of a democratic organization. Telling me, George Proper, 'You have the power, why don't you do something?' is like telling the mayor, 'You've got the power, why don't you clean up Telegraph Avenue?' She works within her system. I work within my system." Unfortunately, Proper's system has shown itself largely unable to deal with Barrington's drug problem.

An unpleasant consequence of the suit is an attempt to prove that "corporate officers or employees intentionally use unlawful drugs for the purpose of demonstrating their acceptance of the drug habits of the members of the cooperative or for the purpose of maintaining their image of credibility with its members." In order to do so, petty examples of drug use by USCA managers and officials are being dredged up for public view: who smoked a joint, who asked whom to buy mushrooms, who grew pot in their backyard.

We're not the only house with neighbor complaints, not the only house with drug use, certainly not the dirtiest house, certainly not the most uncooperative. We are freely accepting of everything that goes on in the USCA, but because of our house culture, we're going to be to the ones watched for it.

These allegations sound trivial, but they point out the uncertain line drawn in Berkeley between acceptable and unacceptable drug use. "There are a lot of people in Berkeley," says Driscoll, "who believe that if somebody wants to use a drug, he should be allowed to use it, whether that drug is LSD or heroin or whatever. I think the people running the USCA have, at the very least, been highly sympathetic to the view that it should be a person's choice to use whatever drug." The issue was made even more pointed when the Daily Cal revealed that Potter and Orfali, the couple suing Barrington over drug use, had themselves written a number of "how-to" books on marijuana and cocaine, with titles like *Marijuana Potency* and *Psychedelic Chemistry.*

During one point in Bob Bonneau's recent eviction case, he found himself alone in the judge's chambers with a USCA lawyer.

You're in Berkeley,' he said. 'It's a drug town. You have a City Council that legalizes marijuana, and this judiciary is not an anti-drug judiciary. It's stacked against you; you should just move out of Berkeley.' I said I didn't feel like being run out of town by drug dealers."

According to Bonneau, the attorney told him that he was making a martyr of himself:" 'You're in Berkeley,' he said. 'It's a drug town. You have a City Council that legalizes marijuana, and this judiciary is not an anti-drug judiciary. It's stacked against you; you should just move out of Berkeley.' I said I didn't feel like being run out of town by drug dealers.

"People dabble with marijuana, they dabble with mushrooms and acid. I felt that anybody in their right mind would draw the line somewhere—short of heroin."

The USCA has taken a mixed approach to the suit. Proper quotes

the USCA's top-drawer San Francisco lawyer, Ephraim Margolin, as calling it "a $10,000 nuisance case." The suit is presented to the membership as far-fetched and ridiculous—but not so ridiculous that they'll feel bad about paying Margolin nearly a quarter of a million dollars so far to defend themselves against it. (The USCA has budgeted up to half a million to fight the suit through to the finish.) The USCA's line towards the various suits it faces was shown in this summer's series of bulletins from the executive committee, which included regular "Lawsuit Updates":

June 22: "We are still waiting for Bev and Sebastian's lawyer, Don Driscoll, to give us the evidence he plans to use against us, and to reveal a list of all people who are informing on us."

August 3: "Driscoll was so busy... that he must have forgotten to answer our interrogatories (questions intended to clarify his unbelievably vague suit like WHEN did we deal with the Hell's Angels and WHO is Skateboard Kenny)."

According to Driscoll, the reference to the Hell's Angels which USCA members find so ludicrous comes from a former dope dealer at Barrington, who bragged that her supply of meth was protected by the motorcycle gang. If it is substantiated, this would also provide another link to interstate commerce, so the suit can be filed under RICO, the federal anti-racketeering statutes. As for Skateboard Kenny, he was listed on Barrington's own PNG list as a well-known heroin dealer.

Each side is now accusing the other of stalling. The USCA says that Driscoll has been unable to produce evidence to back his charges, while Driscoll accuses the USCA of using its greater financial resources to delay in hopes that his clients will drop the suit. Meanwhile, Barringtonians' reactions to the suit have included spray painting insults about their antagonists on the outside of their building.

Illegal subletting in Barrington during the summer of 1989 once again attracted the attention of anti-Barrington activists within the USCA. Then came the final straw: on September 23, almost two years to the day after the 1987 acid punch party, Barrington held another party at which LSD was publicly distributed by three elected house officials. During a subsequent USCA investigation of the affair, Barrington's house managers threatened the finance manager in an attempt to prevent her from showing the house's books. A Barrington member who was falsely accused of having informed on the house management was harassed and threatened; both he and the bookkeeper canceled their contracts and left the USCA.

The investigation found that while the acid had apparently been purchased privately, house funds had been used to purchase nitrous oxide for a "New Members' Disorientation" party earlier in the semester. The three Barrington officials involved in the LSD party were kicked out of the organization.

While not as egregious as other incidents in the past, the September 23 incident came at a badtime; because the law-suit was open-ended, the plaintiffs could include anything in it from 1985 to the present moment. "If you put yourself in Driscoll's shoes," said Carlos Cabana at a September 28 board meeting, "look at the incident from the eyes of a sleazebag who is gifted at manipulating the press; we'll be hammered. There is no way to save Barrington. We can save the USCA or we can let both suffer. Our only chance is to save the USCA." Almost immediately, Barrington foes began circulating a petition to close the house.

Predictably,Barringtonians called foul. "This really came as a shock to us," Barrington's diplomatic president, Todd Siders, told me. "This whole semester has been like a nightmare. The overwhelming majority, 150, maybe upwards of 160, had no knowledge whatsoever of any distribution.... I'm not going to deny that there's drug use in Barrington; that would be stupid. But our house is. at a level with other houses. We're not the only house with neighbor complaints, not the only house with drug use, certainly not the dirtiest house, certainly not the most uncooperative. We are freely accepting of everything that goes on in the USCA, but because of our house culture, we're going to be the ones watched for it."

Unlike previous referendum, this time Barrington was faced by a united and well-organized opposition from a number of other houses. In addition, the USCA management went all out in support of the referendum, with each manager personally signing an argument for closing Barrington. At its base, the debate was over the meaning of history. "Judging us by our history is ridiculous and unfounded," Barringtonians argued in the 1989 pro/con packet. "[Only] six people who were members when the incidents provoking the last referendum occurred still live in Barrington.... New members live in Barrington. Closure of Barrington punishes them and hurts the USCA as a whole, without helping our chances in the lawsuit."

"Judging us by our history is ridiculous and unfounded,"

Barrington's opponents argued that "History does matter because Barrington is already on probation. It is the responsibility of Barringtonians to prevent the recurrence of problems, not to defend them after the fact."

For once, Barrington lost. "They turned the tables on us," admits Siders. "They had a membership referendum so that there would be no way that we could overturn it." Barringtonians have not proven to be gracious losers.. In addition to the vandalism in their own house and at the central office, some organizers of the referendum have received death threats.

On Monday, November 13, Stebbins Hall, home of referendum organizers Dan Ban and Scott Fitz, was besieged by a crowd of twenty to thirty Barringtonians. "It was like something out of a horror movie," said Fitz, who happened to be in the kitchen at the time. "I tried to shut the door—they surged forward, and I had to hold the door with all my strength. Dan was about fifteen feet away—he ran as fast as he could, and slammed into the door. Dan is short but built like a football player; we would have got it shut except one of them stuck his skateboard in enough to block it." There stood Ban and Fitz like the Spartans at Thermopylae; in this case, however, reinforcements arrived in the form of the Berkeley the vandalism in their own house and at the central office, some organizers of the referendum have received death threats.

On Monday, November 13, Stebbins Hall, home of referendum organizers Dan Ban and Scott Fitz, was besieged by a crowd of twenty to thirty Barringtonians. "It was like something out of a horror movie," said Fitz, who happened to be in the kitchen at the time. "I tried to shut the door—they surged forward, and I had to hold the door with all my strength. Dan was about fifteen feet away—he ran as fast as he could, and slammed into the door. Dan is short but built like a football player; we would have got it shut except one of them stuck his skateboard in enough to block it." There stood Ban and Fitz like the Spartans at Thermopylae; in this case, however, reinforcements arrived in the form of the Berkeley police. One woman who was let in to use the bathroom immediately painted an Onngh Yanngh symbol on the wall and was arrested. A few days later, Stebbins Hall received a bomb threat.

Organizers of the referendum have received death threats.

Barrington residents continue to paint themselves as the victims. "We're the ones who are being threatened," says Siders. "We lost our home. The referendum is creating conditions that put Barrington in a situation where it will come close to living up to all the things that the referendum was supposed to have cured.

"I don't like threatening people. But I'm also quite aware of the fact that we're a house of 166 people. The house council cannot adequately control the house; if one person wants to do something stupid, that's life."

Within days of the referendum, T-shirts were appearing on Telegraph Avenue with an Onngh Yanngh symbol and the slogan "Squat or Rot." George Proper is well aware of the threats by some thirty Barringtonians to refuse to move out after the building is closed December 20. "We'll do whatever is legal, but nothing less and nothing more," he says. "We're landlords, so we know what it means to evict someone. We're in Berkeley, so we know what mass action is. We might get a taste of dealing with them simultaneously." Some of the potential squatters reportedly have attorney parents who may get involved in the dispute, promising a long, expensive fight to empty the hall. Nothing has yet been decided about what to do with the building in the future; the popular option of turning it into married student housing would be extremely expensive. A more likely possibility is to use Barrington as housing for entry-level co-op members only, with a complete turnover every year—and theoretically no time for weird house cultures to develop.

A large clothes dryer was thrown off the roof and into Beverly Potter and Sebastian Orfali's yard. When they complained to Barrington's management, a washing machine soon joined the dryer.

On Saturday, December 2, Barrington held what may be its last hurrah. Invitations to the enormous party were even sent out to its neighbors: "Satan's Village invites you to a wine dinner." One participant estimated upwards of one thousand participants at the event, at which speed and LSD were widely (if not publicly) available. The facilities apparently being overtaxed, neighbors reported a row of partygoers urinating off the roof. A large clothes dryer was thrown off the roof onto Beverly Potter and Sebastian Orfali's yard. When they complained to Barrington's management, a washing machine soon joined the dryer.

What will happen next? At the memorable November 9 board meeting in Barrington, a house alumnus from the 1984 period rose to make an inspirational speech. "After this semester the building will close," he declaimed, "but Onngh Yanngh will never die! What I want to know is, what are you going to do about that?"

The naked Barringtonians who filled the hall clapped and cheered. "We're not telling!" they yelled.

Those who know don't tell, and those who tell don't know.

THE DAILY CALIFORNIAN
Berkeley's Independent Daily Established 1871
VOLUME XXV, NO. 2 WEDNESDAY, JANUARY 17, 1990 BERKELEY, CALIFORNIA

Monday, December 11, 1989

Barringtonians pelt co-op board with stink bombs, paint-filled balloons, fire crackers, eggs, golf balls and smoke bombs.

Court orders Barrington to stop hurling appliances, paint from roof

The injunction forbids inhabitants from throwing clothes dryers, paint, and other items off the Barington premises. However the judge did not comply with Driscol's request that they restrain from urinating out of the former residence hall or spray print adjacent properties.

"They keep on painting '*Beverly gives good head*,'" said Orfali, referring to the message written about Potter.

THE DAILY CALIFORNIAN

Berkeley's Independent Daily; Established 1871

VOLUME XXV, NO. 2 WEDNESDAY, JANUARY 17, 1990 BERKELEY, CALIFORNIA

Barrington Injunction

Paint thrown December 29, 1989

"It looks like they were trying to throw it - the clothes dryer - on our skylight...."said Orfali.

"The USCA is going to spend thousands of bucks to (allow co-op members) to write obscenities on the side of Barrington Hall," the lawyer said.

Photo by Bart

Onngh Yanngh

Getting away seemed to be my forte, and I think I learned that if outright escape wasn't possible, and lying didn't work, then somehow grace would intervene; the grace of Onngh Yanngh. Someone in Barrington had invented a faith for a Spiritual Anthropology class or something and called it Onngh Yaangh. Onngh Yaangh had all the necessary requirements for a religion, and icon, a mudra, a tenet, a comic book and a T-shirt.

It had its vaguely cultish feel, based simply on the nature of its devotees, who were Barringtonian freaks, but it was more of a simple faith, based on the tenet, "Those who know don't tell, those who tell don't know." I eventually realized that this idea was lifted pretty directly from the Tao Te Ching, and is about as simple a truth as the world holds, but it held an essential quality for a community of dope dealers.

OY was also a respectable looking icon, a flat headed alien looking dude who first appeared in the comic strip that described his origin. Flashing the Onngh Yaangh sign and repeating his name just gave you the sense that everything would be cool, which it was.

I was sitting in my room one night, studying, when my dad came in. "I want to look at your eyes." he said. "Huh?" I mumbled "Let me look at your eyes." he replied. "What for?" I asked. "I want to see if you've been doing any drugs." he said.

He took this flashlight and shined it in my eyes, searching for some reaction that he probably wasn't really aware of. Oddly enough he picked the rare night that I wasn't high, so I just acted resentful, and by the grace of Onggh Yaangh, things pretty much went on as they had. —Sheldon Norberg, Author,

Confessions of a Dope Dealer

Healing Houses

Legend has it that in 1974 Bill D. a maintenance manager whose name is said to be enshrined in the alleyway in cement, is reputed to have been inspired by the Hare Krishna movement to invent Onngh Yanngh. It's cult appeal grew. To celebrate Barringtonians stole bananas from Chateau and other Houses to use in a candlelight ceremony they called "Onngh Yanngh Day". Later Cloyne built a huge banana that was displayed at Wine Dinners. Subsequently Barringtonians created a cement version of the big banana. Where is it today?

Those who know don't tell;
Those who tell don't know.

INTERNATIONAL SOCIETY FOR

ONNGH YANNGH

ENLIGHTENMENT

KELEY

3-6551

Better Living Through Chemistry

Welcome to Barrington, kids! Please keep your hands and arms inside the ride at all times.

—Graffiti at the entrance of Barrington Hall

Scott Kelly: Barrington was one of those mind-blowing experiences. I had never come across a place like that before. It was supposed to be a college dormitory and there's a 40-year-old biker fixing his fuckin' Triumph in the front room, just tweaking balls. As far as I could tell, no one that lived there went to school. I remember thinking, "How does this happen?"

Ray Fanell: It was a Berkeley campus housing unit. Everybody played there. All the bands from L.A. Anyone that had a San Francisco gig would come to Barrington.

Dean Washington: Dead Kennedys, Flipper, Black Flag, you name it— right there in the dining hall.

Jason Lockwood: They would lose power so the room would go dark, which was great. You would be thrashing around, floors painted with beer, with people slipping every which way.

Scott Kelly: We were walking down the hallway one day, and this guy with a big vial of liquid acid said, "Want some acid?" I say, "Sure." And he sprayed some fuckin' liquid acid in my eye. By the time I hit Telegraph I couldn't even feel my legs.

Nosmo King: A guy goes, "Okay, we've got a keg on number three and four. If

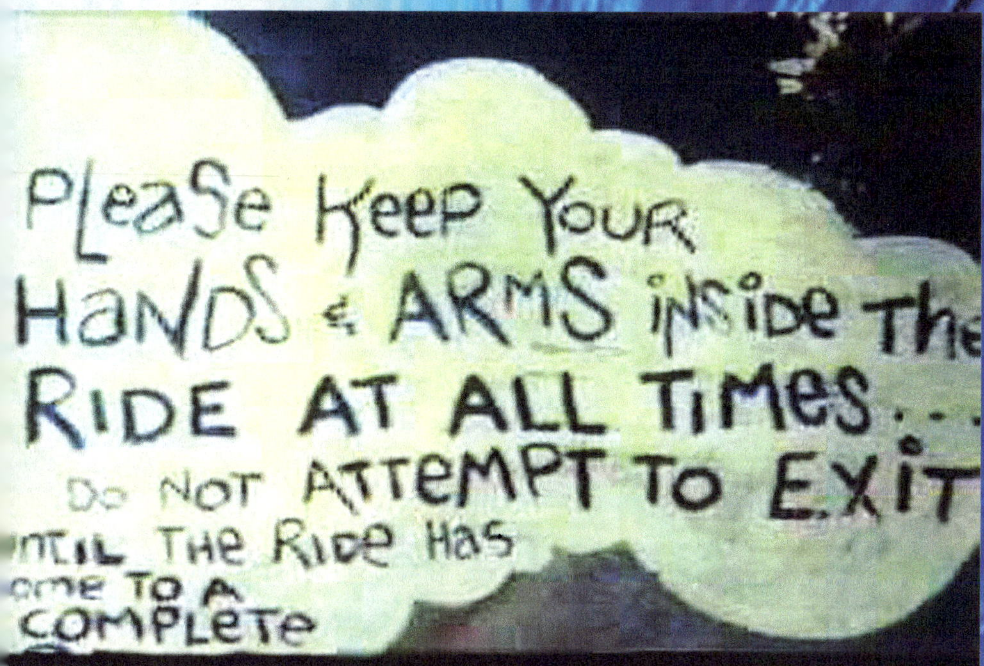

you're into speed, that's on five, and there's acid on six." I was still in high school then and I was thinking, "Wow, this is what college is like?"

Jason lockwood: It was a co-op. Nobody was responsible for anything, because everybody was.

Dan Rathbun: It was a four-story building, a block long. And off of each hall were like 13 suites of rooms and each suite had anywhere from three to five bedrooms and a bathroom.

Nils Frykdahl: I was going to school at Berkeley and wanted to live in the co-ops. I went to the co-op office and they had a little catalog. All the co-ops had little pictures and descriptions of their gardens and other attractive things. When I got to Barrington, there was no picture, no description, it just said, "We suggest you visit for yourself." I said, "Yeah, what about this place?" And they said, "Oh, you don't wanna go there. Everybody just leaves."

Rachel Rudnick: My first punk show was probably '82, '83 at Barrington Hall. I was 12 or 13. It was Trial, Atrocity, Deadly Reign, and 13. I remember going up these dingy staircases and there was a big shit in the middle of a step, and I thought, "No dog is stupid enough to do that."

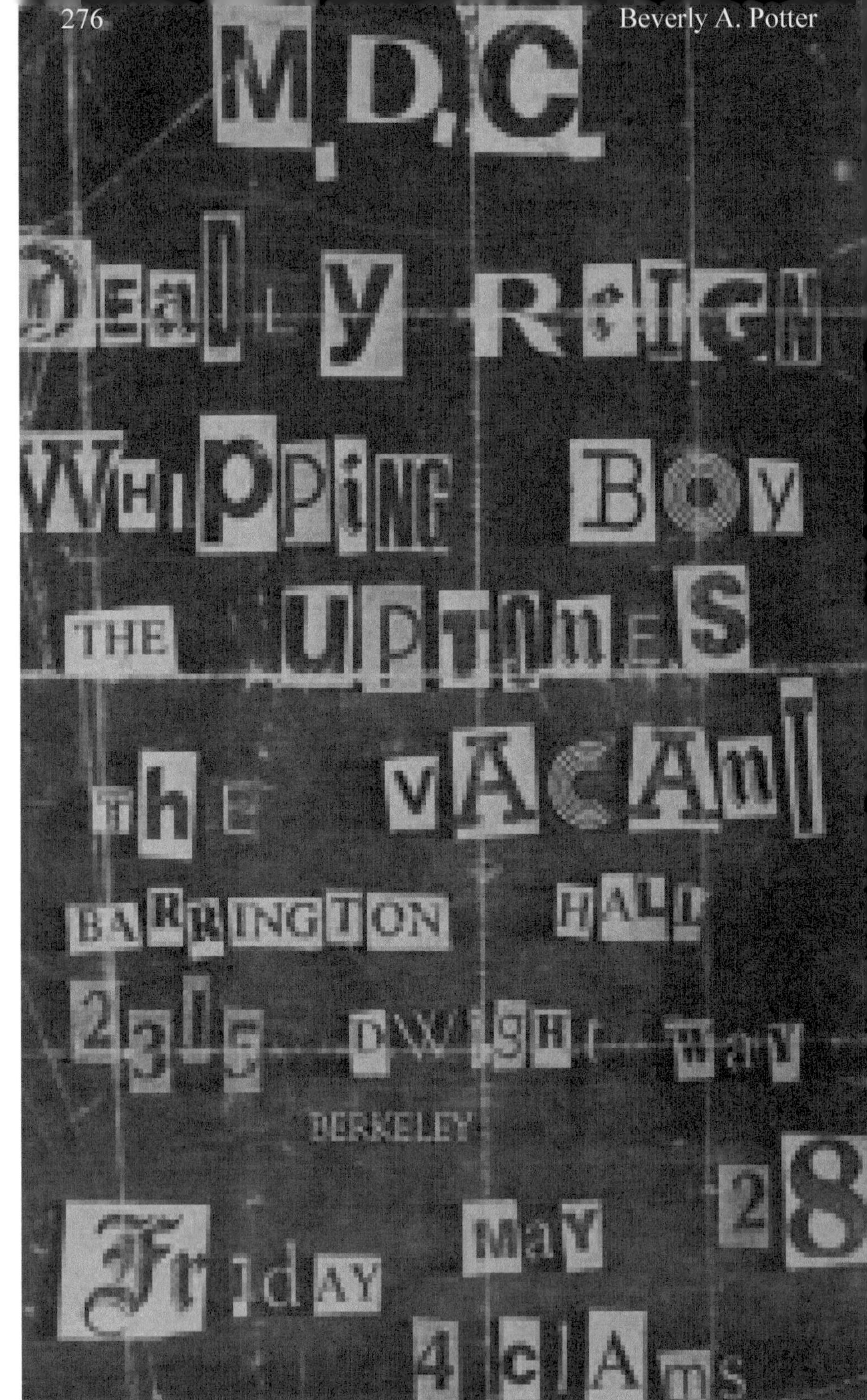
M.D.C
Deally Reich
Whipping Boy
The Uptimes
The Vacant
Barrington Hall
2315 Dwight Way
Berkeley
Friday May 28
4 clAms

You can't fist fuck with nuclear arms

—Graffiti from Barrington Hall

Dean Washington: My buddy Adam had a gutter rat named Lucifer. He became semi-domestic. The rat was huge. Lucifer drank EKU beer, which was really strong. Lucifer inhaled pot all day. As long as someone was smoking, he wanted some. He'd act a fool in his cage if you weren't blowing a cloud his way. Back then, Adam was a heavy doser of acid, so he'd give Lucifer hits every now and then. Lucifer was pretty much the devil himself, really.

Jason Lockwood: The cops would raid that place constantly 'cause it was just rampant with drugs. When the cops came all the windows toward the parking lot would fly open and drugs and needles would come sailing out of the windows. It was just ridiculous.

Dean Washington: They'd have "wine dinners" and the house would vote on what the theme drug was gonna be for the party.

Nils Frykdahl: That was the euphemism for our acid parties, "wine dinners." It sounded very respectable.

Anna Brown: We went to lots of wine dinners. I remember coming out of there with Katie once and we could not find the car, we were so high. We had to walk home.

Scott Kelly: The hippies paved the way for the whole drug market in Berkeley. When you can go to the high school where Jimi Hendrix played, it gives you a different perspective on things. LSD was a huge part of our very specific scene because of the availability and quality.

Nils Frykdahi: Berkeley Bob lived in the closet of the study room. Berkeley Bob was a very sweet guy, but a schizophrenic or something. He had really involved conversations with himself. Like three-person conversations in different voices. This was supposed to be the room where you were gonna work on writing your papers or whatever, and, from the closet, you heard, "Listen! Don't you tell him not to talk." Which implies three people, you know.

There were little quotes from Berkeley Bob all over the walls. There was a whole mock Cult of Bob with the older members who had degenerated into pure stonerdom. They had recorded Bob at one point on a cassette and had memorized long chunks. They would sit around [bubbling bong sounds], and go into it, something like, "Uh,

2315 Dwight Way, don't you tell him not to talk. Listen, this isn't the only pig iron in the business ..." They would fire off these Bob rants in unison. Initially I was very impressed with those guys. But they listened to the Grateful Dead all the time.

You're persona non grata in my hippy van, bitch

—Graffiti from Barrington Hall

Jesse Luscious: I had been squatting in West Philly so I was pretty used to a really radical living situation. I felt really at home. Onng Yanngh was, I don't really know what you'd call it—the entity, the symbol, the embodiment of the house. You'd see it on stickers everywhere. I would call it a religious icon but I don't know if the people who lived there would. You still see it every once in awhile. People from bands have tattoos of it.

Fraggie: There was that pagan organization, OBOD—Order of Bards, Ovates and Druids. They had a bunch of parties there. They would have their ritual bell-ringing, and there would be a band playing, and naked people walking around covered with red paint.

THE ORDER OF BARDS, OVATES AND DRUIDS

Nils Frykdahl: Wes Anderson came to Barrington with his punk band Slaughter of Small Animals. One of the party coordinators had brought some skinned goat heads from a Chinatown butcher. Skinned and mounted on stakes on either end of the stage. It was a gruesome spectacle.

Dan Rathbun: This was Halloween.

Lis Frykdahl: And my brother Per, in an inspired moment, went up and started French-kissing the goat heads, and ended up ripping the tongue out of the head with his teeth. It stopped the band. He grossed out Slaughter of Small Animals. This was a hardcore band from Oakland.

Bean Washington: Everyone looked forward to summer, because the actual students that went to school would leave and sublet their rooms. All us punks would have full control of the building. So

Nils Frykdahl guitarist of Acid Rain,
an indigious Barrington Punk Rock Group.

it was the Barrington Compound. We had a full kitchen, and we made meals-well, when we weren't grinding teeth, or something else.

Nils Frykdahl: The Acid Rain Ensemble was the official name of our band. We started out playing Barrington's wine dinners, which were big costumed affairs, so we dressed up in ridiculous outfits right from the get-go. Not necessarily good costumes but certainly

face paint and garbage bags or whatever we could come up with. That often spilled over into class. I remember meeting each other in the morning, "Hey, let's wear garbage bags to school today" And then we'd see each other between classes wearing garbage bags. Or wearing spikes up to the elbows in music class just bristling. I hope that people are still doing retarded stuff around the UC Berkeley campus.

Dave Chavez: Black Flag with Dez, Flipper and Sick Pleasure. That show was just insane. Somebody kicked in my speaker while we were playing and I got really upset. I had steel-toe boots on. So I just started kicking these bikes until they wrapped around a pole. It was in the air, the violence of the night. Everyone was acting like that. Everybody was pissed off and wanted to throw something. I'm surprised that nobody lit the place on fire. It was the craziest show probably of its time in Berkeley.

Karen McKnight: A friend of ours got killed at Barrington. We believed that he was pushed by the cops. This was around the time that Bush Sr. was visiting San Francisco. He had helped us organize for that protest.

Nils Frykdahl: There were protest movements going on, some of them had their zines based out of Barrington. So there was the political edge and there was the musical, artistic edge, and some extra sort of edge because it was surrounded by this new conservatism within Berkeley.

Karen McKnight. For a long time, Barrington Hall was at the center of the anti-Apartheid movement. We would meet at Barrington and organize, fill containers with gasoline. It was the '80s, no one went anywhere without a can of spray paint.

Nick Frabasillo: The first issue of *Slingshot* was published at Barrington, as were all issues of the *Biko Plaza News, Slingshot's* forerunner, during the anti-Apartheid sit-in.

Robert Eggplant: *Slingshot* gets its name from the Palestinian resistance people shooting slingshots against heavy artillery weapons.

PB Floyd: The first issue was just one sheet of 11 x 17 white copier paper, folded in half. It was raw and militant, with handwritten headlines and hilarious seditious graphics. *Slingshot* looked like it was put together in the backseat of a getaway car after some really cool revolutionary act.

Robert Eggplant: One of the fights that the Slingshot Collective was involved with, besides diversity in education and homosexual rights, was trying to save Barrington.

> During the fall [of 1989], with the war on drugs in full swing, students held a smoke-in on Sproul Plaza that attracted 2000, the largest event of the semester. Barrington Hall, a student co-op that helped organize the smoke-in and that had long provided a haven for activists and organizing efforts ... was threatened with closure from a vote within the co-op system. There had been several other votes over the years to try to close Barrington and in November, the referendum passed.
>
> —*The People's History of Berkeley*

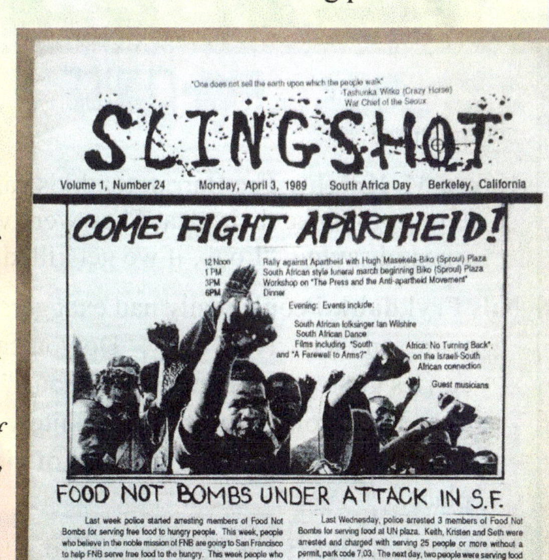
"One does not sell the earth upon which the people walk"
Tashunka Witko (Crazy Horse)
War Chief of the Seoux

SLINGSHOT

Volume 1, Number 24 Monday, April 3, 1989 South Africa Day Berkeley, California

COME FIGHT APARTHEID!

12 Noon Rally against Apartheid with Hugh Masekela-Biko (Sproul) Plaza
1 PM South African style funeral march beginning Biko (Sproul) Plaza
3PM Workshop on "The Press and the Anti-apartheid Movement"
6PM Dinner

Evening: Events include:

South African folksinger Ian Wilshire
South African Dance
Films including "South Africa: No Turning Back", and "A Farewell to Arms?" on the Israeli-South African connection

Guest musicians

FOOD NOT BOMBS UNDER ATTACK IN S.F.

Last week police started arresting members of Food Not Bombs for serving free food to hungry people. This week, people who believe in the noble mission of FNB are going to San Francisco to help FNB serve free food to the hungry. This week people who believe hunger is the crime, not free food, are going to help defend Food Not Bombs and are going to tell Mayor Agnos and his thugs that we will not be frightened, we will not back down and we will not go away.

If you want to help Food Not Bombs, gather at the Federal Building in SF (Golden Gate & Larkin), where they have served food for the past year, on Tuesday at 11. Or, gather at the Farmers Market at UN Plaza (Hyde & Market) at 11 on Wednesday. (Both are at the Civic Center BART stop.) These are the two areas where they are most likely to face arrest and continued police harassment this week.

Last Wednesday, police arrested 3 members of Food Not Bombs for serving food at UN plaza. Keith, Kristen and Seth were arrested and charged with serving 25 people or more without a permit, park code 7.03. The next day, two people were serving food in front of City Hall. Around 5 police arrested Keith again and this time, confiscated his truck. The charge was the same.

Why did the city decide to again arrest Food Not Bombs for their valuable work? Last August, the city tried to stop FNB from serving food in Golden Gate Park. A yuppie landowner organization near the park convinced the city to stop FNB because they said it was bringing poor people to the park. (Somehow they thought free food created the hungry, not the other way around.) At that time, a series of protests and over 100 arrests forced the city to give in and allow food to be served in the park.

Continued on page 8

Karen McKnight: My friends at Barrington put out flyers and showed up at Sproul

Plaza with shoeboxes full of shake joints. Of course, this massive crowd formed. It was a big spectacle. My brother was on the way to class and ended up on the front page of the *Daily Cal,* smoking a joint with a latte in his hand.

Nils Frykdahl: There were always a lot of threats in that direction. Every year, "Oh, the council is voting to close . . ." And we'd all get up in arms and we'd go around to other co-ops and bring guitars like, "Hey, we're from Barrington Hall and we're here to sing some songs for you guys tonight while you eat dinner." As a goodwill gesture.

Karen McKnight: The Barrington kids came around to all the other co-ops to make their plea. They were very emotional. I remember one kid saying, "Look, if we get killed, it's on your hands."

Nils Frykdahl: People really had exaggerated notions of what was going on there. They'd say, "Do you carry a gun? I hear everybody carries guns and it's really dangerous." Or, "I hear everybody's addicted to heroin." There was definitely plenty of drugs and plenty of ruined lives. So from the point of view of parents, it was a bad place.

Karen McKnight: The neighbors sued. They had a lot of documentation about the shows and the parties, people throwing washing machines off the roof.

Finally in March [of 1990], a poetry reading was declared illegal by police who cleared the building by force. A crowd developed which built fires and resisted the police. Finally police attacked, badly beating and arresting many residents and bystanders and trashing the house. Eventually, the house was sold to a private landlord.

—*The People's History of Berkeley*

Karen McKnight: I was told the police formed a gauntlet and beat all the kids as they ran down the hall when they came to throw the squatters out. I went to the courthouse to support all my comrades. We cheered when they were brought out in their jumpsuits. I was so sad to see it close. It's a pathetic piece of nothing now.

Dean Washington: Barrington Hall was like a rainbow in the sky, when you walked through that door. It was a beautiful place.

Time is a crutch, eat mandarin oranges

—Graffiti from Barrington Hall

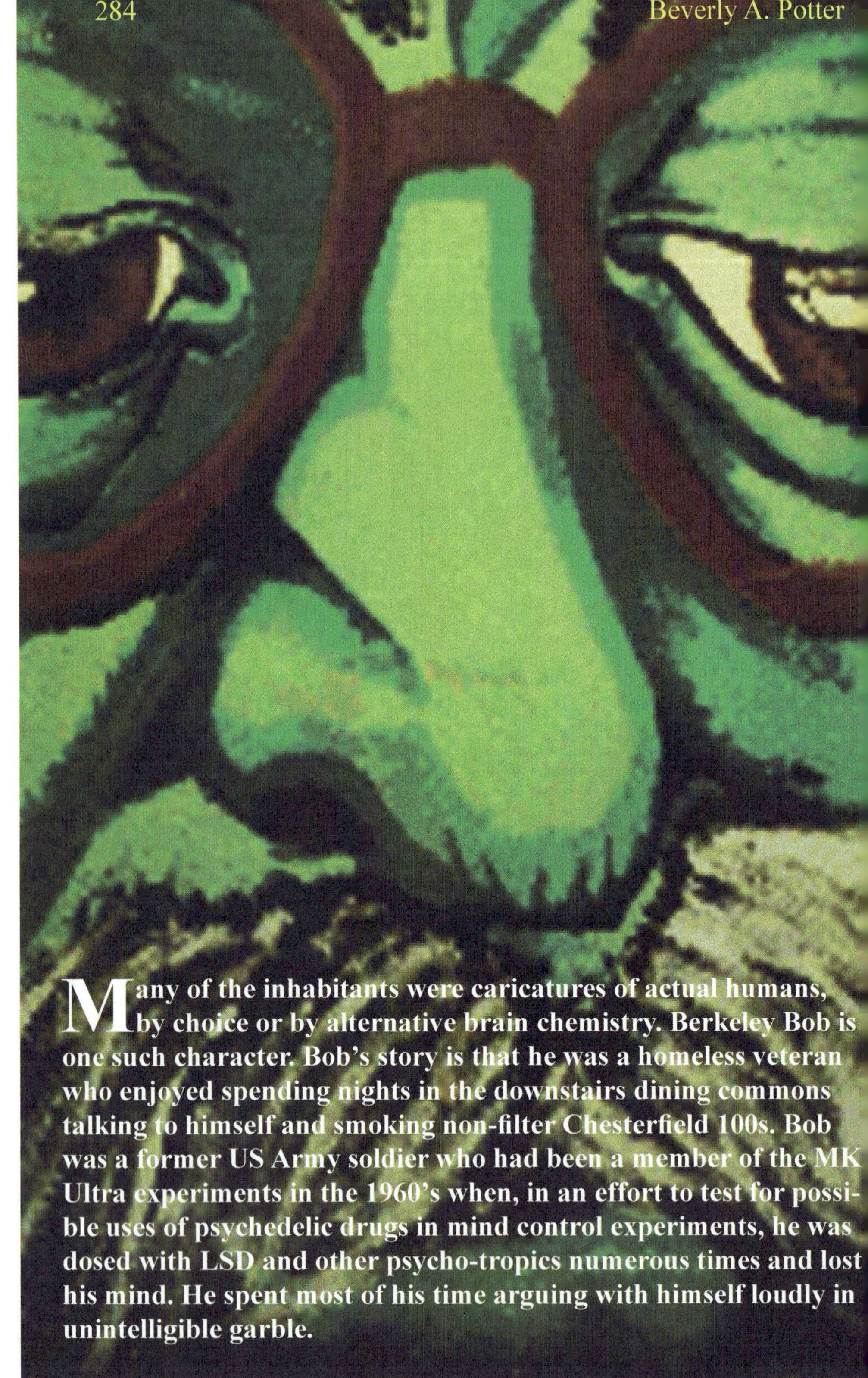

Many of the inhabitants were caricatures of actual humans, by choice or by alternative brain chemistry. Berkeley Bob is one such character. Bob's story is that he was a homeless veteran who enjoyed spending nights in the downstairs dining commons talking to himself and smoking non-filter Chesterfield 100s. Bob was a former US Army soldier who had been a member of the MK Ultra experiments in the 1960's when, in an effort to test for possible uses of psychedelic drugs in mind control experiments, he was dosed with LSD and other psycho-tropics numerous times and lost his mind. He spent most of his time arguing with himself loudly in unintelligible garble.

Berkeley Bob

I attended a house meeting and explained I enjoyed living in the co-op and wanted to stay on.

They allowed me to stay with the stipulation that I might be reassigned to different rooms as the UC students moved in and out. Because I was not paying rent, I did not mind being shuffled around. Nevertheless, I was particularly grossed out by one room that had the stench of vomit so deeply ingrained into the patina of the floor that it could never be washed out.

Only students matriculated at UC Berkeley were supposed to live in the co-ops. I was not the only outsider who lived at Barrington for free. A mentally ill homeless man named Berkeley Bob had crashed there for decades. Berkeley Bob was a parasite who never contributed anything in exchange for his room and board. He was a low-level drug dealer who spent most of his time sitting on the sidewalk on Telegraph Avenue slouched against the outside of Moe's Bookstore. He was so spaced out that he sold methamphetamine to the same narc three times, never remembering that this was the same undercover officer who had already busted him. With the exception of these three stints in prison, he had mooched off the generosity of the Barringtonians without showing any gratitude and often having psychotic outbursts that were quite disruptive.

Once while browsing through the minutes of a general meeting from the early 70s, one of the topics the Barringtonianas had discussed was "We just gotta figure out some way to get rid of Berkeley Bob." There was even a huge mural of his face that stretched from floor to ceiling. The caption read, "Berkeley Bob: Wingnut or Prophet, You be the judge."

Reid Stuart
Author: Triumph of the Green Man

The Security Guards

The U.S.C.A. hired security guards in an attempt to secure the building. At first entry level Brink's Security Guards were called in. But with larger scale vandalism of the house, Phoenix Security guards who carried firearms appeared. The feeling of the house held hostage was intense for all involved.

Barrington Hall Event Chronology

1971 High vacancies provoke "Barrington Hall Feasibility Study" of alternative uses.

1976: Rate differential begins—Barrington is cheaper than other houses

1982 Member falls down airshaft, sues, gets settlement Insurance inspections begin.

1983: Barrington insurance canceled. Barrington Study Committee formed—recommends rehab which is completed for $400K. Rate differential phase-out begins. East side neighbors sue, ask DA to declare "Public Nuisance"

1984 Binding arbitration betw/ Barr and East side neighbors. Kitchen put on probation by City.

1985: "Hell Summer"—crasher, vandalism, graffiti. Gen Mgr recommend closure; BarrCom formed, meets weekly; Crisis in Fall—media blitz; West Side neighbor sues, gets settlement; Many vacancies; Insurance canceled again; City inspects room-by-room; City Task Force named.

1986: Board votes to sell Barrington; Board votes to keep Barrington and put it on probation; Professional manager hired; Singles conversions occurs.

1987: End professional manager hired; "Acid-Punch" party occurs, several are hospitalized; Manger fired by CLMT; Insurance canceled again; City Task force starts up again; City Council members are agitated; Board votes for 100% turnover.

1988: Professional manager idea abandoned; westside neighborhood sue, ask for dissolution o co-op; Referendum on 100% turnover is held;

1989: Board votes to close Barrington and evict all members. House has one last Wine Dinner, throw washing machine on westside house, Attorney gets injunction from being on the roof. Security guard at $40K month.

1990: Residents evicted; 18 hold-overs refuse to leave; Security hired to keep Barringtonians off the roof; Poetry reading turns into riot with police. Barrington trashed, with fires on Haste St. Member falls or is thrown off the roof. Hold overs leave and Barrington is boarded up.

THE DAILY CALIFORNIAN

Berkeley's Independent Daily; Established 1871

VOLUME BERKELEY, CALIFORNIA

Mystery of Barrington's Missing Doors Stumps Police

by Patricia Jacobus
^Staff Writer

Berkeley police are searching for 47 bedroom doors reported missing Monday from the former Barrington Hall student cooperative.

The University Students' Cooperative Association received a judgment on Monday that granted it permission to lock bedroom doors of dwellers who were staying in the building illegally, USCA President said.

Last week Michael Mastronardo, general manager of the USCA, placed locks on the first floor of the 2315 Dwight Way building and was scheduled to lock bedroom doors on the second and third floors Monday, but found no doors to secure when he returned.

Four security guards patrol the house 24 hours a day, seven days a week and were present at the time the doors were unhinged, said Kim Stafford, client/service manager of Burns Security in Richmond. Proper said he does not believe the doors were stolen fro the building.

"I don't think the doors were stolen, I think they are in the building somewhere," Proper said. "whatever the guards do there I think they would have noticed 47 doors being removed (from the building), he said.

USCA officials said they hired security guards at the end of January to protect the building from damage, keep non-residents out and keep the holdovers off the roof.

Co-op spokesperson Derek Glass said he thought it was "just another publicity stunt (from the holdovers) to harass our operation at the USCA." Cooperative members voted to close Barrington Hall Nov. 8 and scheduled formal eviction of the house's residents at the end of last month.

Eighteen people have opposed the eviction and may continue living in the house until the courts decide whether the USCA is acting legally. Many of the remaining students legally occupying the premises continuously change rooms within the house so co-op managers will not know which rooms to lock up, Proper said.

"They refuse to tell us where they are," Proper said. "I don't know why they are doing this, but they don't want us to know where they are. Residents of the former co-op have claimed that their eviction is illegal and are fighting in Berkeley/Albany Municipal Court for the right to remain in the co-op.

February 28, 1990

From Poetry to Rioting

Three months into the standoff on a Friday night in March 1990, the security guards called George Proper, asking if they should allow The Holdover to have a small, quiet poetry reading. Proper said they could allow the poetry reading.

At eight o'clock, Proper got another call telling him that the poetry reading was out of control. As George approached on Dwight Way, he saw police cars lining the streets for several blocks. Blasting noise from the amplified music almost knocked George down as he got out of his car. The police were lined up in front Barrington in riot gear.

George tried to negotiate with the partiers for an hour. People ran through the halls screaming and yelling. When Geroge told them to shut the party down, they escalated yelling and spitting at him. It was chaotic. The police gave George an ultimatum of shutting the party down or they would leave and not return. George told them to shut it down.

The police formed a riot line at one end of the dinning room. About a hundred party goers stood at the other end of the room. George and Neil Huston, the U.S.C.A. physical plant manager, were behind the police line.

The Holdovers and their guests Barringtonians began chanting, "We want George, give us George," and threw beer bottles towards George, thought not trying to hit him, he later claimed.

The police moved in unison toward the partygoers and as they got closer, the partiers panicked and ran out of the dining room into the rest of the house as the riot began.

I'm On Sound

by The Lemmings

About Barrington

There's a place in town
Where the people hang
around
Not far from the school
Close to the avenue
There's a hundred rooms
Everyone's playing tunes
When you walk in the door
They know what you're looking
for
Those that know don't say
Those that say don't know
Those that know don't say
Those that say don't know
When you walk down the hall
You see murals on the wall
When you turn your head
Someone's listening from the bed
There's a scene going here
But the direction seems weird
When the clever hang around
Will they ever go down?
Those that know don't say
Those that say don't know
Those that know don't say
Those that say don't know

by Guy and Charlie

By 1982, The Lemmings was playing east bay clubs, co-ops, and Greek parties around UC Berkeley. Several members of the band and the sound man lived in Barrington Hall, where The Lemmings played often throughout the 1980s. Think laughing gas and LSD and you get a pretty good picture. They had a monthly event called "Wine Dinner", which was a big party with a hot band and LSD-spiked punch. The Lemmings did a lot of these parties. They played the Starry Plough and the Berkeley Square often and opened for Wall of Voodoo at the old Stone in Palo Alto (now The Edge) and a ton of other shows. The song, *I'm On Sound* is referred to by many as "The Onngh Yanngh" song. *Last Big Blast* was written for Barrington's last big blast played during the "hold-over" party, when Barrington was shut down.

Engineered by: Richie Moore (Toast, Running, Lost Not Plost)
Jeff Kliment (Brains, Walk Along)
Matt Brady (Murphy's Law)
Live Sound: Grey Wicker
Guy Brenner: Guitar, Vocal
Tom Dean: Bass, Vocal
Kurt Schleunes: Drums, Percussion
Jeff Silberman: Piano, Organ
Chris Walcott: Drums
Charlie Walter: Guitar, Saxophone

Bev, The Cop Trainer

In the late 70's I hooked up with a group of psychologist in LETRA—Law Enforcement Training Associates. Except for the psychologist, aka mind-fuckers, this was a great gig. I loved working with cops, who are like teenage boys. I love teenage boys.

One really fun thing was creating scenarios of cops acting badly, which we would roleplay while videoing to create tailored to that department training tapes. When we were living in a hotel in Rochester, I played the role of a prostitute in the hotel lobby. My hair over one eye, in my hippy fur coat slumped off my shoulders, pulling my skirt above my knee, *"Hey, Copper!"* I whispered in a sultry tone and waylaid him as his partner went up to the disturbance and got shot! In another, I was a teen in pigtails who was being punished by my abusive father. Cops came and interviewed only the father, as I twirled my hair. As the cops left, the mean father said gruffly, *"Get in your room!"*

We had a room set up like a living room with a 2-way mirror where the class sat to observe. My call was *"Man with a gun"*. I had on my cop costume, sans gun. Me and my cop partner had to enter the room with people running around and yelling. We had to get them under control and then interview each using the LETRA process to find out the nature and scope of the problem. Then mediate an action and leave—all in 10 minutes. Playing with cops was soooo fun.

Then we'd all hit the bar to down a few beers. I rode around in squad cars on the beat. Being a cop is a great gig. Most of the time you are on your own with a partner, never knowing what the next call will bring. Having to live by your wits.

I was the instigator who started the water fights, throwing glasses of water, shrieking and racing around. I was the black sheep of LETRA. They said I was immature! Yeah, Baby!! Cops are great. Real men. Black or white. You always know where you stand with a cop. Unlike with the sickologists who give the shit eating grin, talk in PC-babble and mind-fuck. Psychologists are up there with lawyers on my hit list.

The Rochester PD class

One day I looked around the training site and saw no staff. Hummm. I went down the hall to Don Liberman's (who changed his name to Hatha Surrenda) room, paused at the door to hear voices. They were all in there roasting Bev. A "No! No!" as psychologists are to be open and authentic—not back biting harpies.

I knocked. Silence. *"Come in."* Ah Ha! Caught in the act. I stood by the door and ran their interview process on them, forcing each to tell me what they couldn't stand about me. Then I said, *"I'll consider that"* and left the room. My favorite kind of one-upsmanship!

Later I had other cop gigs. I taught cops getting their masters while on the job. In my first class one guy taunted me, *"Bill asked our last teacher how she looking in a nighty and she left crying."* Soon all the classes with cops were assigned to me. Few prof-types, esp women, can deal with them. Whenever there are cops, they were all heaped onto me. I understand them intuitively, being quasi-military. They require authority! As long as I am THE authority, which I am willing to exercise, I do great with cops. If I'm stopped on the highway, I instantly flip into respect mode: Approaching my car, *"Officer, I have two dogs in the car." "Yes, Officer", "No, Officer."* Automatic. Always give cops facts, let them draw conclusions.

From Home Video
Police Sweeping Halls

Cops Hate Poetry

Police Riot at Barrington

On March 1, 1990 the University Students Co-op Association—USCA—received a temporary injunction prohibiting public gatherings that Barrington Hall. On Friday, March 2, a poetry reading was scheduled to happen in the downstairs area. The USCA, at 4:30 p.m., replaced unarmed Burns security guards with the elite force the Phoenix guards, who are off-duty San Francisco police officers and armed with clubs and automatic pistols. We had a party the weekend before with the more peaceful Burns security guards completely without incident.

The poetry reading began around 8:30. There were around 40 people in the downstairs peacefully reading poetry. At some point the Phoenix guards, acting on USDA general manager George Proper's orders, decided the poetry reading was no longer a small private gathering and that it was a party. They first called the Berkeley police and then Proper. When he arrived, there were already more than a dozen police cars outside of the building. This was between 9:30 and 10 p.m.

Police Arrive–Violence Begins

A resident from Barrington, Pete Ibrahim, had gone outside to peacefully negotiate with the police. Without provocation, a Phoenix security guard told the police to arrest him. He was placed under arrest, handcuffed and placed in the back of the squad car.

Slingshot

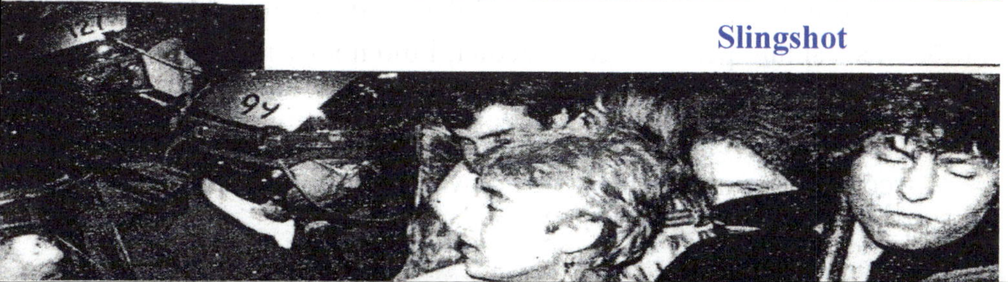

Approximately half a dozen police officers entered the downstairs area without making an announcement. Several people witnessed the police surreptitiously spraying mace in the downstairs area. Everyone in the downstairs smelled and felt the mace burning in their noses and throats. The police then walked outside. When asked why they were leaving, they said, "to get some fresh air."

Inside, the gathering was playing non-amplified music, playing banjos, guitars and drums. After 20 minutes, Proper entered the downstairs and 30 police officers—in full riot gear—lined one edge of the room. Proper made an announcement that the gathering was illegal and we had to disperse or we would be arrested. Several minutes later the police officer in charge made a similar announcement. Because I was a legal tenant in Barrington pending the outcome of the unlawful detainer case, and knew the gathering was not in violation of the court injunction because it was a small, peaceful get-together, I did not believe the police had a right to force me to leave.

The police began sleeping the downstairs shortly after the second announcement. It was now around 10:30. When the po-

lice reached us we stood our ground. After pushing us about five feet towards the Dwight Way entrance, the police were ordered to assume jabbing motion (a position that was illegal for the SF riot police since the maiming of Dolores Huerta by the same jabbing motion).

The police began jabbing at our heads and abdomens. Immediately, I saw one woman crumpled to the ground after being struck in the forehead. Several people were randomly pulled behind police lines, thrown to the ground and beaten. I saw another friend of mine shortly afterwards, with blood pouring out of the back of his head. We were beaten out of the downstairs. The whole time, we were non-violently resisting.

While this was happening, another legal tenant, Jennifer Contreas-Danner, attempted to get upstairs to retrieve her asthma medicine. Jen has a very serious asthma condition and could not breathe because of the mace the downstairs. She was blocked from walking to her room by a police officer on the second floor, even after insisting that she had to retrieve her medicine.

Serious Injuries

She continued to insist, and the police officer ended up grabbing this 5'2" woman by her pony-tail and slamming her head repeatedly into the wall. Another woman, Laura Nicodemus, was holding the door open so that Jen could not be beaten without witnesses. The police bashed the door off its hinges and it landed on Laura's leg. Laura was taken to the hospital and given 25 stitches on her leg from the resulting huge gash. Jen was later taken to the hospital for multiple head injuries.

After we were forced out of the building, police left the building under the control of the Phoenix security guards, who refused to let legal residents of Barrington into the house. Two legal residents, Moniker Bhushan and Julia Eisenberg, tried to get back into a side door. The cops wouldn't let them in and instead beat both of them.

By this time it was about 11:30. We were so enraged by the police action that we built a bonfire on Haste Street between Dana and Ellsworth in front of Barrington—and Beverly and Sebastian's house. About 400 people gathered on the street around the fire. The crowd consisted of those who had been at the poetry reading, former Barrington residents, neighbors and community activists.

Before midnight, a police line formed on Haste and Dana and moved down the street. The crowd threw bottles at them as they swept Haste Street to the corner Haste and Ellsworth. People went around the block and return to the fire in front of Barrington.

After 1 a.m., a fire truck arrived to put out the fire. After extinguishing the fire several times only to have it restarted by the crowd, the fire department turned the water on the crowd itself, using the hoses as a water cannon. The crowd threw bottles and bricks at the fire truck and a cop station in the parking garage facing Barrington.

The Invasion

At 2:15 a.m., the police charged from the garage and into Barrington, screaming. I ran into my room with seven other people and locked the suite door and my room door. We turned out the

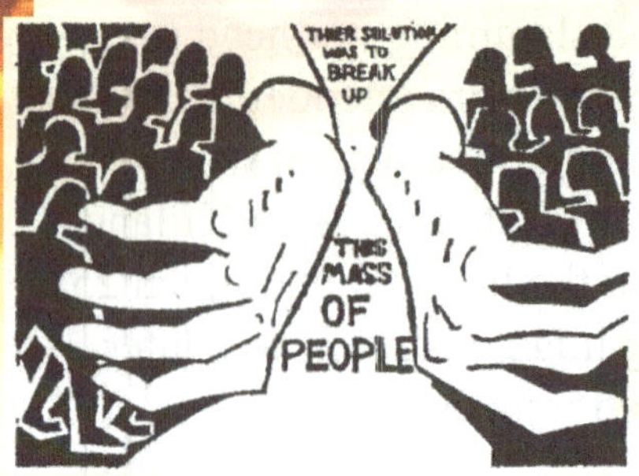

light and kept very quiet. The police conducted an unannounced, room-by-room search, kicking in doors to gain access.

First my suite door was kicked in, and then my room door. The police beat the person closest to the door. They ordered us out, and ran us through a gauntlet of at least seven officers, each of whom we hit us and then threw ice down the fire escape.

Others had similar and worst experiences. One black student, Zappa, was isolated in the hallway and knocked to the ground by several officers. He was punched and kicked repeatedly in the head and the cops threatened to throw him out the window. An unidentified woman was also beaten alone in the bathroom. Another Barrington resident, Julia Eisenberg, was dragged out of her room, beaten and arrested in a bathrobe with no shoes on. At the same time people were climbing down the outside of the building and out the third-floor windows onto the fire escape in order to escape the police. The police forced everyone out of the building, including legal residents.

After we were forced out of the building, a crowd milled about on Dwight Way. Done with their beatings inside Barrington, a couple of cops briefly emerged on the third-floor fire escape and threw several bottles and one brick at us. At this point, some people, angered by the beatings, smashed the front windshield of an empty police car. Other people threw bottles and debris at Berkeley cop stationed that at Dwight and Ellsworth.

Shortly after 3 a.m., another police line formed up the street and forced us down the street to the Ellsworth intersection, meeting little resistance. They continued swinging the club's and jabbing motions, hitting one young man in the ribs. They also swung at an older black man's head, narrowly missing him. Once pushed into the Ellsworth/Dwight Way intersection, the crowd dispersed.

Aftermath

The next morning, when legal tenants were finally allowed back to Barrington, we found an $800 stereo with speakers kicked in and the CD amplifier smash. A computer monitor, keyboard and printer were destroyed. Two guitars and the radio had been smashed. A $4000 computer, a CD player, $1000 from the Barrington cash box and an answering machine were all missing–stolen by police. All the doors in the house had been kicked in by police and would no longer close. Many rooms had been ransacked and various other items had been destroyed by the police.

There were 17 arrests made the evening of the riot and at least 2 more made the next day. Barrington residents, co-op members and neighbors were hospitalized, some with concussions and one student with a broken knee-cap, broken ribs and a broken arm in which he has no feeling in his fingers.

For three days following these events, only the 18 legal residents, but no guests, were allowed in the building. After that the guards would only let a limited number of guests in. All of the legal residents, particularly the women, were living in great fear, following an incident with the Phoenix security guard on Sunday morning.

Before dawn, one of the security guards, not in uniform, shined his flash-light into a room where three women were sleeping. They were all sleeping together because none of the doors locked and many did not close after being kicked in on Friday night.

When the women in the room saw the light they lept up to tell the security guard he had no right to enter their room or their suite. He responded by saying, “Eat it, Bitch!” and walked down the hall. The guard was 6’ 5” tall, the women barely over 5’. The women followed the guard down the hall, telling him not to go into any of the other rooms. He grabbed Monika Bhushan, with two hands by the throat and threw her against the wall. Jennifer Danner told him to stop and he hit her in the head. Neither the president Linc Madison found the incident significant enough to respond adequately. The guard remained in the building at the end of his shift.

The hold-overs were living in a constant state of fear in Barrington with little protection against the aggressive Phoenix security guards or the Berkeley Police. —Guy Fox

The people fight back

"MOVE YOU ASSHOLES"

I, too, was at Barrington Friday night. After watching ahearing of the police brutality occurring my friends and I decided our best option was to barricade ourselves into our room. Two sheets of plywood, nails and bricks, couldn't stop the cops from breaking down our suite door. Then the couch, headbolts and chair couldn't keep them from breaking down the room door. The barricade and 20 min. delays still wasn't enough to cool down the cops machismo or.

After discovering the dozen of us cowering in the back they barked out the order to "move you assholes!" As my friends were lined against the wall I got thrown against the wall by one cop, onto and breaking a table by another and then thrown so that I tripped over a chair by a third. But cops still weren't finished.

I got thrown into the foyer falling on top of the door and barricades they had destroyed, was jabbed with bull clubs while on the ground, and then kicked into the hallway. For the next 20 min. I knelt on the ground with my hands behind my head ("fingers interlaced" the cop yelled) while not 10 feet away, they proceeded to smash my $800 stereo. Once I was notified that they had "taught me a lesson" I was told to "count my blessings and never come back" and released into the cold night, homeless.

—Leonard Carrillo

HOW BPD "coöperates"

My name is Kyle Stuart Miller and I have been arrested for assault with a deadly weapon (rocks and bottles) is on the police officer. I do not attempt to persuade you of my innocence with these words but report how the police treat a citizen who they accuse of violence. When arrested the first thing I did was declare that I would "fully cooperate" and made every attempt not to struggle. The first thing 9 or 10 peace officers did

was hit me in the stomach and then in the head. They grabbed my hair and led me away from any other citizens where I was thrown against the wall and then the ground. Hands on my back and face down I was kicked in the side and head while one of the officers knees held my neck.

Is there some new definition of the word cooperate with the police and the USDA share? At the end of my dramatic abduction four felony assault and two assaults with a deadly weapon were committed upon me by the respectable police officers of Berkeley. Even if I were guilty of one count of assault charged to me, does that just the six combined felonious actions committed by the protectors of all citizens?? FIGHT THE POWER!!!

Berkeley Police War Mentality

Berkeley Police have a war mentality. The WBar on Drugs, Cleanup on Southside, Crackdown on Civil Disobedience on manifestations of this war mentality. Us versus them; a white male power structure versus whoever gets in their way. War mentality.

And they will pick us all off, beat us up, and arrest us one by one until they control all our lives or until we stop them. We have their laws, they have their guns, and they are ready to fight. War mentality

And now I am charged with assault with a deadly weapon on a police officer for throwing rocks and bottles. That the entire night I do nothing. I am a prize to make up for their losses. Berkeley Police War Mentality. And they are on the attack.

—Patrick McIlrath. USCA member, ex-Barringtonian.

THE BLUES

Blue
Blue and Red
Blue: Shut up, I'll beat your head
'Til it's red

Blue
I'll beat you
I'll beat you black, brown,m yellow, white
I'll beat you tonight

Blue
Black and blue bruises
on bodies
all colors
Red fear
Red terror
Terror wears a blue suit with a helmet

Blue says "Eat it bitch"
Blue shoves his stick down your throat,
Smashes your house, smashes your being...

Man
Big strong man in blue
See only a thing to be beaten into submission
When he looks at you.

Blue says he's your protector
Just call 911

—Allison Shore

— *Slingshot*
November, 1989

WE OWN IT GEORGE RUNS IT

The University Students Cooperative Association has a slogan: "We own it, we run it." The Coop's 18 houses are owned jointly by it approximately 1400 members. Each house elects, each semester, one or more (depending on the size of the house) representatives to the Board of Directors. The Board reps supposedly represent their houses' collective opinions. The Board is said to be "the governing body of the USCA."

Alongside the board operates the Central Level Management Team (CLMT) composed of the Board-Elect President and Vice-President and several hired professional managers. The CLMT is headed by USCA General Manager George Proper. The job of CLMT is supposedly to deal with the administrative details of running the Coop, as directed by the Board. The CLMT is supposedly to be the members' employees, not the boss

But let's look at what's really going on here. Is "We own it, we run it" at all accurate? Do the members really run the Coop? Is the Coop really a coop? Fuck no!

First let's look at the Board of Directors. For one thing, they don't always represent the feelings of their houses' members. The majority of the Board reps just make a decision (often based on questionable sources such as the Daily Cal) and stick with it, despite any logical arguments for or against the proposal. But this isn't even the main problem. The big problem is that the board is really just a puppet of the CLMT. Especially George Proper. The Board is George's puppet.

Yes, it's true: the Board of Directors is spineless. Instead of representing their houses, they basically do whatever the CLMT and he tells them to do. If George backs a proposal, it goes through. If he doesn't, it doesn't.

It's very simple: this CLMT has way too much power. The Coops bylaws state that this CLMT has the power to make whatever decisions it needs to "when the board is not in session." Board meets for about 3 - 7 hours every 2 weeks. The rest of the time it's not in session. What this means is that most of the time explanation the CLMT can do pretty much anything it wants!

Likely, the CLMT has been seriously abusing this power. They hired the original Burns security guards at Barrington, costing $10,000 per week, without consulting the Board in all. Now they have stepped up this security by hiring the Phoenix "ultra-security" guards: off-duty S.F. Police with guns and clubs. These guards are costing the Coop about $30,000 per week. The change from Burns to Phoenix was again made by the CLMT without consulting with the Board.

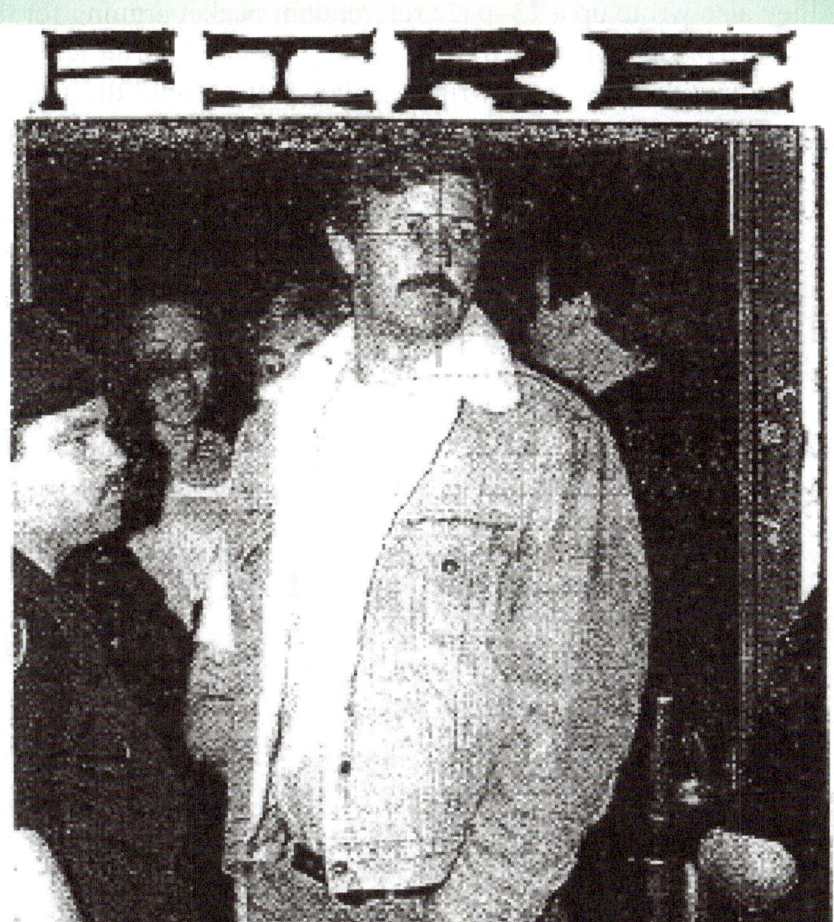

And now George is gone too fucking far. On Friday night he ordered the cops to disperse the crowd. He is responsible for the violence that followed—George isn't stupid, he knew we would resist being kicked out of our house. There is blood on George Proper's hands. And he was not in any way carrying out the directions of the Board.

There is another way that the CLMT has abused its power. During the recent referendum to close Barrington, to CLMT, which is supposed to be a neutral body (don't laugh, it is really supposed to) came out aggressively in favor of closure. Not only did they speak out for closure at numerous membership forums, they also wrote up a **23**–page referendum packet arguing for the closure of Barrington. They used co-op money to print it up and even paid themselves to write it. When they weren't discussing the packet before writing it up, they asked then USCA President Paige Wolverton, the only student present at the time, to leave.

So the Coop is fucked up. So the Coop isn't really a Coop. What are we going to do about it? Well, the first thing we need to do is fire the CLMT. If not the whole team, we should at least fire George and impeach President Linc Madison and Vice-President Tom Utiger.

Another idea is to have the CLMT managers elected by the membership. Each manager could be limited to one term to prevent them from becoming entrenched and gaining too much pow-

er. We also need some kind of review committee to evaluate the conduct of the CLMT.

But the biggest problem is that the USCA is too big. What has allowed the USCA to become so uncooperative is that power is too centralized. The houses need more autonomy. How can a centralized body make good decisions that affect the lives of people they have never met? People should have control over their own lives.

I don't know whether we have to go this far or not. But maybe we need to split up the USCA into smaller units. This may be the only way to avoid the kind of centralization of power we have in the co-op now. –Dinsdale Pirranha

The Holdovers

All but eighteen "holdovers" protesting the closure moved out of Barrington in the spring of 1990. The U.S.C.A. issued member contracts for an entire school year, i.e., for both fall and spring semesters. When the U.S.C.A. membership opted to shut Barrington down before the spring semester started, they canceled the residents' contracts. Legally the holdovers were contesting their contract cancellation, and could stay in the building until they had been formally evicted. These holdover exercised their rights as squatters while they appealed eviction.

For the first few weeks of the "holdovers" threw massive, loud 500-person parties every weekend as they methodically destroyed the house. Vandalism planned. Barringtonians climbed onto the roof, ran a fire hose down a light shaft that provided air circulation to a column of bathrooms, turned it om, flooding and destroying the dining room.

Hoping they would win the eviction appeal and Barrington would continue as their counter cultural haven. The anarchy was exptreme. Ex-Barringtonians tried to organize to purchase the house from the U.S.C.A. The Barrington members felt a strong commitment, which most was multiplied by the drive to kick them out.

POETIC INJUSTICE

When I was invited to read poetry at Barrington Hall on Friday, March 2nd, I was more than happy to do so. I had followed Barrington's saga from a comfortable distance and felt that any good energy I could give it would be the least I could do to help out. If I had known every detail of what would happen later–a police riot which would leave me with scars and leave other people and the Hall itself disfigure–I would have come and read anyway. I knew this was too important to miss.

Entering the Hall I immediately felt utter wrongness of Barrington's occupation by the security guards. This was not some paranoid–filled compartmentalization box of strangers who do not trust each other. True anarchy requires no guards. Hence their only purpose is to oppress the residents and guests. Their mere presence is violence. But if we lack the spirit to stand up in the face of that, we are lost. So, I prepared myself as I would for any poetry reading, clearing my mind, talking poetry, awaiting the

Barrington Haste
Street Door

Light on Bev & Seb's House

Neighbor Video Haste Street

Muse. The meeting began. Though I was still conscious of the security guards, I've read three short poems and one long poem from my forthcoming book and made a couple of jokes about getting money to print it. The poems were communicating themselves, but there was a feeling of confrontation in the air–not between the people present, but against all of us. John–Michael read his work, drawing out the confrontation to stark relief. We finished reading and everyone went let the energy out with joyful noise and dancing. Indigenous people have done this for tens of thousands of years, long before the invention of the mace the police hit us with as we dance. It was history in miniature, like an indigenous village in the way of the colonialists, we were poisoned and pushed out by the mercenaries. Mercenaries have historically targeted women in their attacks, and this was no exception; it is no accident that a woman was pushed out and beaten by the Berkeley Police Department.

The indigenous culture does not want violence, despite our differences we need each other to stay alive. It is the colonizer who provokes an attack, who uses force for the sake of force. We nonviolently protested this outrage against us cries of anger and a bonfire in the street. The mercenaries responded by forming a line of attack and deploying a water cannon. We stood our ground, armed only with bottles, while the police, in full riot gear, carried pistols. From the Caribbean to Vietnam and back again, the colonizer has never understood the resisting power of the people of the land. It doesn't fit in with the cop game. The cop game is that the cop is always right. The cop game is that you run while the cop chases you until you give up and the cop wins. Cops need criminals, and criminals need the cops. Get it? But we don't play that game. So they did what they do to punish any of us who don't play; they charged us and tried to beat us into submission. I saw the rampaging flanks of cops running up the street and felt the tiny fragment of nameless terror indigenous peoples around the world feel when an Army helicopter sweeps in on their village. Some tried to flee the building; others, including myself, hid in rooms. The police clubbed every moving target. They kicked in every door. The hate in their eyes was so strong you could taste it like poison. And as an African-American who stared that hatred in the eye, I was thrown down, handcuffed, club, cursed at, and arrested

Jail is a sequence of small rooms, one leading into another, none leading to freedom. You never see the sun. You never see trees. You never feel eldritch breeze electrify your skin under a full moon. This is the colonizer's world, the world where th cops masturbate to themes of power, and where the criminals playing along. If you don't want to live there, fight back today.

Police Water Cannon—
Neighbor Video

Riot Squad in front of Bev & Seb's house

WHAT ARE PEOPLE GOING TO DO ABOUT IT ?
KEEP OUT.

Police Press Conference

The day after the riot the Berkeley Police held a Press Conference in City Hall to explain Police actions at Barrington, the night before. A crowd of Barringtonians, their supporters and neighbors gathered to hear what the police had to say. Seb and I are standing in left corner, listening to Captain Miller.

Capt. Bobby Miller: "The Police were called to protect the Firemen trying to put the fire out and ran into problems with people throwing rocks and bottles and bricks at them. One fire fighter was hurt and ten police officers were injured.

TV cameramen moved about filming angry Barringtonians and supporters on the stairs waving signs and chanting.

As Capt. Miller, completed his remarks, a bold Barringtonian leaped into the empty chair next to him. With considerable confidence, he took over the Press Conference and relayed, "The Police formed a line downstairs, pulled out their clubs and began sweeping the downstairs. The Sergeant in charge said, 'Put your clubs in jabbing motion'. Then they proceeded to jab people really hard. They pushed us and beat us and clubbed us. We were being completely non-violent."

City Hall was undergoing a face lift. The Main Entrance, exterior stairs, and front sidewalk were an enclosed walkway in plastic to protect pedestrians from the construction. Exiting, the crowd had to squeeze

Capt. Bobby Miller of Berkeley Police Department explained police actions.

together to get into the plastic exit shoot—which could have been a disaster. Had someone a knife, it would have been easy to enact revenge. We didn't think of things like that in 1990, which was before empting our pocket for security at the doors of public buildings, and having to take off our shoes at the airport.

As we squeezed through the front door of City Hall, pressing together, I saw Banjo Boy who was smiling at me. Banjo Boy called out over several heads, "Bev, are you on our side now?" Standing with him, Juan Mendoza called out, "Are *you* Bev?" I laughed and nodded, "I've heard the legend of Bev!" he continued,

Unnamed Barringtonian "holdover", wearing an onngh yanngh + anarchy tee-shirt, took over Press Conference to recount Police brutalilty.

March 10, 1990, 3:05 a.m.

Sebastian! Sebastian! What's that smell? I mumbled as I awoke to a strong, strange smell in our bedroom. I looked at the clock. 3:05 a.m. So strong was the smell that I rolled out of bed to stumble into the kitchen to check if the gas stove were leaking. The stove, of course, was fine. Looking at the clock again: 3:06 a.m. as my head hit the pillow. I rarely awoke in the night. What was going on? What was that smell?

Imagine my shock the next morning as I read *The Daily Cal* to learn that Juan Mendoza was found by a passer-byer in a pool of blood in the Barrington parking lot, 25 feet from the building *at 3:10 a.m.* and pronounced dead by Alta Bates Hospital at 3:33 a.m.

Clairalience – Psychic Smell

Distinctive smells have long been associated with a variety of paranormal and psychic phenomena. Many mediums specifically rely on their ability to 'smell spírit' in order to validate loved ones who have crossed over, or to identify the presence of spíritual entities. —*Psychic Blogger*

The smell dissipated by the time I got back into bed. I don't know if Sebastian also smelled the strange strong odor. I do know this. Whatever it was, it was so strong that it woke me out of a deep sleep. And it happened virtually at the moment of Juan's death. I believe it was a visitation. Whatever could it possible be? And just a few days earlier he'd waved at me, saying, "*I've heard the Legend of Bev.*" And now he was dead.

If it were Juan, why visit me upon transitioning to the Other Side?!!!

THE DAILY CALIFORNIAN
Berkeley's Independent Daily; Established 1871
VOLUME
BERKELEY, CALIFORNIA

Barrington Death Still a Mystery; Probe Urged

By Joshua B. Good

Barrington Hall residents are calling for an independent investigation into the Saturday morning death of a fellow resident who plummeted four floors from the top of the embattled student cooperative.

Juan Mendoza, a 20-year-old UC Berkeley junior died from head, shoulder and chest injuries suffered as a result of the fall, the Alameda County Coroner's office said.

An unidentified passer-by discovered the body in the parking lot of the 2315 Dwight Way house at 3:10 a.m. Saturday, police and neighbors said.

"A lot of people here at Barrington don't trust the police," said Daniel Miller, a Barrington resident. "We've asked (Berkeley City Council member Don Jelinek to request) that someone outside the police department investigate it."

Jelinek could not be reached for comment before press time Sunday night.

Mendoza's death comes one week after a riot at the co-op that started when Berkeley police broke up a party there. Seventeen people were arrested, and more than 20 people suffered injuries during the five-hour-long conflict.

The Barrington resident was pronounced dead at 3:33 a.m. at Alta Bates Hospital Saturday. Berkeley police are still investigating the cause of his death and have not ruled out suicide.

The coroner's office said they would know if Mendoza had any drugs in his system when the final toxicology report is finished within three weeks.

But current and former Barrington residents who knew Mendoza said he showed no sign of wanting to take his own life.

"Juan was not the type of guy that would have thrown himself off the roof," Miller said.

Mendoza was an avid rock climber who sometimes practiced by scaling the Barrington walls, friends said.

He climbed out a third story window onto the roof, said Miller, adding that he and other residents did not know what had happened until police arrived.

Miller said, "We're pretty much in the dark."

Mendoza was found lying in a pool of blood about 25 feet from the building.

"I saw him lying there on his back," Miller said. "It was a really, really shocking sight. The image is burned into my mind."

One of the police investigators at the scene said none of the Barrington residents knew exactly how Mendoza died.

"I don't believe anyone at Barrington was aware of it," said Berkeley police Sgt. Alek Boga.

But Robert Maloney, the department's homicide inspector, said Mendoza's death came from either slipping or jumping off the building. "The wounds are consistent with falling from the building," Maloney said.

Doctors at Alta Bates hospital were unable to revive Mendoza and pronounced him dead at 3:33 a.m. Mendoza was unconscious at the scene, the coroner's office said.

Another of Mendoza's friends, Leonard Carrillo, said Mendoza was upset because of last week's riot. "He was pretty enraged about (the riot)," said Carrillo, a former Barrington resident. "He said he was sick and tired of the cops beating him up."

Although Mendoza was involved in last week's altercation with police, he was not arrested.

A neighbor who lives across the street said he did not hear anything unusual coming from the Barrington parking lot until Mendoza's body was found.

March 12, 1990

March 15, 1990

CONFIDENTIAL

TO: Shirley Dean
City Council, City of Berkeley Berkeley, CA

FROM: Beverly Potter

At your request I am providing a summary of my conversation with Mark Romero, the step-father of Juan Mendoza who died in a fall from Barrington Hall last Saturday morning.

Mr. Romero said that Juan had called his mother 3 days before he died and said something like, "Mom, if something happens to me make sure you investigate." Then he went on to talk about the riots, police brutality and problems with the guards. Mr. Romero asked me if I knew of a Phoenix guard named Rodrigez. I said I did not know any of the guards or their names. He said that Juan had specifically mentioned a problem or confrontation with such a guard.

Mr. Romero said that he had been told by someone, I believe the coroner, that "metal fragments" were found in Juan's head. During the conversation Mr. Romero twice said he wondered if it was a bullet and was waiting the results of the analysis.

Mr. Romero said, "He was a leader. There's no way he killed himself." He said that Juan had a fractured leg and landed on his head.

Mr. Romero's brother is a Deputy District Attorney in Contra Costa County. He said that his brother was not permitted to view the body. So he went to Taos and viewed it before the burial yesterday.

Later Mr. Tom Romero, the brother called me. He gave me very little information and asked a lot of questions. He said Juan's mother and father are still very upset.

It is my understanding that students were told that Juan's parents were traveling in Europe. However, Tom Romero indicated that they had not been traveling.

For further inquiry:
Mark & Judy Romero: PO Box , Taos, NM 87571, 505/phone
Tom Romero, home: 707/phone, Vallejo, Ca.

East Bay
EXPRESS

Sticks and Stones **March 16, 1990**

Paul Rauber

Did He Fall Or Was He Pushed?

How did **Juan Mendoza** die? Mendoza was one of the 18 tenants of Harrington Hall who was resisting eviction attempts by the University Students Cooperative Association (USCA). *At* 3:10 a.m. Saturday morning, his body was found in the parking lot next to the building in a pool of blood; twenty minutes later he was declared dead at Alta Bates.

Mendoza was a rock climber who was known to scale Barrington's walls for practice. (While 3:00 a.m. would normally be considered an odd time for mountaineering exercises, Barringtbnians are known for the odd hours they keep.) A passer-byer—the same one who later discovered the body—has told Berkeley police that he saw Mendoza climbing on the building. Mendoza was known to be upset by the March 2 riot at Barrington; some USCA members hypothesize that he had climbed up to the roof to be by himself, and slipped as he tried to climb bads: down again over the building's eaves.

There remains, however, the anomalous position of Mendoza's body, which was found a full 25 feet away from the building's wall. One theory is that Mendoza's efforts to grab hold of the building actually propelled him away from it, and that his body bounced after falling from such a height. Another theory calculates that Mendoza would have had to be moving at a rate of 10 mph away from the building to achieve such a distance, a theory consistent with the victim running—or being chased off—Barrington's roof.

One Barrington resident, **Kibi Schultz,** has reported hearing noises on the roof, and suspects foul play. Barrington residents are currently enjoined by court order from being on the roof; there are security guards patrolling the building who are charged with enforcing that order.

With the coroner's report not yet in, Berkeley Police homicide inspector **Robert Maloney** is only able to say that Mendoza's wounds were consistent with those "resulting from falling, jumping, or being thrown" off the roof.

Requiem

We had some beautiful quality time together when Juan was home at Christmas, which I shall always treasure. Juan spent a great deal of time with his father who is a classical guitarist. He had recently decided to major in music and practiced the guitar for long hours.

Juan was a beautiful loving person. He loved skiing, rock

climbing, soccer, music and Reese's Peanut Butter Cups. He loved his friends, his family and especially his little sister Sophia. His reasons for fighting for Barrington were those of love—not for a building or a life style but because he loved the people he lived with. He felt a deep loyalty to them because they were dedicated, honest and sincere. They were accepting of others and non-judgmental.

Juan hated bigotry, racism and injustice. "Mom," he told me after a USCA meeting regarding Barrington, "I was accused of things and called horrible names by people who don't even know me. They hate me not because of who I am, or what I am, but simply because of where I live." Another reason for fighting for Barrington was his outrage about the injustices heaped upon Barringtonians.

Juan touched the lives of many people and at his funeral there were family and friends from across the United States—Washington, Oregon, Berkeley and Los Angeles on the West Coast to Chicago in the center and Boston on the East Coast. It is only through the support of this varied and wonderful group of people that I am able to make it from one day to the next.

Even George Proper, while admitting that he and Juan were adversaries, called to tell me that I had a son to be proud of. Other comments from those closer to Juan were: "Juan was a joy to be around." "Juan had a gift of making us feel as though we were his best friend." "He always cheered up people with his great sense of humor and great personality." "I will miss Juan's sense of humor and refreshing honesty." "He was one of the few people I could talk with openly." "Juan was one of the sweetest, nicest people I know. He always had a smile for everyone and deeply cared for everyone he knew."

And my favorite—"The boy/man with the electric eyes and constant grin is well loved by his friends in Berkeley. He made the grayest days seem laughable and the sunniest days brighter."

The prayer of St. Francis of Assisi blessed Juan's funeral. It begins—"Lord, make me an instrument of your peace . Where there is hatred let me sow love ..." Juan did sow love. Juan was love and those of us who were lucky enough to have shared in that love are forever richer for it

— Judy Romero
Juan's mother

Who Killed Juan Medoza?

Here's what I "imagine" happened: Mendoza had been disputing with the security guards and just couldn't leave it. He climbed up on the roof where he figured he'd find his adversaries. He did. He probably taunted them from afar.

Enraged, they grabbed him. He struggled and scratched. (The autopsy found blood under his nails.) Being only 5' 4" and 145 lbs, Juan was easily overpowered. They got him face down, each taking one arm and one leg, swinging him back, while running to the edge of the roof, and flung him off—face first. A witness reported hearing running on the roof at that time.

The force of the swing with two large men throwing the smaller teen could account for his landing 25 feet from building, at the 10 miles an hour that Rauber of the *EastBay Express* speculated about in Sticks and Stones. He hit his left face and head, smashing in his nose and eye and skull, and sliding, causing the scrapes on left side described in the autopsy.

> "*....obvious asymmetry of the head with palpable fracturing . . . prominent on the left side....there is a laceration measuring about 1 inch in length and gaping to about ½ inch....linear scratch-like abrasions...adjacent to the left eye and measure about 2 inches in length . . .contusion around both eyelids bilaterally measuring about 2 inches horizontally . . . the left eye appears somewhat sunken . . . and there is a contusion on the left bridge of the nose. ." "...there is extensive traumatic injury to the brain. The frontal lobes show extensive traumatic pulverization . . . back to almost the level of the basal ganglia on the left...*

The force of gravity plus the force of the throw combined so that as he hit ground his lower body came down very hard, possibly bouncing, to break both knees and the left femur, as noted in the autopsy.

Fully conscious, Juan had a terror ride. Flying down to his death, he experienced "expanded time" where everything slows down, as the mind speeds up. Juan *knew* he was going to die. THIS IS WHEN HE CAME INTO MY ROOM, which I detected in the form of the intense smell. Perhaps he had an out-of-body experience, as is often reported by people with NDE—near-death experiences. At any rate, I believe Juan's energy, spirit—whatever—came into my room at the moment of his death. Why?

The "investigation" was cursory. His death was blown off. I made a complaint with the Police Review Commission, which I was later pressured me into withdrawing because his mother hand filed one, they said.

It's not credible that Juan could propel himself 25 feet from the building. And, of course, he showed no sign of depression. I continue to believe that Juan was murdered—thrown from the roof by Phoenix guards. I recall a story about two unaccounted for guards, who claimed they were getting coffee at the 7-11—only the 7-11 wasn't open at 3 am. That implicated the guards—and the Co-op by association. The Co-op was happy to have Juan's death fade. They certainly didn't want another law suit.

I've learned that the Phoenix Security were permitted to carry guns, and were off-duty police. Recall that just a week before the Barringtonian-holdovers, of which Juan was one, had ignited a full riot with the riot squad. The Berkeley PD took a lot of criticism for brutality and had no sympathy for Barrington-holdovers. The notion that Juan was thrown from the roof by police opens a whole host of possibilities. We've all heard of the "code of silence".

The autopsy is curious. There is no mention, for example, of Juan being found 25 feet from the building. Yet in a Supplemental entry on 3/**23**/90 (there's that '23' again) that Investigator Maloney said he was viewing the case as "Accident vs Suicide pending tox."… because the "deceased was alleged to have taken" LSD the day of the "accident". The "Death certification would be 'pending' until tox is complete". A "urine LSD" was added to the tox on 3/29/90, with the result being "presumptive positive".

BPD refused to give me copy of the Police Report, saying it was in storage.

That same Supplemental particulars noted that "Maloney said that the deceased did not fall while climbing the building but crawled out a third floor window and scaled the building using 1 ½ inch electrical conduit on the north side of the building and he fell/jumped from the south side of the building." Duh? Barrington runs through the block North to South, with the parking lots on the east and west sides?

Who is powerful enough to quell investigation into such a high-profile "unnatural" death, as it was classified on the autopsy?

After all, Juan Mendoza was a *only a useless* "Barringtonian"—and a criminal holdover at that! Everyone *knew* Barringtonians were *always* on acid. So obviously Juan, high on acid, flew off the roof, thinking he was a bird – as he "committed" suicide.

Well, he *did* commit suicide – considering that he said to his mother three days earlier, "Mama, if anything happens to me, make sure to investigate." He went up on to that roof where he "knew" he would encounter his adversaries—dick-headed pigs—and he went up anyway. So, yes, he "committed suicide by cop". Well, it is as good an explana-

Wednesday, March 14,1990

THE TRIBUNE

Moms Tell Barrington Horror Stories

***By William Brand** The Tribune*

BERKELEY - A group of angry mothers — from all over the East bay — along with residents of the neighborhood around Barrington Hall, the riot-torn student co-op, accused the City Council last night of ignoring problems at the four-story south campus rooming house.

The mothers are members of Parents and Community Together, a Berkeley-based organization of parents of children with drug problems. Barrington, at 2315 Dwight Way, has been a haven for juvenile runaways for years.

Susanne DeWitt of Berkeley said she and other mothers whose children had hidden out in Barrington, out of reach of the law and parents, had complained to the city many times.

The death this weekend of a Barrington resident, who apparently fell from the roof, is a direct result of the city and the coop's long-standing policy of doing nothing, the mothers and neighbors charged.

The complaints came during the same "open mike" period that angry residents of Barrington used at last Tuesday night's council meeting to assail police brutality.

"No one ever does anything," DeWitt said.

The residents and their supporters—who call themselves 'Barringtonians'—were complaining about a night of violence that broke out the previous Friday evening as police ended a poetry reading. Under a restraining order, the event was not allowed.

Before the night ended, police arrested 17 people; 10 officers and a firefighter were injured.

The more than 1,200 members of the University Students Cooperative Association, who live in 18 non-university owned dorms around Berkeley, voted in November to close Barrington.

However, 17 residents remain while they are fighting their eviction in court.

Derek Glass, a spokesman for the co-op, said the cooperative is proceeding with eviction as fast as the law allows. He said a summary eviction hearing has been set in Berkeley-Albany Municipal Court on Friday morning.

If the co-op prevails, the last residents could be forcibly evicted March 23.

The co-op hasn't decided what to do with Barrington. Choices range from selling it to converting it to another use.

"When is this city ever going to listen?"

In interviews during the City Council meeting, two mothers, who asked that their names not be used, said their children obtained drugs in recent years at Barrington.

"My son is off drugs now," an Oakland mother said. "But I feel that part of his downfall was due to his interaction with Barrington people,"

It was difficult, a Berkeley mother, said. "I found out later that they'd go over there and hide out for three or four days or a week at a time."

Nancy Barnes, another mother in the group, said juveniles from El Cerrito, Richmond and other cities in the East bay know to come to Barrington to get drugs.

Neighbors of Barrington, many of whom are involved in lawsuits against the co-op, were not as soft-spoken as the mothers.

"... they'd go over there and hide out for three or four days or a week at a time." a Berkeley mother said.

"We were here last week when all the students were yelling," one neighbor said. "Now they're gone. But we're still here. When is this city ever going to listen?"

Investigator Maloney said that the deceased did not fall while climbing the building but crawled out a third floor window and scaled the building using a 1 ½ inch electrical conduit on the north side of the building and he fell/ jumped from the south side of the building.

—Alameda County Coroner

Duh? The sides of the building are West and East, Inspector!!!

The Plywood Goes Up

My Daily Fix

Each morning I ran down to the Roxy Market (does every neighborhood have a Roxy?) at the corner of Shattuck and Ashby to get *The Daily Cal,* which I called my "Daily Fix", to see what they had said about Barrington and our lawsuit *today!*

I read about Christian Soto being a heroin addict and jumping off of Barrows, and noted that as an immigrant he was "one of the 24 best high school students in the bay area" after only 5 years in USA. I wondered how does one the best students in the Bay Area become a junkie? I've asked friends who are "hip", "If you wanted to buy heroin do you know where to get it?" I always get a perplexed look, with "No!" in an "are you crazy?" tone.

Heroin resides down the Rabbit Hole. *Christian Soto must have been in Barrington,* I speculated. I tracked down his sister, Sandra, who confirmed my suspicion. Indeed, his roommate was a heroin pusher. The tragedy! And the intense shame he must have experienced, being the son that his entire family had sacrificed for to give him a leg up. Then he becomes a junkie!!!!.

This is the underside of Barrington—the dark side. Yes, it fostered free expression. But it was also a door to the dark side where Satan resides. "Satan's Village" How devastating for his family.

Sandra Soto gave me a video tape from among Christians things. Several images have been included: There was the Onngh-yanngh-a-trong and the Big Rapper—*"Come one come all to see the dopers and pushers in Barrington Hall . . ."* The video also showed the President of Barrington bragging about how he lied at the City Council Task Force, saying there was no heroin.

The world of drug rehab is rigid and brutal. Attacking and breaking the addict down into compliance. Minuscule transgressions become the basis of brutal "treatment". A "threat" could be a little as point a finger and speaking angrily.

The group takes on incredible power. In one hour from being thrown out—which was unconscionable—Christian threw himself off of Barrows. He must have raced at top speed, in a crazed panic to be rid of his failure self. What a tragedy! Juan. Now Christian. How many others were scared by Barrington?

Barrows Hall

THE DAILY CALIFORNIAN
Berkeley's Independent Daily; Established 1871
VOLUME BERKELEY, CALIFORNIA

Suicide blamed on New Bridge

July 18, 1990

By Patricia Jacobus
Staff Writer

After many years of battling a heroin addiction problem, Christian G. Soto finally succeeded, his father said.

Soto joined a local drug treatment program as an alternative to jail in a federal drug case against him nine months ago. "He was happy again," said his father, Juan Soto.

But the 23-year-old violated house rules and was discharged Wednesday from the program. Less than an hour later he jumped to his death from the eighth floor of UC Berkeley's Barrows Hall, investigators said.

Discharge from the program could have meant that he would be sent to federal prison for three years, an attorney close to the family said.

The victim's father said that the program, New Bridge Foundation located at 1820 Scenic Ave., did not follow safety procedures when they discharged his son.

"They don't do the right thing," Juan Soto said. "How can they throw people out like that? He may have had no drugs but he was still sick."

The suicide victim apparently threatened another patient twice, a serious violation of the program's rules.

Peter Budlong, the program's director, said he could not comment on the suicide, citing patient confidentiality rules. He said, however, that threats can be grounds for discharge from the New Bridge Foundation.

"In general, when people are discharged, they are allowed to make phone calls," Budlong said. "But we would never discharge anyone if there was evidence of suicidal tendencies."

The father made several attempts-to contact his son earlier last week, in efforts to remind him to register for fall classes.

The student's family discovered he was expelled only after he jumped, his sister, Sandra, said.

"He was put out on the street with a BART ticket, without his family or the police being notified, even though legally he was still in federal custody," she wrote in a letter to The Daily Californian.

Soto was born and raised in Valparaiso, Chile and moved to California with his father in 1984. Several years later his sisters and mother emigrated to the United-States.

"Chris helped me enroll into Berkeley, and help me learn to speak English," his sister Sandra, said. "He used to give dictionaries to our mother to encourage her to learn to speak English too."

Soto received a scholarship to UC Berk in 1985 for being one of the 24 best high school students in the Bay Area, said Sandra Soto.

He dropped out of college to deal with his drug addiciton which caused repeated trouble wiht the police. However, Soto was registered for the fall semester and enrolled in prerequisite courses for the College of Environmental Design, his sister said.

Soto was interested in architecture. "He was very sensitive, creative and artistic," Sandra Soto said.

"My brother never liked to see anybody alone. He would always bring people over to the house and make sure that his friends had a warm bed.

East Bay

EXPRESS

Paul Rauber
Sticks and Stones
Aug 3, 1991

What a Racket!

Barrington Hall may be no longer with us, but its legacy is fated to last in the courts far into the future. Last Friday, the Distric Court of Appeals, San. Francisco ruled that Barrington's former neighbors Charles Spinosa and Ruth Oscar could indeed file suits against the University Students Cooperative Association under the federal Racketeering Influenced Corrupt Organizations Act, or RICO. While the dailies reveled in recounting the nude gatherings, drug parties, and other lurid details of Barrington's past, they missed the other shoe: the Appeals Court ruling came only days after USCA executive director George Proper filed a suit for malicious prosecution against Spinosa and Oscar, separate plaintiffs Beverly Potter and Sebastian OrfaU, and their lawyer Don Driscoll. Proper's suit (which amounts to between $1.8 and $5 million, depending on whether the damages being asked are individual or collective) came as a surprise to the defendants, who were served papers in the midst of settlement negotiations. All bets are now off, and we may finally learn in court the extent of the USCA's knowledge of drug dealing in Barrington. Onngh Yanngh will never die!

THERECORDER

California Daily Service
5930-5933
Ninth Circuit Court of Appeals
Decided June 4, 1992

Cite as 91 C.D.O.S. 5930

RUTH E. OSCAR; CHARLES SPINOSA,
Plaintiffs-Appellants,
v. UNIVERSITY STUDENTS CO-OPERATIVE ASSOCIATION, GEORGE PROPER, et aL,
Defendants-Appellees.

No. 9015750
D.C. No. CV-89-2117-SAW
Appeal from the United States District Court for the Northern District of California, Stanley A. Weigel, District Judge, Presiding
Argued and Submitted June 13,1991
Before: BRUNETTI, KOZINSKI, and RYMER, Circuit Judges
Counsel: Donald P. Driscoll, San Francisco, California, for the plaintiffs-appellants. Arthur Brunwasser, San Francisco, California, for the defendants-appellees. Filed July 26,1991

KOZINSKI, Circuit Judge:

If Berkeley, California was the last bastion of sixties counterculture, Barrington House, the city's oldest and largest student housing co-operative, was surely the last rampart. While much of Berkeley became stuffy and conventional, the residents of Barrington House clung to their freewheeling ways. A bit too free-wheeling according to two of Barrington's neighbors. They claim that the co-op's denizens engaged in massive drug-law violations, turning the neighborhood into a drug-enterprise zone. This, they allege, interfered with the quiet enjoyment of their property. We consider whether they state a claim under RICO, 18 U.S.C. §§ 1961-1968.[1]

FACTS Barrington House's reputation was larger than life,

even by California standards. Known across the country as a "drug den and anarchist household," Barrington House prided itself on fostering alternative lifestyles, S.F. Chronicle, April 9,1990, at B3, col.l. Its bizarre and irreverent rituals included nude dinners with themes

1. **1. For the sake of brevity, we refer to the residents of Barrington House and defendants together as Barrington House. At this stage, there is no reason to distinguish between them: If the complaint's allegation of conspiracy and aiding and abetting are taken as true, see Third Amended Complaint §§ 7-20, ER 3-7, defendants and Barrington House's resident are liable for each other's conduct 18 U.S.C. § 1962(d) (conspiracy to violate RICO unlawful); Petro-Tech, Inc. v. Western Co., 824 F.2d 1349,1356-62 (3d Cir. 1978) (aiders and abettors liable under civil RICO as principals).**

2. Property interest in their apartments. *Venuto* v. *Owens-Corning Fiberglass Corp.,* 22 Cal. App. 3d 116,125,99 Cal. Rptr. 350,356 (1971); see W.P. Keeton, et al., *Prosser and Keeton on the Law of Tom* § 87, at 621 (5th ed. 1984) (any interest sufficient to be dignified as a property right - including a tenancy for a term or a week-to-week tenancy — will support action for interference with its enjoyment). Not even the landlord may lawfully interfere with that property right. See *Brown Derby Hollywood Corp. v. Hatton,* 61 Cal. 2d 855, 858, 395 P.2d 896, 898, 40 Cal. Rptr. 848, 850 (1964) (tenant right to possession and enjoyment). This makes sense. One who has paid to use and possess property — even if only for a limited time — is entitled to it for that period and state law protects that right from unjustified interference.[2]

3. 3. Of course, the limited nature of plaintiffs' property right will affect the amount of their recovery; they are entitled to compensation only for the loss of "market value of [their] term, but not for that of the reversion, in which [they had] no interest." W.P. Keeton, *supra* § 87, at 621 (footnotes omitted). But that's a question of damages; it doesn't affect whether there was a property interest in the first place.

4. 4. B. Defendants have a back-up argument, however: Even if plaintiffs had a property interest, it wasn't the type of interest RICO protects. RICO, they claim, protects only business property; it doesn't extend to property owned for non commercial purposes. See *Van Schaick v. Church of Scientology,* 535 F. Supp. 1125, 1136(D. Mass 1982). The language of the statute is to the contrary; it requires an injury to "business *or* property." 18 U.S.C. § 1964(c) (emphasis added). Nothing in the statute requires that the property be commercial. Indeed by referring to business or property in the disjunctive, Congress must have meant for the terms to cover different (though perhaps overlapping) concepts. Under defendants' proffered reading, the term property would be subsumed entirely withinthe term business and the disjunctive "or" would be rendered meaningless. Normal principles of statutory construction preclude suchan interpretation. See *Nieto* v. *Ecker*, 845 F.2d 868,873 (9th Cir.1988); 2A N. Singer, *Sutherland Statutory Construction* § 46.06 (4thed. 1984).[3]

5. 5. C. So we turn to defendants' back-up to their back-up argument, which runs something like this: Plaintiffs didn't lose the right to live in their apartments; they just lost a portion of the enjoyment they would normally derive from living there. This, defendants contend, is not the loss of a property right at all; it is merely a personal injury. And the established law of this circuit is that personal injury alone will not support a RICO claim, *Berg* v. *First State Ins.Co.*, 915 F.2d 460,464 (9th Cir. 1990).

6. 6. *Berg* does not control this case. The plaintiffs in *Berg* claimed that the defendants had caused their insurance policy to be cancelled. *Id.* even though the policy was property, we concluded that the plaintiffs suffered no financial harm: They paid no damages while uninsured and then replaced the policy at no extra cost. *Id.* at 465. What they sought was compensation for the stress of having been without insurance. *Id.* at 464. This, we held, was personal injury not damage to property, and therefore not cognizable under RICO. *Id.*

7. 7. In contrast, plaintiffs here do not seek RICO damages for emotional distress, loss of sleep or any other personal injury caused by Barrington House's activity. Their loss is economic: They paid good money for their leasehold

1. interests, which included a right of quiet enjoyment W.P. Keeton, *supra* § 87, at 619 (undisturbed enjoyment inseparable from ownership of property); see also *Brown Derby Hollywood Corp.*, 395 P.2d at 898. But, as a result of defendants' alleged racketeering activity, they were denied one of the

2. 8. Plaintiffs have alleged other types of property damages as well. For example, they claim that persons acting on behalf of defendants wrote "Go Die" in indelible ink on plaintiff Oscar's car. Third Amended Complaint § 73, ER 19. However, these allegations don't appear in the RICO portion of the complaint The complaint also fails to allege that the acts were connected with the racketeering activity. Accordingly, we infer that the loss of quiet enjoyment is the only injury to property plaintiffs allege under RICO.
3. 9. Defendants' position is remarkably like that of the dissent in Sedima, 473 U.S. at 521
4. (arguing that only businesses may bring RICO claims.)

like Satan's Village Wine Dinner and the Cannibal Wine Dinner — the latter complete with body-part shaped food. "It was hard on us vegetarians." sniffed one former resident. Id at B4, col. 1.

These bacchanalian festivals often turned riotous. Objects, ranging from bottles to clothes dryers, were thrown out of the building into the yards and homes of neighbors. And in keeping with the counterculture motif, drug use and distribution were common: Plaintiffs allege that no fewer than 19 different enterprises and individuals — with colorful names like "Mushroom Dave," "Icepick Al," "Onngh Yanngh," and "Marybeth (a.ka. Scarymeth)" — used Barrington House as a base for dealing drugs such as LSD, heroin and methamphetamine. Third Amended Complaint *fl* 21-39, ER 7-11; see also S.F. Chronicle, April 9,1990, at B4, cols. 1-3 (mentioning the presence of drugs at Barrington House).

Even as Berkeley gentrified and grew more conservative, Barrington House remained "a place where revolutionary expression was encouraged and often taken to the extreme." *Id.* at B3, col.l. Barrington House was, according to the graffiti on its walls, "An Oasis of Madness in a World Gone Sane." *Id.* at col. 2-3 (photo).

The neighbors were not amused. They blame Barrington House for all sorts of social problems, including crime and litter. They also claim that the co-op's residents conducted drug deals and posted look-outs in front of plaintiffs' apartments, bothering them and making it look like they, too, were dealing drugs; and that Barrington's residents, to avoid publicity and conceal their illegal activity, regularly dumped the bodies of persons suffering drug overdoses onto the sidewalks, near neighboring apartments.

Two neighbors, plaintiffs Ruth Oscar and Charles Spinosa, filed this suit, charging that the drug-dealing constituted a racketeering enterprise which injured their property. They asked for triple damages under RICO plus recovery on an assortment of pendent state claims. Barrington House itself has since gone the way of love-ins and strawberry wine: Defendant University Students Co-operative Association, which owned and operated Barrington House, closed the co-op's doors in December of 1989. S.F. Chronicle, July 10, 1990, at A3, col. 1: But this suit remains, proving once again that there is strife after death.

DISCUSSION

Under civil RICO, persons injured in their "business or property" by a pattern of racketeering activity can recover treble damages and the cost of suit, including attorney's fees. 18 U.S.C. §§ 1962(c), 1964(c). Everyone agrees that the repeated sales of narcotics alleged by plaintiffs amounts to a "pattern of racketeering activity." See 18 U.S.C. §§ 1961(1)(D), (5). Defendants dispute, however, whether plaintiffs adequately pleaded an injury to business or property, and whether their injury was caused by the racketeering activity. The district court agreed with defendants that causation was not sufficiently pleaded and dismissed the complaint. Plaintiffs declined the opportunity to amend and brought this appeal instead.

The first question is whether plaintiffs have alleged an injury to "business or property" that will support a RICO claim. 18 U.S.C. § 1964(c); see *Sedima, S.P.R.L* v. *Imrex Co.,* 473 U.S. 479,495 (1985).

A. Defendants claim that Plaintiffs had no property interest at all, much less one that was injured. They point out that plaintiffs didn't own their apartments; they merely rented them. See Third Amended Complaint §§ 51-55, ER 14-15 (alleging that plaintiffs have leasehold interest in their apartments and parking spaces). According to defendants, this means that plaintiffs had no property interest mat could have been harmed.

While federal law controls most questions under RICO, whether a particular interest amounts to property is quintessentially a question of state law. See *Logan* v. *Zimmerman Brush Co.,* 455 U.S. 422, 430 (1982) ("The hallmark of property ... is an individual entitlement grounded in state law . . . ."); *Board of Regents* v. *Roth,* 408 U.S. 564, 577 (1972) (property interests "are created and their dimensions are defined by" sources "such as state law."); *Milens* v. *Richmond Redev. Agency,* 665 F.2d 906, 909 (9th Cir. 1982) ("We look to local state law to determine what property rights exist. . . ."). Under California law, lessees such as plaintiffs do have a prop—sticks in the bundle which made up their property — the right of quiet enjoyment. Indeed, the right of quiet enjoyment is itself considered property. *Hart v. Buckner,* 54 F. 925, 930 (5th Cir. 1982) ("[T]he right of access and the right of quiet enjoyment... are property ...."); see also *United States* v. *Causby,* 328 U.S. 256, 266-67 (1946) (overflight of aircraft "so low and so frequent as to be a direct and immediate interference with the enjoyment and use of the land" is a taking of property). And the loss of that right is clearly economic: There can be no doubt that a leasehold in an ordinary apartment is worth more than a leasehold in a unit besieged by narcotics traffickers.

Plaintiffs' injury is conceptually no different than if a portion of their apartments had been flooded or damaged by fire. It would be possible, in either of these cases, to characterize the injury as merely psychic: The lessees are still entitled to live there; they just won't enjoy it as much. Indeed, just about any injury to property (except tneft of the property itself) could be characterized the same way: You still own the pile of scrap metal lying by the side of the freeway, but you won't derive the same pleasure from it as when it was a brand-new Maserati.

This argument need not detain us. Even if the harm inflicted by the damage to property is psychological to some extent, the victim can still bring a RICO claim for the injury to the property itself; although the emotional injury is not compensable, the loss of or damage to property is. Thus, RICO entitles the owner of the Maserati to recover triple the value of the ruined car; but it gives him nothing for the pain and suffering of having watched his dream machine reduced to a heap of rubble. Similarly, plaintiffs cannot recover under RICO for their suffering and emotional distress. But they *can* recover for the diminution of the fair market value of their property interest.[4] They ask for no more, see Third Amended Complaint § 53, ER 15; and they're entitled to no less.[5]

Having concluded that plaintiffs sufficiently pleaded an injury to business or property, we now address the issue of causation. In doing so, we note that plaintiffs have alleged the type of unlawful conduct that lies at the heart of RICO: The sale of illegal drugs and the crime and violence associated therewith. This is not a case where an enterprising lawyer has converted a business tort into a federal case; nor is it an ordinary landlord-tenant dispute run amok. Instead, plaintiffs allege precisely the type of conduct RICO was meant to deter — the continuous operation of a drug distribution enterprise. See 18 U.S.C. §§ 1961(l)(d), (5).

A. Plaintiffs blame the occupants of Barrington House for a multitude of misdeeds, from assault to vandalism;[6] their complaint reads more like an enumeration of the ten plagues than a pleading in federal court. Obviously, defendants aren't liable for every social ill in the neighborhood; RICO liability is expansive, not unlimited. Under RICO, defendants are liable only for the harm inflicted "by reason of" the racketeering activity, 18 U.S.C. § 1964(c); RICO does not afford compensation for injuries caused by other conduct or other persons. *Sedima,* 473 U.S. at 496-97; see *Brandenburg v. Seidel,* 859 F.2d 1179, 1187 (4th Cir. 1988) (plaintiff must adequately plead causal nexus between harm and racketeering activity). Thus, although Barrington House may have been noisy, thrown

Some of the alleged actions may have caused both psychic and property damage. Thus, plaintiffs allege that various defendants threatened them in order to protect the racketeering enterprise. Third Amended Complaint § 16 ER 4-5. To the extent these threats interfered with plaintiffs' enjoyment of their property and decreased its fair market value, they are cognizable under RICO; to the extent they merely caused plaintiff's emotional distress, RICO does not provide a remedy.

Defendants also argue that plaintiff's harm is not financial because Berkeley's rent control ordinance prohibited plaintiffs from selling their interests. But the requirement that plaintiff have a financial interest has no independent statutory significance; it is merely another way of articulating the requirement that plaintiff must suffer an injury to property. Under California law, a thing may be property even if it is not marketable and has no exchange value. 4 B.E. Witkin, Summary of California

have already concluded, plaintiffs interest does amount to a property interest under the applicable state law.

Apparently plaintiffs were unable to come up with any injuries or crimes that begin with the letters w, x, y and z.

wild parties and otherwise been less than an ideal neighbor, RICO does not afford plaintiffs a remedy for those wrongs. It provides compensation only for injuries caused by the racketeering conduct.

B. The complaint alleges that residents of Barrington House conducted drug sales and posted look-outs in front of plaintiffs' apartments and in their carports. This, they contend, interfered with the quiet enjoyment of their property by making them fear for their safety and by making it appear that their apartments were a source of drugs. Third Amended Complaint 1 55, ER 15-16. In addition, they claim that Barrington House's residents regularly disposed of overdose victims by dumping them in front of the building insteadof summoning emergency assistance, all in an effort to conceal their nefarious activities. *Id.* J 15, ER 4.

Plaintiff's pleadings are no model, but this much is clear: The racketeering conduct complained of was the direct cause of the alleged injuries. According to the complaint, the racketeers themselves interfered with plaintiffs' quiet enjoyment by distributing narcotics on and around plaintiffs' property. Furthermore, plaintiffs alleged that overdose victims languished about the neighborhood because the racketeers were trying to conceal their illegal conduct. The injury was thus the direct consequence of the racketeering activity; there were no intervening causes or actors; and the harm was strictly foreseeable. The blighting of a neighborhood by the fallout from a racketeering enterprise seems to be the type of harm well within the contemplation of the statutory drafters. Causation was adequately pleaded.

C. The same cannot be said of plaintiffs' other allegations. Without doubt, plaintiffs found it unpleasant to live amidst "filth, risk of disease, and noise." Third Amended Complaint 1 56, ER 16. We also agree that they should not have had to tolerate "violence, [the] throwing of garbage on [their] property, [people] urinating on carsparked at [their property], vandalism," *id.*, and burglary, *id.* 154,ER 15. But RICO doesn't provide a remedy for unneighborly conduct; it provides compensation only for damages caused by racketeering activity.

Plaintiffs have failed to allege sufficient facts to demonstrate that these problems were caused by Barrington's narcotics activity. First of all, the complaint never explains who committed the alleged wrongs. Of course, the culprits might have been customers of the racketeering enterprise, or even the racketeers themselves; but plaintiffs don't say so. Based on the complaint, it's just as likely that the perpetrators were totally unconnected to Barrington House or its racketeering. Certainly, defendants are not liable under RICO for every misdeed ever committed in the neighborhood. In fact, defendants aren't even liable under RICO for the conduct of their social visitors — unless their bad acts can somehow be connected to the racketeering.

Furthermore, the complaint fails to allege *how* Barrington House's racketeering activity caused the culprits — whoever they were — to commit the listed offenses. It's certainly possible that Barrington's racketeering drew the perpetrators to the area and encouraged them to commit the offenses; but plaintiffs made no such allegation. Accordingly, the district court did not err in dismissing those portions of the complaint that allege harms but fail to link them to the racketeering activity.[7]

CONCLUSION

We reverse in part, affirm in part, and remand for further proceedings.

RYMER, Circuit Judge, dissenting:

I have no quarrel with the notion that these aggrieved plaintiffs may have some state law cause of action against "the last rampart"

7. Plaintiffs also claim that discarded hypodermic needles posed a threat to their safety and interfered with their quiet enjoyment Third Amended Complaint 156, ER 16. One could easily infer that the needles were provided by Barrington House or were used to inject drugs purchased at Barrington House; an allegation to that effect would have'sufficiently stated the causal nexus between the racketeering activity and the harm. But plaintiffs made no such allegation and declined to amend the complaint. We defer to the district court's sound discretion on remand as to whether the inference of causation should be drawn from plaintiffs' pleadings or whether plaintiffs should be given opportunity to amend their complaint in light of our opinion.

of sixties counterculture. I dissent because I am convinced that their inability to allege *financial* harm sinks their civil RICO claim.

The majority correctly concludes that RICO's requirement of an injury to "business *or* property" does not require a plaintiff to plead injury to "business property". Nevertheless, invocation of the talismanic phrase "property interest" does not suffice to satisfy the statute's requirement of injury to property. In this circuit, we require civil RICO plaintiffs to allege that they have suffered a "financial loss or injury." *Berg* v. *First State Ins. Co.,* 915 F.2d 460, ;464 (9th Cir. 1990); *First Pac. Bancorp, Inc. v. Bm,* 847 F.2d 542,547 & n.12 (9th Cir. 1988). The proper focus is on the nature of the *loss* these plaintiffs have suffered, *not* whether a "property right" exists. Even assuming that these plaintiffs have suffered some harm to a property interest, I fail to see how they have contended that harm is *financial* in nature. Their complaint, therefore, cannot survive a motion to dismiss. *Cf. Berg,* 915 F.2d at 464 & n.4 (civil RICO action by pjaintiff who had "property interest" in insurance policy could not survive summary judgment because harm from cancellation of policy was not "financial").

The majority reasons that defendants allegedly infringed upon plaintiffs' right to quiet enjoyment of their leasehold—one of the "bundle of sticks" making up their property right. Not according to California law, they didn't. A tenant's right to quiet enjoyment is a warranty by a lessor against her own acts, not against those of strangers. *Merches* v. *Standard Realty and Dev. Co.,* 74 Cal. App. 3d 142,148,141 Cal. Rptr. 370,374 (1977) (citing *Carry* v. *Blauth,* 169 Cal. 713, 717, 147 P. 949 (1915); *Lost Key Mines. Inc. v. Hamilton,* 109 Cal. App. 2d 569,573,241 P.2d 273 (1952)). Thus, disturbance by a neighbor cannot support a lessee's claim of impairment of his right to quietly enjoy his lease.

Plaintiffs' claims sound if anywhere, in nuisance.[1] Assuming the alleged nuisance here could be characterized as private,[2] it is true that" 'any interest sufficient to be dignified as a property right' " will support the action, including "a tenancy for a term." *Venuto* v. *Owens-Corning Fiberglas Corp.,* 22 Cal. App. 3d 116,125,99 Cal. Rptr. 350,356 (1971) (quoting Prosser on Torts 613-14 (3d ed.)). I agree that these plaintiffs' property interest is sufficient to confer standing to bring a state law nuisance suit See *Stoiber* v. *Honey-chuck,* 101 Cal. App. 3d 903,920, 162 Cal. Rptr. 194,202 (1980) ("tenancy is a sufficient proprietary interest to give [plaintiff] *standing* to bring an action based on nuisance." (emphasis added)). For purposes of this case, though, the proper focus is not on the nature of plaintiff's property rights to determine standing but on the nature of the *damage* they suffered.

In general, there are two types of damages a plaintiff may recover for nuisance: (1) loss of value of property and (2) loss of use and enjoyment of property. 9 H. Miller & M. Starr, Current Law of California Real Estate §§ 29:14-15 (2d ed. 1990). The existence of a "property interest" does not automatically entitle a plaintiff to both types of damages. Rather, a plaintiff's measure of damages in a nuisance action is "only an amount sufficient to compensate him for his actual detriment." *Coats* v. *Atchison,* T. & S.F. Ry., 1 Cal. App. 441, 444, 82 P. 640 (1905); see also Cal. Civ. Code § 3333 (West 1970) (measure of damages is "detriment proximately caused" by defendants' action). We must therefore examine the nature of plaintiffs' "actual detriment."

When a nuisance is continuing, rather than permanent,[3] the usual measure of the first category of damages (loss of value of prop-

Generally, under California law, the definition of a nuisance includes "[a]ny-thing which is... offensive to the senses, or an obstruction to the free use of property, so as to interfere with the comfortable enjoyment of life or property ..." Cal. Civ. Code § 3479 (West 1970).

That assumption is not at all clearly warranted. The ills of which plaintiffs complain sound more lite a public nuisance, which is defined by California law as "one which affects at the same time an entire community or neighborhood, or any considerable number of persons, although the extent of the annoyance or damage inflicted upon individuals may be unequal." Cal. Civ. Code § 3480 (West 1970). All other nuisances are considered "private." Cal. Civ. Code § 3481 (West 1970). See Venuto v. Owens-Coming Fiberglas Corp., 22 Cal. App. 3d 116,123-26,99 Cal. Rptr. 350, 355-57 (1971) (distinguishing private actions based upon public nuisances, which require an injury different in kind from the injuries suffered by the general public, from private nuisances). Plaintiffs in this case have not alleged that their injuries are any different in kind from other residents of their neighborhood.

erty) that an owner of property may assert is loss of rental value. *Guttinger v. Calaveras Cement Co.,* 105 Cal. App. 2d 382, 387, 233 P.2d 914, 917 (1951); *Ingram* v. *City ofGridley.* 100 Cal. App. 2d 815,820,224 P.2d 798,801 (1950) (citation omitted).[4] That type of loss would qualify as financial. In this case, though, plaintiffs have not sustained that type of injury because they have not alleged that they are even legally capable of renting their property interests to others, much less rent them for higher prices than they were paying their lessors.[5] The rental value to plaintiffs, therefore, is zero and cannot be diminished any further. Plaintiffs in this case differ from other plaintiffs in California cases who were capable of renting their interests and therefore could claim actual, financial injury from a nuisance diminishing that rental value. See, *e.g., Quails v. Smyth,* 148 Cal. App. 2d 635,637-38,307 R2d 29,30 (1957) (measure of owner's "value of property" damage from periodic "turkey dust"that wafted over from neighboring farm "was the depreciation of the rental or use value of the property"); *Spaulding* v. *Cameron* 127 Cal. App. 2d 698,706,274 P. 2d 177,182 (1954) (owner who lived in premises during period of nuisance received damages for loss of rental value); *Guttinger,* 105 Cal. App. 2d at 387, 233 P.2d at 917; *Ingram,* 100 Cal. App. 2d at 820,224 P.2d at 801.

There are other types of loss of value of property that are financial in nature and would therefore arguably be cognizable under RICO, for example, "actual injuries to the land" and "costs of minimizing future damages." *City of San Jose* v. *Superior Court,* 12 Ca. 3d 447,464,525 P.2d 701,712,115 Cal. Rptr. 797,808 (1974) (citation omitted). Another example would be a tenant who loses rental money because a nuisance forces abandonment of the premises with time still left on a lease for a given term (and therefore money still owed to the lessor). See *Kishlar v. Southern Pac. R.R.,* 134 Cal. 636,66 P. 848 (1901) (recovery for lost value when nuisance compelled lessee to vacate before the lease ended and building stood idle for over nine months). Plaintiffs in this case have alleged none of these other types of financial loss. They are not out one cent from defendants' alleged acts, either in foregone opportunity or money owed or damage needing repair. In short, they have alleged no financial loss at all.[8]

Instead, plaintiffs' allegations implicate the second type of nuisance injury: loss of use and enjoyment That is a perfectly proper thing to allege in a nuisance action, and there need not be actual loss of value in order to sustain a nuisance claim for annoyance, inconvenience, discomfort, mental distress or the like. See *City of San Jose,* 12 Cal. 3d at 464, 525 P.2d at 712, 115 Cal. Rptr. at 808; *Acadia, Cal., Ud. v. Herbert,* 54 Cal. 2d 328, 337, 353 P.2d 294, 299, 5 Cal. Rptr. 686,691 (1960); *Smith v. County of Los Angeles,* 214 Cal. App. 3d 266, 287-88, 262 Cal. Rptr. 754, 766 (1989); *Quails,* 148 Cal. App. 2d at 637-38, 307 P.2d at 30; *Spaulding,* 127 Cal. App. 2d at 706, 274 P.2d at 182; *Alonso v. Hills,* 95 Cal. App. 2d 778, 788, 214 P.2d 50,57 (1950). Yet even'if such damage is labeled an "injur[y] to real property." *City of San Jose,* 12 Cal. 3d at 464,525 P.2d at 712, ,115 Cal. Rptr. at 808, it is not a financial loss. "Personal discomfort and annoyance to which a person has been subjected by a nuisance on adjoining property," which describes this second

A nuisance that will presumably continue indefinitely is considered permanent; one that may be discontinued at any time is continuing. Phillips v. City of Pasadena, 27 Cal. 2d 104,107,162 P.2d 625, 626 (1945). Because the alleged nuisance in this case has stopped, obviously it was continuing rather than permanent while it lasted.

Rental value is different from market value, which is the measure of damages when the nuisance is of a permanent character. Ingram, 100 Cal. App. 2d at 820,224 P.2d at 801 (citation omitted).

They allege only that "[a] reasonable person would have a reduced desire to rent plaintiffs' apartments" in general, not that the plaintiffs themselves were actually legally capable of renting. Indeed, given that the apartments were rent-controlled, the plaintiffs likely could not sublease them.

The majority reasons that plaintiffs' loss is "economic" because their leases are "worth less." Ante at 9332. They may be "worth less" in a lay understanding, but the characterization is legally immaterial. The leases have no quantifiable "worth" to the plaintiffs to begin with, so the leases legal value to them has not been diminished, at least given the absence of an alleged capability to earn something from the property. The majority dignifies potential recovery for an abstract loss-a diminished "market value" in general—even though as to these plaintiffs, who are incapable of marketing the property at all, it has no legal rental value. There is no such thing as market value "in the air," as it were.

type of nuisance damage, "is like that claimed by the plaintiff in a personal injury action." *Ingram,* 100 Cal. App. 2d at 823,224 P.2d at 803. It is settled that personal injuries are not financial losses compensable under RICO. *Berg,* 915 F.2d at 464.

JUDGEMENT: If defendants diminished plaintiffs' enjoyment of their property, then plaintiffs may sue to their hearts' content—in state court, alleging nuisance. But in my view, this complaint was in the wrong court under the wrong statute and the district court properly dismissed it.[7]

Orfali Potter settle suit with USCA 7/30/92
Supreme Court declined to hear Oscar/Spinosa 12/7/82

He Had Agreements

Being from the Middle East, Seb's diet wasn't the greatest. He always had painful teeth problems, namely root canals. One particularly painful one had to be redone for more torture. Later we learned he had a "silver point" procedure when a small silver wire protruded from the root had actually become a "battery" giving off a current. This is probably what caused the cancer on his tongue right next to that tooth.

It started with a violent kind of headache. I heard a bunch of banging in the kitchen, and suddenly Seb came flying out, as if he had dived, like a stunt man. He landed on the floor, then stood up and ran into the door, and fell back on the floor. As he lay there, with me screaming. That was Headache A. After that he didn't thrash, instead it overcame him like a kind of migraine. Then came Headache B, which was a constant, unrelenting head pain.

Headache B stopped, on his birthday, August 26, just as the dentist, Steve Baldwin, pulled the tooth loose of the socket. From that moment, he got better and better.

I didn't want him to do it, but Seb did the traditional treatment, including radiation. During which a pimple developed on his neck at one of the beam points for the radiation. Previously they had cut off half his tongue and removed some huge number of lymph nodes in his neck and shoulder, essentially raping his immune system.

At the BEA Book Convention we learned that a famous alternative doctor, Douglas Brodie, was right in Reno. Few know there's a health mecca in Reno, Las Vegas and Tijuana—all just across from California the Big Brother of Medicine. It was in Reno that Seb's electric tooth was discovered. We had a lot of fun. It was an adventure. We

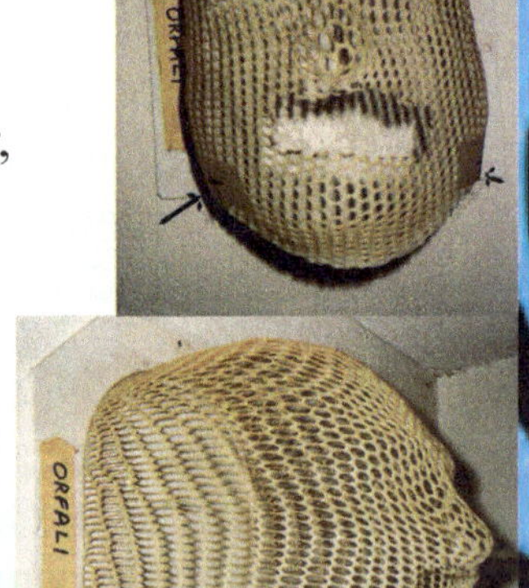

Radiation mask

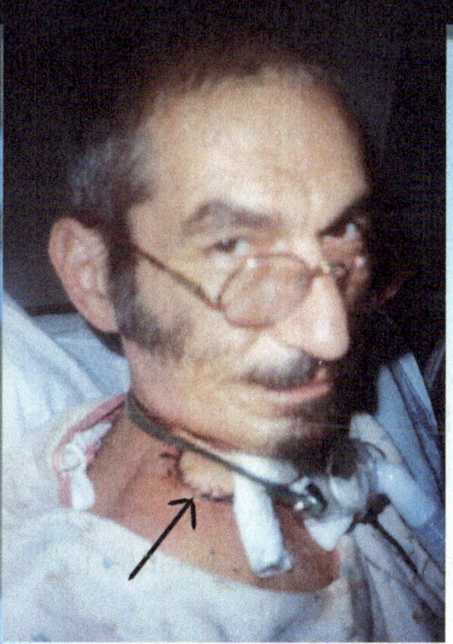

Seb looking like Steve Job. Arrow points to hole.

went to tour of the cancer hospitals in Mexico and had our minds blown! Seb began getting treatment from Dr. Brodie. First we had a "dark screen" which was our living blood blown up upon the computer screen. That's when I realized that Sebastian was sick. While my blood was filled with fat globs from the huge Reno ranch breakfast I'd just eaten, his was filled with fungus. The "treatment", which could be taken with or without chemo of varying strengths, was an intervenous chemical cocktail drip. Dr. Brodie created a special drip for me and I sat with Seb and the other cancer patients getting our infusions. The clinic drove him to and from his condo, which was only $175 week where he stayed during the week and I'd go up on the weekend.

Sebastian became obsessed with a pimple on his neck from the radiation and began putting hydrogen peroxide into it—full strength. The more it opened into a kind of channel, the more fixated he became. He would lie with his head off the side of the couch, holding a mirror as he poured in the H_2O_2. Eventually he carved out the carotid artery at the back of the channel. He kept it covered with a wide clothy band-aid and loved saying to someone, *"Hey, look at this!"* then he'd whip the band aid to the side, the person's face would contort in shock and horror. He thought that that was hysterical. Last year I found one of those band aids among the rocks in the driveway at the cabin.

The Kaiser doctor convinced Seb to have an operation to close up the hole. The day before the operation Seb was on TV 2 Special talking about managing one's health team. I'd been telling the Ch-2 producer about the alternative treatment in Reno. Looking small and weak, in his old man's hat, Seb

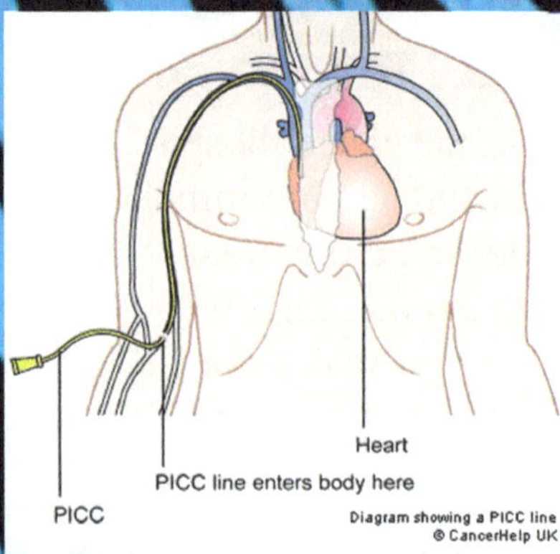

PIC delivers medicine into top of heart.

blabbed on and on with bravado, exaggerating how much his Kaiser treatment was costing. And, horrors, big brass from Kaiser where also on the special.

When he was in the hospital horrific things happened. It's not clear why, but they did a tracheotomy, which is a surgical hole through the front of his windpipe with a device in the hole. Because of it, he couldn't eat and lost 25 pounds in five days in the hospital and was suddenly frail.

One night he was so scared, he called after mid-night. He could only tap on the phone, *"Huh? Oh, it's Sebastian." "OMG, I'll be right there!!!"* I sneaked in the service entry of Kaiser Hospital and raced up to his room. The docs were certainly surprised to find me in bed with Seb when they did their rounds at 6 am. From that moment, things changed. I demanded a feeding tube immediately. Later at home we had a blast with it, when celebrating with a bottle of Champaign. He drank some, opened the tub and could hear it bubbling around. This was hysterical!! Then we just poured the champaign directly into the tube.

The surgery to close the hole didn't work. The muscle they wove up from his chest to pop into the hole came out. I had to stuff the hole a few times a day with a gauze dipped in Mercurochrome. As I did I could see the carotid artery and—to my horror—there were cuts in the shape of a tic-tact-toe on it. *"Yes, I've seen it",* Seb said.

We went to see Dr. Brodie in Reno. He saw the cuts, too. Dr. Brodie installed a PIC - peripheral intravenous catheter, which would enable him to administer the life-reviving medicine at home by just plugging into the PIC. Then we would receive the bags of treatment fluids by FedEx for less than $200 week. I would have paid anything, of course. Seb's PIC got stuck. Dr. Brodie told him to go to emergency and they would fix it. I begged Seb to go to Alta Bates—I'd pay. I didn't care what it would cost—and not Kaiser where he had to pay only five dollars.

When the Kaiser emergency room doctor saw the PIC, we were taken into a separate room where he began yelling and pointing at the PIC, demanding "*Where did you get THAT? Where did you get THAT?!!!" "Huh?"* There was nothing illegal about the PIC. We had paid for it.

The doctor left and a male nurse came in, who walked around behaving oddly, taking very deep breaths, while stretching his arms downward and stretching out his hand and fingers and then sucking in. In hindsight, it seemed like he was building up to "do" something.

The mean doctor came back and he stood at the end of the room watching, as the nurse sat and took Seb's arm with the PIC between his knees. He took hold of the PIC, twisting it hard, pulled it off. "*Oh, it broke off at then entry site"*, he gasped. The PIC is connected to a small tube in Seb's artery that goes up, across his shoulder and to the top of his heart. Before what our eye had seen could sink in, the nurse put his thumbs together and began needing the tube up Seb's arm. *"Oh, it's moved up from the entry site",* he gasped again. We were in a state of disbelief. People in white smocks are suppose to help, not harm—not murder you!

The mean doctor said, *"Take them to X-Ray"* and abruptly left the room. As the nurse was taking us down the hall, he asked, *"Is it okay if I talk to my mentor about what I just did?"* As I nodded *"Okay"* I felt like I'd entered a dark tale, an alternative reality populated by demons.

The mean doctor put the X-ray up on a light screen. Seb's body looked like the picture here, with the tube loose in his vein. I gaped at it in horror. The doctor told us to go home and return tomorrow to have it fixed. His attitude was "No big deal." No appointment set. Come in the early afternoon he advised. "*But doctor,"* I worried, *"what if it moves more?" "Oh, it won't. Can't!"* He sent us off, gruffly, with a diabolical air. Right before he walked out he stopped and looked at

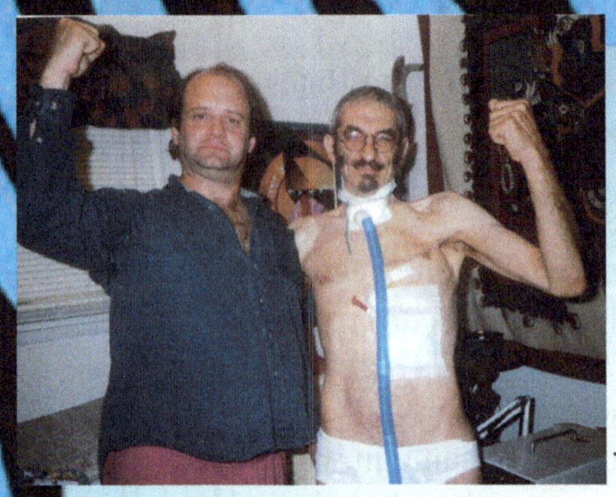

Seb with Dan Joy showing off his Halloween Ccostume

us intently and he said ominously, *"When you do the right thing for the wrong reasons, anything can happen."* Halloween was in two days.

Terrified, Sebastian could hardly sleep. I raced him to Kaiser at 6 am. *The tube was just about to go into his heart.* They raced him into one of those tube machine where they view your whole body. They went up through his groin, *through his heart, (!!!)* grabbed the tube and pulled it out. Sebastian was saved!!!

And then what did they do? They gave him a new PIC and sent him home. They must have pumped him up with fluids to remove the tube. But no one advised that we wait before giving him an infusion at home. We were elated. Seb has his first infusion at home. The PIC worked beautifully. His veins were really pumped. We'd forgotten all about the cuts on his carotid artery

We were so relieved. Everything would be okay now. I remember him running the coffee grinder. Just like normal. I still run that grinder every morning and often remember thinking, everything is normal again. For the first time in two and a half weeks, I felt I didn't have to watch him *every minute*. He was fiddling with his mirror and the hole in his neck when I went to bed.

In that twilight place just before sleep, I imagined that my arm was glowing with a white light. When Seb came to bed, I took hold of his arm, interlocking so I was holding his arm and he was holding mine. Half asleep I said, *"Do you feel that energy in my arm?"*, referring to the light. He indicated that he did. *"Take it,"* I said. *"Take it."* I awoke a little later. Seb was sleeping. His curly hair, which I loved, was growing back from the chemo. Inexplicably, because it was not at all like me, I made a fist with my right hand, reached over, and rubbed the top of head back and forth with my knuckles. right on what I later learned was the "crown chakra", through which the Soul goes when leaving the body.

When I awoke again, Seb was gone. Figuratively and literally! I jumped up and as I walked to the kitchen I saw blood spray om the carpet, by the time I got to the kitchen entry, I saw large blood drops, then I saw the red hand mark on the wall by the light switch. I turned and there was Seb, lifeless, hanging forward in "my chair". There was a big pool of blood under the chair with the mirror on the counter and a second pool under him in my chair. He must have gone to the mirror, saw the blood spouting in the mirror. Then gotten up. There was a crease in the side of his forehead. He must have fallen from weakness, hitting his head on the edge of the table, then dragged himself up into my chair. The expression on his face showed that he had had an ecstatic experience at the moment of his death. His eyebrows were raised, his eyes wide open and mouth in an "Oh Wow!" expression. (His eyes are closed in the death picture.)

Research has shown that we experience a "near-death"-like experience when the brain is deprived of oxygen, which triggers a flood of glutamate that kills brain cells. Dr. Karl Jansen believes that natural occurring ketamine-like substances in the brain, work to prevent the flood, in an effort to preserve the brain. Out of this struggle to live comes hallucinations, seeing a tunnel and white light often reported in near-death experiences. Whatever the biology, I have no doubt that Sebastian's exit was ecstatic—as he bled to death in the kitchen early Halloween. He died around 1:08 am 10/31/97.

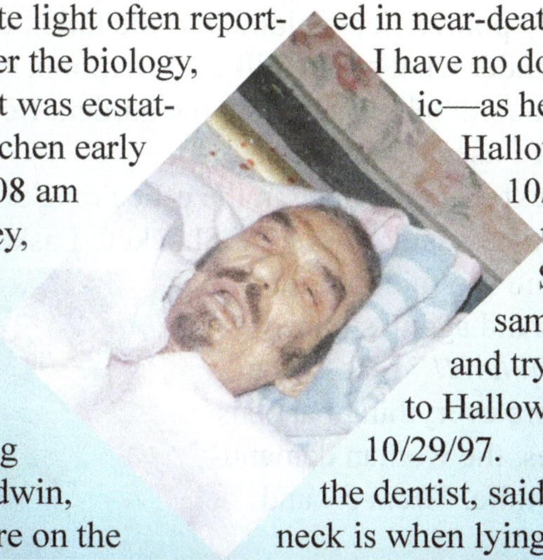

Anton Lavey, the famous San Francisco Satanist, who died that same weekend, was trying and trying to hold on to make it to Halloween. He failed, departing 10/29/97.

Steven Baldwin, the dentist, said that the greatest pressure on the neck is when lying down, especially on a pillow. Perhaps had he sat up all night, he may have survived.

Sebastian's attachment to St. Sebastian came out. People sent me stories about St. Sebastian. Amazing. Though he had been obsessed enough to change his name to Sebastian as a child, yet he didn't know the full story. Sebastian thought that St. Sebastian had evaded death. He hadn't.

We were working on *Healing Magic of Cannabis,* he suggested including "create your own healing prayer". He chose to pray to St. Sebastian because he thought he overcame death. When I met Seb and he showed me a drawing of St. Sebastian tied to a tree with arrows, I couldn't "get" it. At death, he re-enacted St. Sebastian. There he was with the medical slings and arrows in his body. Earlier he and Dan Joy had pranced around with Seb showing off his "Halloween Costume".

St. Sebastian was a Centurion who would heal people and then convert them to Christianity. He healed the Mayor of Rome. This pissed off the Caesar who sent his Centurions out to kill Sebastian. They tied him to a tree and shot him with arrows, then left him for dead. But Irene came along, cut Sebastian down, dragged him home and nursed him back to life. Sebastian was not content to live in exile. He went back to Rome and waited on a bridge for Caesar, who became enraged and ordered him beaten to death and his body thrown into the sewer.

I nearly poured Seb's blood into the toilet, but went out in the back under what seemed like a full moon, early on Halloween and poured Seb's blood into the garden. Recently I noticed the bucket I used out in the back lot.

The next day the phone in the office rang and the woman very insistently said, *"Irene!"*. Shocked, I asked, *"Who?!!"* A second time she said insistently, *"Irene?"* And again, stunned, I asked, *"Who?!!"* Like in the Bible where everything happens three times, the woman demanded a third time, *"Irene?"* and

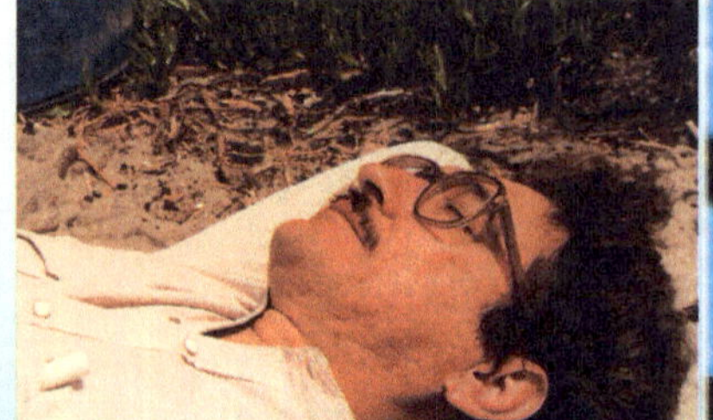

a third time I asked, *"Who?"* She mumbled, *"Oh, I'm, sorry, I mean Beverly?"* Weird. Just too weird. This was just like Seb!!!

For the next year and a half until I could get out of there, I sat in "my" chair, where I had found Seb and looked out into the kitchen to notice blood spots I'd not seen before. I am forever grateful that he did not bleed to death in the bed.

There was a book show in San Francisco the next weekend where we had a booth. Somehow I got all the books over there and set up. Sitting in the mausoleum of Sebastian's life work—a woman peered over at me. *"Where's Sebastian?"* she asked. *"Oh, he died."* I whispered. "*Ooooh, no wonder I got a message to come here today."* She said.

This was Karen, one of the mediums who attended Seb's how to get published classes. Turned out we have the same birthday, March 3, tho different years. I went to her home for a private seance and took her medium classes. It was awesome. I was told to go to a place in my old office to find something from Seb that was handmade with a photo. Right after, I went to the airport to pick up my old Syracuse roommate, Sharon Townshend, who had just flown in.

Going into my cluttered, packed with stuff old office that I called "The Archaeological Dig" with Sha, I said, *"There's the painting and it is to be to the right, on a shelf."* There was a stack of forgotten papers, about eight inches high, where I kept putting things to get back to but never did so. A tiny corner of a paper about a third of the way down caught my eye and I pulled it out. "WAMB!" Incredible!!! It was a handmade Christmas card David Shaw from Stanford had sent. It had a cut out photo of Seb in the RV pasted on the corner like a mailing stamp. Hand made. A photo. Incredible!!! I opened it and there was a blond Angel sitting in a half moon with my name with a bubble saying something and an owl, symbol of death, with Seb's name. Incredible.

Weird things kept happening. Noises. Radio coming on. Book falling open. There was only one explanation. Sebastian!!!

Bev in Joan of Arc tunic at Rennissance Faire where she and Mark had 4 booths

Another medium called and asked if I would like her to do a reading. *"Yes, Please do so!"* I regret not keeping it. But it is burned into my mind. The front of the card had the same illustration as on David's Christmas card in the paper stack. Colored balloon on strings hovering together.

He wants you to know that he's okay. He had agreements and designed his own death which he wasn't going to let anyone take away from him.

I remembered a Halloween two years earlier when I'd heard on the radio about a costume party at a bar. Rummaging through my costume box, Seb pulled out a devil costume, with tail and feet and devil face. I found the Joan of Arc tunic I'd bought at an MGM costume sale years earlier when my brother and I had booths in the Renaissance Pleasure Faire. We won first prize! The bar owner loved our theme "The Saint and The Sinner"

Then I remember Seb telling me about being in school in Jerusalem when the nuns told about evil Satan. Joe (he wasn't yet "Sebastian") held up his hand and said, *"Everyone hates Satan. I will love Satan"*, which brought much consternation, as you might guess.

The lawyer told me to make a list of Seb's aliases. Aliases? Well, yes, he DID use various names: JS Orfali, Seb, Sebastian Orfali, So and So. And . . . Sebastian was not his birth name. In musing, I realized that he used the various names for various purposes, such as JS Orfali for signing contracts. Sebastian Orfali for introducing himself. I realized I did not know who this man was?

What agreements? Agreements having to do with Barrington? Agreements he had failed to keep, and therefore had to die?

I developed a fantasy that Seb was next to Barrington for a dark purpose—to help capture young Souls. BUT he had taken up with "The Exorcist"—psychologist, exorcist, not so far fetched—who diverted him from his purpose. I continue to believe this fantasy. I also suspect that I may have, indeed, been Irene.

Contributors

My Father's Prostitute
Story of a Stolen Childhood
Steven Whitacre

Confessions of a Dope Dealing
Sheldon Norberg

Healing Houses
Transforming Sick Houses into Healthy Homes
Sheldon Norberg

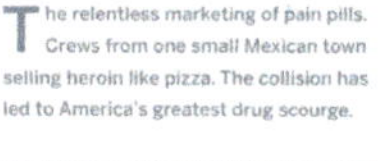

Dreamland
The True Tale of America's Opiate Epidemic
Sam Quinones

Insect Phenotypic Plasticity
Dougles Whitman

Reid Stuart
Triumph of the Green Man

iNK BARREL
video networks
Stewart Huntington
525 University Loop, Suite 120
Rapid City, SD 57701

CPSIA information can be obtained at www.ICGtesting.com
Printed in the USA
LVOW01s1816290615

444255LV00004B/9/P

9 781579 511937